Post-war British Theatre Criticism

Post-war British Theatre Criticism

Routledge & Kegan Paul
London, Boston and Henley

by
John Elsom

with drawings by Feliks Topolski

First published in 1981
by Routledge & Kegan Paul Ltd
39 Store Street, London WC1E 7DD,
9 Park Street, Boston, Mass. 02108, USA and
Broadway House, Newtown Road,
Henley-on-Thames, Oxon RG9 1EN
Set in 10pt Times by
Computacomp (UK) Ltd, Fort William, Scotland
and printed in Great Britain by
Whitstable Litho Ltd, Whitstable, Kent

British Library Cataloguing in Publication Data

Elsom, John

Post-war British theatre criticism.
1. Theatre – Great Britain – Reviews
I. Title
792'.0941   PN2595   81–40668

ISBN 0 7100 0535 0
ISBN 0 7100 0536 9 Pbk

Contents

Introduction

In this book, I have not tried to present British theatre criticism at its best, or at its worst. There are many learned, and even thoughtful, articles in monthly magazines and books which I have wittingly ignored; because my main purpose has been to illustrate the general, not-too-specialised, receptions given to some fifty post-war productions. For that reason, I have concentrated on the daily and weekly theatre columns, occasionally straying from the professional critics to quote from news items, fashion columns, leading articles and even *Hansard*. The focus, however, is upon those journalists whose opinions are thought to affect box-office trade.

British theatre critics have never had the categoric power of the Butchers of Broadway. None of us can kill a show overnight, or guarantee a smash-hit. The circumstances governing British and American theatres (as well as their newspapers) are too different. The investment stakes in West End productions tend to be smaller than on Broadway, and so the need for instant success is less acute. Impresarios can wait for the weeklies to redress any unfair impressions left by the dailies, although, if their resources are running out, they may not wish to do so. *The Birthday Party* in its original production was off before the only really enthusiastic review (in the *Sunday Times*) appeared. By contrast a musical like *Charlie Girl*, which had damning reviews, was nursed into a long-running success.

Nevertheless, critics do have considerable power over the commercial success, or otherwise, of productions; and I suspect that, for most people working within the theatre, that is their chief importance. Critics are not to be valued for their opinions but for their impact upon trade; whereas critics like to believe the reverse – that their views are respected and the commercial consequences stemming from them are not of great importance. Directors see critics as rather unpredictable pawns in the publicity game; whereas critics see directors as talented students who need the benefit of objective advice.

The strength of British theatre criticism, such as it is, lies in its variety. There are more theatre critics in London than New York; and, taken together, their columns represent a wider range of views. If Oxbridge liberalism sets the tone in the weightier papers, as Jonathan Hammond once suggested in *Plays and Players* (November, 1974), fringe directors had the comfort of knowing that two sentences in *Time Out* during the 1970s were of more practical use to them than a column in *The Times*. Actors and directors often believe that there is a conspiracy of critics, who meet in shady pubs adjoining the theatres, swop notes and rush off rudely before the final applause. When the reviews are uniformly good, bad or just imperceptive, they find it hard to believe that there has not been some kind of ganging-up from the press. Usually, however, critics do not discuss what they are about to write amongst themselves, except perhaps to clarify a point which they may have missed. They tend to be over-protective of their opinions, making up their minds in secret, so that they can display the results in their full glory publicly.

Nor, in Britain, does a particular sort of person became a critic. In some European countries, critics are trained within the drama schools. Students have to decide whether or not they wish to become critics; and this choice represents a certain mental attitude – preferring to be a commentator rather than a participant. They also learn at college what the role of the commentator should be; and such images of a critic's job can involve some challengeable assumptions. In the various deliberations of the International Association of Theatre Critics, there is often a clear division between those who believe that their task is to state, objectively and precisely, what happens on the stage; and those who interpret their role more subjectively – as a sounding board for theatrical experiences. On one side, the academics seek for criticism the exactitude of a science; while on the other, there are those who argue that 'scientism' is in itself a cultural phenomenon and that while a critic's job may be to tell the truth (for critics usually agree that they should not tell lies), this involves a wider sensitivity than mere documentary reporting. In some countries, theatre is seen as part of a wider political process, that of educating people into the aims and responsibilities of socialism. With that assumption, a critic's duty is to explain the ideological 'correctness' (or otherwise) of a production.

But in Britain, few start out their professional lives intending to be critics. They have usually drifted into their profession by accident, without specific training as critics, although they may have received a general arts education. Some start out by being journalists, while others may have wanted to be actors, playwrights or directors. There is a tradition in Britain of practitioner critics, of which Shaw is a good example; and among the critics quoted in this book, Irving Wardle and Frank Marcus are dramatists, Robert Cushman, Michael Billington and Kenneth Tynan have been directors, and others have had practical theatre experience of one sort or another. They are not, therefore, 'eunuchs in a harem', although they could be failed or embryonic sultans.

There are advantages and disadvantages in having professional experience in the art which one happens to be criticising. It is always helpful to know how a play gets put on, the difficulties of working on this or that kind of stage, the problems of casting, the limitations of budgets and the opportunities seized or missed. Theatre critics always have the problem, particularly with new plays, of trying to assess where the real credit lies – with the directors, actors or writers. Many second-rate plays have received bubble reputations through the work of imaginative directors. Critics must learn how not to be dazzled by wealth and how to steel their hearts against excessive displays of poverty. It is salutary for them also to feel what it is like to be on the target end of criticism, how painful it can be to receive a really unjust, dismissive review (perhaps misinformed, too). A bad review can affect not just box-offices, but the whole careers of actors and directors. Conscientious critics may have small nightmares about the mistakes which they perpetrate; but those whose talents are damned by such errors are faced with worse trials than a sharp twinge of conscience.

But there are also drawbacks to practitioner criticism. The theatre can easily become a very inbred activity, with the same people talking about the same things in the same way. A critic can easily get sucked into a self-perpetuating folly which carries the name of art but which relates to nothing but itself. Failed practitioners who turn critics can also carry with them some of their lost ambitions; and that can have unfortunate consequences – at worst, an underlying tone of 'sour grapes', or, more frequently, a readiness to praise those who are doing what they originally wanted to achieve or to blame those who are not.

No critic, of course, can be totally unprejudiced. However hard he may try for that multifarious receptiveness which only Indian mystics and High Court judges are supposed to possess, he is inevitably biased, as all human beings are. But even prejudices are not absolute. A telling production can conquer them; and good critics are aware of their familiar tastes and, indeed, are prepared to subject them to continuous self-examination. The discussion of 'values' is the critic's stock-in-trade; and this involves worrying about why one prefers this kind of production to that. Critics, however, often tend to worry about values in a rather abstract way; whereas often their values are subtly determined by what could be called their allegiances.

Critics usually start by having a double allegiance – to their papers (and thus to their readers) and to the theatre. Some (particularly non-practitioner) critics assert that they really have only one allegiance, to their papers. They are, first and foremost, journalists; but journalists who specialise, whether in politics or the theatre, cannot be indifferent to the activity about which they are writing. If they are bored with the theatre, then they are likely to write boring columns, unless, of course, they regard the whole critical activity as an excuse to display their own verbal brilliance. Ambitious journalists will want to write longer and more eye-catching articles; and so, in the scramble for space in a paper, they will try to persuade their editors that the theatre is really a very important cultural phenomenon, worthy of special attention. They may not succeed, but they have to try; and thus they have a vested career interest in maintaining the health of the theatre.

Among the mass-circulation popular dailies and tabloids, very little space is usually given to the theatre, because it is considered to be a minority interest. The journalist is forced to condense his opinions into very few words, with little analysis to support them; and often he can do little more than to recommend or discourage. Since he is also looking for bright copy, he will be drawn into the 'smash-hit', 'disaster' and 'scandal' pattern; and, to that extent, his allegiance to his paper starts to determine the nature of his responses. This book could easily have been just a parade of hyperbole; and the reader may consider that it is sometimes in danger of being so.

In other papers, however, where the editors assume that their readers do regularly go to the theatre or, if not, like to know what is in fashion, the journalist-critic is given a considerable amount of space, and accordingly can develop his or her views. But more space does not mean less allegiance, nor should it. I am not suggesting that

Fleet Street editors seek to dictate editorial lines to their critics; nor do I wish to stress that familiar point that the capitalistic ownership of papers inevitably affects the tenor and content of what we read. That kind of allegiance, as far as theatre critics are concerned, is not the chief problem. But papers do have general images to maintain, which can be expressed in broadly political or class terms – left-wing productions do not usually receive such sympathetic treatment in the *Daily Telegraph* as in the *Guardian* – or in such matters as tone and emphasis. You do not read *The Times* to find out what is happening at the Talk of the Town or Raymond's Revuebar.

A paper's image is important, for that is what attracts regular readers; but it is not fixed. It varies from editor to editor, and from critic to critic; but it usually fluctuates within certain limits. A critic is usually not employed in the first place unless it is thought that he will somehow fit into the editorial grand scheme. I have never quite understood what skills an editor looks for when selecting a critic, but I would imagine that they consist mainly of an ability to write in the style to which the editor has become accustomed, a good knowledge of the theatre and a wide appreciation of our culture. Other qualities could also be valuable – such as imagination and stamina, a talent to write in the dark (in more senses than one) and a high boredom threshold, for, however attractive it may seem to spend five evenings or so at the theatre in a week, the routine can pall.

Another attribute could be added to this list – a readiness to enter into a public debate about the kinds of lives we lead, the society we live in and the alternatives which do, or could, exist. A critic has to have an appetite for speculation, not gullible or utopian, but constructively thoughtful. A critic has to enjoy the process of testing one theatrical vision against another, to understand and appreciate them all on many levels – of fashion, politics, psychological and spiritual insights. He should be impatient when the theatre narrows its range to the expression of very simple or familiar attitudes, but be responsive to new ideas from whatever quarter they may come. There is no such thing, in abstract, as 'good theatre'; for you can see highly skilled acting, beautiful sets and competent directing and still leave the theatre feeling that the experience has been a waste of time. Theatrical excellence lies as much in the quality of the debate as in the techniques of presentation, although often form and content cannot and should not be separated.

Critics who care about maintaining the health of the theatre, are particularly concerned with furthering the debate; but how can they do so, for they are not principal speakers? Some try to encourage the newcomers – every critic likes to talent-spot – while others look at the theatre system as a whole, to see where and how talent is being frustrated. Others still seek to twist the debate, perhaps towards politics, religion or even Wagnerian opera; and sometimes their preoccupations with what ought to be said in the theatre can blind them to what actually is. The debate goes through fashions. During the 1950s, the concern with Christianity, social propriety and existentialism was very evident in the more serious-minded reviews, just as, in the 1960s, a rebellion against propriety was equally prominent.

Theatre criticism on this level is essentially ephemeral, tied to particular productions, times and places; and one purpose in compiling this book is to show how fashions in theatre criticism change. What have changed very little, however, are the physical circumstances in which critics write their reviews; and I admire the sheer proficiency and intelligence of those daily reviewers, such as Irving Wardle of *The Times*, who manage regularly to produce sensible articles within a couple of hours of the final curtain. I have been lucky enough mainly to work with weekly or monthly columns; but I can guess at the problems of Mr Wardle's job through my experiences of instant radio reviews – for LBC and *Kaleidoscope*, where I have had, on occasions, to rush from the theatre, writing notes frantically in taxis, before arriving at the broadcasting studio. My most nightmarish experience was in phoning through a radio review of Trevor Nunn's *Macbeth* from a telephone in the RSC's press office, with the actors wandering in and out of the room while I was talking. The most salutary lesson, however, came with two reviews I wrote on John Osborne's *A Bond Honoured* – one overnight for Paramount Pictures and the other for the monthly magazine, *London Magazine*.

These two pieces showed me how much my snap reactions could differ from my more considered opinions. My first impressions of *A Bond Honoured* were very favourable. I enjoyed John Dexter's stylish production, Robert Stephens's athletic performance and the dry wit of Maggie Smith's delivery. I had a good time at the theatre – and said so, for Paramount. For *London Magazine*, I had the opportunity to work more slowly; and so I went back to the original play, Lope de Vega's *La Fianza Satisfecha* on which *A Bond*

Honoured was based, to compare it with Osborne's adaptation. It then became clear that the new version was rather poor; a different kind of play, with a different theme, had been superimposed on the original, with the result that the ending was untidy and perfunctory. Dexter's production had skilfully disguised the weaknesses of Osborne's script.

I have no doubt that the *London Magazine* article was closer to the truth than the assessment for Paramount; but critics rarely have the time or the opportunity for this sort of prolonged consideration. In any case, it could be argued that my initial reaction was more useful than the later one, for if I originally enjoyed the production, other members of the public were also likely to do so. But is the critic's job simply to test the bath water for other people? I don't think it is. Underneath all the surface problems and attractions which beset the work of critics and the productions which they see, there remains a core of reality which critics ought, however dimly, to perceive and to be able, however incoherently, to express. Some plays are better than others: levels of quality do exist. Ultimately, the critic's task – which is a formidable one indeed – is to distinguish between these levels as clearly and accurately as they can. Critics cannot expect many external rewards for what they do – they are neither over-paid nor over-liked. But if they can retain some glimpse of what is good and bad in the theatre, and recognise the degrees of goodness and badness (which is more difficult), their job can be satisfying to themselves and others, even honorable. Within this book, however, I have decided to let the reader be the critic of the critics, although my introductions to the productions may give an indication as to where my sympathies lie.

Collectively, these reviews remind us of the immediacy of the theatrical experience; and I have been fortunate to be able to include some theatre drawings by Feliks Topolski, whose remarkable talent at capturing fleeting dramatic impressions on his sketchpad complements the efforts of others in print. Topolski has been closely involved with British theatre, as observer and designer, since the 1930s; and the full range of his theatrical drawings and paintings require a volume or so to themselves. I am grateful, however, in that he has allowed me to reproduce not only some of his portraits from life but also those evocative sketches, jotted down during performances, from his customary place in the front row of the stalls, where the stage lights reflect down on to his pad.

The Old Vic at the New Theatre (1944–49)

The Old Vic theatre in Waterloo Road was bombed in 1941; but Tyrone Guthrie had kept an Old Vic company together, touring regional theatres from a base in Burnley. In 1944, however, Guthrie and the Vic-Wells governors decided that the Old Vic should return to London. One of the governors, Bronson Albery, was an impresario who owned the New Theatre, which he offered to the company as a temporary London home. Guthrie arranged that a new management team should be formed for the London seasons, consisting of Laurence Olivier and Ralph Richardson, who were both released from the Fleet Air Arm for the purpose, with John Burrell, a young drama producer from the BBC.

The first seasons were triumphant. I doubt whether any British company, before or since, made such an immediate impact on the public mind. Thirty years later, young actors were still mimicking Olivier's Richard III, a performance which they could not have seen except in the screen version. This performance, together with his remarkable double-performances as Hotspur and Justice Shallow in the *Henry IV* plays and as Oedipus and Mr Puff, raised Olivier's reputation as a classical actor above those of his contemporaries, which included John Gielgud and Donald Wolfit. He was widely regarded as the greatest living actor; but he was also a matinée idol – one paper disapproved of the fact that he was being given the kind of reception by teenagers associated with such pop stars as Frank Sinatra – and a patriotic symbol. His film of *Henry V* went on general release in 1945.

Richardson's performances as Peer Gynt, Falstaff and the Inspector in J. B. Priestley's *An Inspector Calls* were also acclaimed; and the Old Vic company included Sybil Thorndike, Miles Malleson, George Relph, Harcourt Williams and Margaret Leighton. The presence of such an acting team in London during the last months of the war was inspirational. British theatre-goers boasted that despite the doodlebugs and flying bombs, London possessed the finest acting company in the world. In 1945, the first formal steps were taken to unite the Old Vic with the Shakespeare Memorial National Theatre

Trust in a joint initiative to establish a British National Theatre, which eventually led to the passing of the first National Theatre Bill in 1949.

In the meantime, the Old Vic in a sense behaved like a national theatre. In 1945, Olivier led the company on a remarkable six-week summer tour of Europe. They were the first foreign company to be invited to play at the Comédie-Française, where they were rapturously received. They also visited Germany where the response, perhaps surprisingly, was not less enthusiastic. The Staatliche Schauspielhaus in Hamburg, which had miraculously survived without too much war damage, was packed with cheering audiences. They also played a matinée for the soldiers whose grim task was to care for the survivors and bury the dead at Belsen. Their Belsen visit was a harrowing experience. 'I'll never get over today,' wrote Sybil Thorndike afterwards, '*never.*'

In preparation for the establishment of the new National Theatre, Olivier, Richardson and Burrell proposed to the Old Vic governors that a training centre should be incorporated into the Old Vic organisation. It was to consist of a children's theatre, a training school for actors and an experimental studio; and two directors associated with the pre-war London Theatre Studio, Michel St Denis and George Devine, were invited to run it with Glen Byam Shaw. According to Irving Wardle's *The Theatres of George Devine*, St Denis, a French director inspired by the work of Jacques Copeau and the *Compagnie des Quinze*, provided the original outlines of the scheme, while Devine was its dogged organiser. Of the three sides to the Old Vic Centre, the actors' training school was probably of greatest long-term value, for it furnished Britain with many of its best actors and directors of the coming generation.

The Old Vic seasons at the New, however, proved to be one of several false dawns for the National Theatre. In 1949, Olivier, in Australia touring with the Old Vic company, and Richardson, who was filming in Hollywood, were curtly informed by the new chairman of the Vic-Wells governors, Lord Esher, that their contracts would not be renewed. It was a great blow from which the Old Vic took years to recover; and indeed it never regained its former pre-eminence. The Old Vic Centre was soon to be disbanded, with Glen Byam Shaw moving to the Shakespeare Memorial Theatre at Stratford, Devine eventually establishing the English Stage Company at the Royal Court Theatre and St Denis accepting an appointment as the director of the Centre Dramatique in Strasbourg.

The precise reasons behind the governors' drastic action have not been fully revealed. There were certainly many motives involved. In 1948, the Old Vic had a bad season, leaving an overdraft of £8000. This was particularly embarrassing in a year when the National Theatre Bill was passing through its various parliamentary phases. The long absences of Olivier and Richardson, touring abroad with the company or filming, had weakened the Old Vic in London, despite the brave efforts of John Burrell to carry on; and artistic standards had fallen. One justification for Olivier's world tours was that they brought much-needed foreign capital to the company and the country; but Guthrie was amongst those who were uneasy at the workings of the triumvirate which he had helped to bring into being. Burrell inevitably was overshadowed by his star associates, who were so much in demand that their professional attentions continually seemed to be drawn away from what Lord Esher regarded as the main purpose of the enterprise, the establishment of a National Theatre. Nor was Esher particularly enthusiastic about the Old Vic Centre, which he regarded as foreign to the traditions of British drama.

The drama director of the Arts Council, Llewellyn Rees, took over as the new administrator of the Old Vic, following the collapse of the old management, with Hugh Hunt as the new artistic director. The theatre in Waterloo Road was rebuilt and the company moved in, with Hunt responsible for the opening season in November 1950. The inspiration, the fervour and pride of the Old Vic seasons at the New during and just after the war were not easily forgotten; and for many years to come, they were cited as an example of what British theatre was like, at its best.

Richard III

13 September 1944

It is the marriage of intellect and dramatic force, of bravura and cold reason, that so distinguishes Mr. Laurence Olivier's study at the New

Theatre. Here indeed we have the true double Gloucester, thinker and doer, mind and mask. Blessedly the actor never counterfeits the deep tragedian, the top-heavy villain weighted by his ponderous and marble jaws. His Richard gives to every speech a fire-new glint. His diction, flexible and swift – often mill-race swift – is bred of a racing brain. If, outwardly, he is a limping panther, there is no lameness in his mind. Other players have achieved the Red King, boar, cockatrice, bottled spider, and developed the part with a burning theatrical imagination; none in recent memory has made us so conscious of the usurper's intellect, made so plausible every move on the board from the great opening challenge to the last despair and death.

J. C. Trewin: *Observer*
17 September 1944

There was a great deal of Irving in Wednesday's performance, in the bite and devilry of it, the sardonic impudence, the superb emphases, the sheer malignity and horror of it. If I have a criticism, it is that Mr. Olivier takes the audience a little too much into his confidence. ... I do not propose to forget its mounting verve and sustained excitement.

James Agate: *Sunday Times*
17 September 1944

As he made his way downstage, very slowly and with odd interruptions in his progress, he seemed malignity incarnate. All the complications of Richard's character – its cruelty, its ambition, its sardonic humour – seemed implicit in his expression and his walk, so that when at last he reached the front of the stage and began his speech, all that he had to say of his evil purpose seemed to us in the audience less like a revelation than a confirmation of something we had already been told.

W. A. Darlington: *Daily Telegraph*
14 September 1944

From a sombre and uninventive production, this brooding, withdrawn player leapt into life, using the circumambient gloom as his springboard. Olivier's Richard eats into the memory like acid into metal, but the total impression is one of lightness and deftness. The whole thing is taken at a speed baffling when one recalls how

Laurence Olivier as Richard III

perfectly, even finically, it is articulated: it is Olivier's trick to treat each speech as a kind of plastic mass, and not as a series of sentences whose import must be precisely communicated to the audience: the method is impressionistic. He will seize on one or two phrases in each paragraph which, properly inserted, will unlock its whole meaning: the rest he discards with exquisite idleness. To do this successfully, he needs other people on the stage with him: to be ignored, stared past, or pushed aside during the lower reaches, and gripped and buttonholed when the wave rises to its crested climax. ...

In this Richard was enshrined Blake's conception of active, energetic evil, in all its wicked richness. A lithe performance, black at heart and most astutely mellow in appearance, it is full of baffling, irrational subtleties which will please while they puzzle me as long as I go to theatres. I remember the deep concern, as of a bustling spinster, with which Olivier grips his brother George and says, with sardonic, effeminate intentness: 'We are not safe, Clarence; we are not *safe*'; while, even as he speaks, the plot is laid which will kill the man. The persistent *bonhomie* of middle age shines in his face as he jests with his chosen victims: how often he skirts the footlights, his eyes turned skyward, on some especially ironic aside: with what icy disregard he slights his too ambitious minion Buckingham! 'I am not in the giving vein today'; the words fall like drops of frozen dew.

Kenneth Tynan: *He That Plays The King*
(Longmans, 1950)

(Tynan reprinted this review in *A View Of The English Stage* (1975, Davis-Poynter) and gives it a date, 1944. From references within the article to the film of *Hamlet* and to the revived *Richard III* production, with Vivien Leigh as Queen Anne, it is clear that Tynan revised the piece for inclusion in his first book. He might have revised it for other reasons too, for in 1944, he was only $17^1/_2$ years old, about to embark on his dazzling career at Oxford. He sent this review, among others, to James Agate, the doyen critic of the *Sunday Times*, who recognised the uncommon eloquence, perception and maturity of this young undergraduate. The descriptions also reveal Tynan's particular appreciation of Olivier's acting, a fascination and respect which later led to their working together at the National Theatre during the 1960s.)

Henry IV, Parts 1 and 2

26 September 1945   3 October 1945

Are Shakespeare's Barons inevitable bores? One has often thought so, as the stuffed breast-plates boomed away, without character or meaning. Recent productions, however, gave this gloomy theory a crack or two. *Henry IV, Part I* at the New smashes it finally. Of course, Ralph Richardson's Falstaff and Laurence Olivier's Hotspur are first-rate company: the essential point is that the company are grand company, too. The baronial halls are packed with humour and humanity; behind the breast-plates are flesh and blood. Now the play soars like an eagle uncaged. ...

... there is a tremendous Falstaff performance. Mr. Richardson grows to obesity downwards; the legs are dropsical trunks, the paunch is sketchy, the head is even and lean. ... No nose-painting here; indeed the neb already is almost as sharp as a pen and pale as a quill. So Falstaff is not just a gigantic purple patch on the fabric of history. He is in the heart of the play, its commentator as well as its cordial, a man of testy, sardonic wit. ...

... Laurence Olivier's Hotspur immediately possesses the audience. Odd, uncouth, now darting of mind and phrase, now almost stammering of speech, sour, fiery – the figure is unforgettable: you watch him at every moment, tenderly domestic, roughly discursive, baiting Glendower, dying with harness on his back and iambics halting on his tongue ... These two portraits, aligned in a notable production, give one high pride in the English theatre, which, amid all the difficulties of our time, is offering, in several quarters, presentations of the classics worthy of a National Theatre. ...

Ivor Brown: *Observer*
30 September 1945

In the past I have occasion to indicate, regretfully, the roles Mr. Richardson could not fill. Roles to which he brought no more than the competence of a fine actor labouring at the uncongenial. Now at last comes the time when I can legitimately quote the great critic [Hazlitt], again on Liston: 'He does some characters but indifferently,

Act 2, Scene 4

OLD VIC
THE New
HENRY IV

Ralph
Richardson
as
Falstaff

Thou knowest me in compound of majesty, by this light, flesh
and corrupt blood, thou art welcome

others respectably; but when he puts himself whole into a jest, it is unrivalled.'

Mr. Richardson put himself whole on Wednesday night into that great joke which is Falstaff. He had everything the part needs – the exuberance, the mischief, the gusto, in a word. Falstaff is more than a 'stuffed cloakbag of guts'. He is also 'reverend vice' and 'grey antiquity'. Meaning two things, first, that the old toper, sorner, fribble still keeps some of his fallen day about him; second, that he is conscious of his own enormities.

James Agate: *Sunday Times*
30 September 1945

On the stage Mr. Richardson creates the illusion of having one of those open personalities through which the true character shines from within, so that we think, 'Ah, I can tell what you're really like, my transparent fellow.' This gift well suits an interpretation of Falstaff, who, with his innocent deceptions and free pleasures, is the purest of Shakespeare's characters, yielding to temptation with such ready grace that he seems the master, not the slave, of passion.

If Mr. Richardson seems to go back to Shakespeare's original, Mr. Olivier just as strikingly creates a new Hotspur, reminding us that Northumberland is of the Border, a soldier of Celtic shyness and taciturnity, through the impediment of whose diffidence the marvellous words break suddenly, in an unpremeditated stream – a daring and successful performance. *Feliciter audax* is, indeed, the phrase for Mr. Burrell's production. Choosing not to adopt the uninterrupted flow of the Elizabethan method, he closes each scene with a dumb-show, shadowy and significant. I shall never forget Glendower, standing at the window (the actor is Harcourt Williams, who knows how to stand) – standing and staring after Hotspur as he gallops away, with the two women weeping at his feet while we know what they guess, that they will never see Hotspur again.

Stephen Potter: *New Statesman*
6 October 1945

Although the performance of *Henry IV* ... may be the best that we shall see in our generation, a production displaying so much talent and enterprise in the service of genius that even the spectators are made to feel they are sharing in the glory, still nothing has been done to make good the chief inferiority of Part II – the fact that much of it is a feeble echo of Part I. The Earl of Northumberland revolts again, with less of a dog's chance than ever. The very life-blood of his enterprise and our interest is infected from the first by the disappearance of Hotspur and Glendower. Soldiers trot still more perfunctorily across the stage to even ungorier battles. ...

This production makes us see more clearly than ever before that Shakespeare in Part II lost interest in the nobles and became absorbed in the character of Falstaff and the study of riotous youth in decay. We see Falstaff brought face to face with the great mysteries, the only solid man, not only in flesh, but in spirit, among the attendant chorus of ghostly eccentrics. It is probably a right decision that to play Pistol, Bardolph and Mrs. Quickly thicker than cardboard is to overlay the stage with character. Mr. Olivier, on the other hand, is tremendously funny as a Shallow for whom the only reality is Falstaff, on whose every word he hangs, and every part of whose life he tries to identify in fantasy with his own. This Shallow, and Miles Malleson's Silence (concentrating so hard upon concentration that he is unable to take anything in), provide the best comic performances in London.

Stephen Potter: *New Statesman*
13 October 1945

Oedipus
(Version by W. B. Yeats)

The Critic : R. B. Sheridan
18 October 1946

At six-thirty on Thursday evening a young man sat in a box at the New Theatre talking rapidly into a microphone.

I thought he was a roving BBC reporter, telling the town that we were a brilliant first-night audience. I have never quite discovered what makes us so brilliant so often.

Later I learned that he was informing the continent of Europe that London was about to witness a play written by a Greek author named Sophocles, directed by a Frenchman named Michel Saint-Denis and acted by a company of British actors.

An hour later Mr. Laurence Olivier as the blinded, bleeding, damned and doomed Oedipus stood, exhausted and crushed, while the cheering audiences acclaimed him as a great tragic actor.

Somewhere around 10.45 p.m., the same Mr. Olivier who had been hilariously wafted to the roof on a piece of ascending scenery and had come sliding down most perilously on the curtain, was cheered by an audience roaring with laughter and delight at a climax which sets a level that will be hard to beat in any of this year's pantomimes.

On the whole I think it as well that the young man with the microphone disappeared when the entertainment began. Europe might have been more than usually puzzled by this expression of British culture, even though Mr. Olivier could argue that in playing Sophocles's Oedipus and Sheridan's Mr. Puff on the same evening, he is in the true Vincent Crummles tradition.

> Beverley Baxter: *Evening Standard*
> 20 October 1945

Yeats's translation of *Oedipus* has Greek simplicity and strength. It follows the original fairly closely yet without a shade of embarrassment and without a single swerve into over-coloured writing.

The action moves swiftly and inevitably to its climax, leaving us with the impression that, for once at any rate, the power of Greek drama has been conveyed into English. Other things contribute to that impression. First and foremost, there is the splendid Oedipus from Mr. Laurence Olivier, an organic personality from the early scenes in which he exercises his authority over the Theban elders with the easy assurance of a king, through the gathering clouds of suspicion and rising, when the last doubt is dispelled, to stage magnificence which exacts no forfeit from the personality portrayed. It is a steely personality which breaks before it bends, and in disaster it loses none of its essential virtues, its courage or its magnanimity.

Around this performance, Mr. Michel Saint-Denis has arranged a production which, though the handling of the Chorus wants flexibility, encompasses the tragedy with its proper dignity and emphasizes the salient lines of the narrative....

> *The Times*
> 19 October 1946

He who enacted Oedipus? I seem to remember a great cry, a swift flight, and a moving episode with some children of a compellingness to make me play with the notion of Mr. Olivier as Great Actor. But something has wiped cry and flight and pathos from my mind. Dame Sybil Thorndike's Jocasta? Mr. Curzon's Creon? Mr. Richardson's Tiresias? Mr. Malleson's Messenger? Mr. Relph's Herdsman? I seem to remember being moved. But by whom, and to what extent, and in what passages, has gone. I think I was tickled by John Piper's decor, and impressed by Mr. Anthony Hopkins's evocative dissonances. But, of the rest, nothing. Dr. Johnson held it to be 'a vain endeavour to cultivate barrenness or to paint vacuity'. Holding that it is equally vain for a critic to write out of an empty mind, I desist and withdraw.

James Agate: *Sunday Times*
21 October 1945

(James Agate disapproved of staging *The Critic* after *Oedipus*. '... these grotesqueries of juxtaposition are not to be tolerated.' He claimed that 'the Sheridan romp successfully dowsed whatever light I had seen the tragedy in.')

Before John Piper's decor, garishly sunset and focused on to a formidable idol, stood Chorus, a cluster of decent eld, forming and reforming themselves as Montague tells us William Poel arranged his chorus in *Samson Agonistes*. Into their midst strode Olivier, black fingercurls surmounting an arrogant, sensitive, built-up nose. Both literally and in Meredith's sense, you saw that he had a leg: it needed no effort of the mind to deduce that, if pricked, he would bleed purple gore, not blood. The thick, intolerant voice syncopated perfectly with the lithe, jungle movements of the man: intellectually and physically, he was equipped for the heaviest suffering: his shoulders could bear disaster. I know that from the first I was waiting for the time when the rack would move into the final notch, and the lyric cry would be released: but I never hoped for so vast an anguish. Olivier's famous 'Oh! Oh!' when the full catalogue of his sin is unfolded must still be resounding in some high recess of the

New Theatre's dome: some stick of wood must still, I feel, be throbbing from it.

Kenneth Tynan: *He That Plays The King*
(Longmans, 1950)

An Inspector Calls

J.B. Priestley
1 October 1946

Priestley's *An Inspector Calls* was first produced in Moscow in 1945, and when it was brought into the Old Vic's programme in 1946, some critics (J. C. Trewin among them) objected to its inclusion. It was variously considered to be a slight play, an over-polemical one and an unlikely fantasy; and it was asked what a new play was doing in any case in a classical repertory programme. *An Inspector Calls* is now accepted as a modern classic, to be set for school examinations; but it seems to me to be a 'period' play, in two senses of the word. It is, of course, set in Edwardian times; but Priestley's gentle moralising – about how the various members of a wealthy, powerful family all indirectly conspire to bring about the death of a poor girl – also recalls a period of innocent, optimistic socialism, before the Cold War set in and the trials which led to the downfall of the postwar Labour government.

The piece shoots its question-marks as the porcupine its quills. Early in the evening we might be sitting at a revival of some doctrinal play of the Manchester school (in the Gaiety's best mood). Presently we ask if the author can be speaking in symbols. Can the Birlings stand for that complacent world of 1912, tottering blindly to its fall? ... Is, then, this omniscient inspector Priestley's idea of the angel with the flaming sword? Who can tell? He comes in such a questionable shape. He may be an embodiment of Conscience or the representative of a Celestial Watch Committee or another version of

J.B. PRIESTLEY

the Examiner from *Outward Bound* – or simply (as he claims) an Inspector Goole. Have it your own way, says Mr. Priestley.

The play, not a long one, could have been stripped to half its length: though their offence is rank we feel that the Birlings are hardly worth this elaboration, this prolonged rattling of skeletons (and, indeed, this high place in the Old Vic's repertory). ...

J. C. Trewin: *Observer*
6 October 1946

Who is the Inspector? Something out of 'The Passing of the Third Floor Back'? Did the dead girl ever exist? The theatre hates indecision. Mr. Priestley, not making up his own mind, does not persuade ours. And Heaven help his chief actor (Mr. Ralph Richardson) for the author won't.

It is an indication of the play's lack of theatrical truth that its author was obliged to put it into an Edwardian scene and costume. Mr. Richardson, looking for something to act in a nebulous part, paraded like some dummy in the Tailoring section of a 'Britain used to make it' Exhibition. A pitiful sight for a fine actor.

And a pitiful play for a dramatist who can write such brilliant introductory scenes for Mr. Basil Dean to direct and for Mr. Alec Guinness and Miss Margaret Leighton to play.

Lionel Hale: *Daily Mail*
2 October 1946

The piece is magnificently played. By Mr. Julian Mitchell who gives the manufacturer a boisterous ebullience that never lets up. By Mr. Alec Guinness who makes of the tragic libertine something that is a long way from being wholly vile. By Mr. Ralph Richardson who gives the Inspector a stern, unangry poise far more effective than all the thunder he obviously has up his sleeve. (I found this performance intensely moving.) But the whole cast is excellent, and it is not until you leave the theatre that you ask yourself by what magic dullness has been kept away from this modern morality in which nobody does anything except talk.

James Agate: *Sunday Times*
6 October 1946

... surely it was wise of Mr. Priestley, standing as he does here in the stupendous context of Shakespeare and Sophocles, to keep this side of Jordan and give us a simple and straightforward example of the beautiful craftsmanship that, in hands like his, the contemporary dramatist can offer. And surely it was the critic, and not Mr. Priestley, who was being politically minded when he dissected the play in the brutal modern manner, by splitting it into Left and Right. ...

... the play holds up completely – indeed at the end of the second act the characters are tied so immovably into their strait-jackets that there seems nothing more to be done. Nevertheless in Act III the cords are unpicked one by one, only to be crushed together again in one suffocating grip by the best *coup de théâtre* of the year.

Stephen Potter: *New Statesman*
12 October 1946

The breaking-up of the Olivier/Richardson/Burrell directorship of the Old Vic caused a considerable amount of press comment and debate. It raised questions concerning the future of the Old Vic, the National Theatre and what was to be the relationship between the artists and the governing boards of subsidised theatres. Cyril Ray in *The Spectator* gave a clear account of the reasons for a change, as he saw them; while Basil Dean in *The New Statesman* put forward the view that the marriage between the Old Vic and the proposed National Theatre was doomed from the start. The correpondence in the *Daily Telegraph* between Stephen Mitchell and Lord Esher suggests the depths of feeling which the controversy aroused, unwelcome in a year when the National Theatre Bill was being debated and damaging to the prospects of the still embryonic Arts Council of Great Britain.

It will be half-a-dozen years or so before the wedding [between the Old Vic and the proposed National Theatre] can take place, but what matters now is how one of the contracting parties – the Old Vic company – faces its forthcoming responsibilities. This is the importance of last week's announcement that when the five year period of office of the present directors – Sir Laurence Olivier, Sir Ralph Richardson and Mr. John Burrell – expires in June, there will be a re-organisation; an administrator will be appointed for the whole complex of activities – Old Vic, Young Vic, the Theatre Centre, and School, and the Bristol Old Vic – and a new director to control the Old Vic Company itself. The change, according to the governors' announcement, was contemplated as long ago as last April and agreed to in July; it was a recognition by the Old Vic of its change of status from Britain's most distinguished repertory theatre to the National Theatre Company-to-be.

But most people will view it in the light of the failure of the Old Vic's current season – a failure so marked that the proposed visit to America by the company now playing at the New Theatre has been hurriedly called off. It is this failure that has exposed the Old Vic's current weaknesses. It is not enough to say that with Sir Laurence or Sir Ralph the Old Vic – in its temporary West End home – is famous and fashionable, and that without them it is a flop. As the governors have said, in announcing the proposed change, the work of the three retiring directors 'has added new lustre to the long and glorious tradition'. What has been wrong, and will have to be put right, is that this surface lustre hid, from most people, the fatal flaws in the structure underneath.

The Old Vic Company is a repertory company, and the lesson every such company must learn ... is that the strength of a repertory company is not in stars but its sense of general purpose and direction. Why has the Old Vic lost both fame and fortune this season? Faced with the fact that Sir Laurence was in Australia, Sir Ralph in Hollywood, it patched away at the holes left in the top when what was needed was vigorous work on strengthening the foundations. 'Names' had brought the theatre both profit and prestige; 'names' were imported to take their place. But Sir Cedric Hardwicke was miscast as Dr. Faustus, and Dame Edith Evans, as Lady Wishford, played Millamant off the stage. The one Old Vic director left in London, Mr. John Burrell, the producer, was overburdened, and his work betrayed it. It is noteworthy that the season's one relative success has been *The Cherry Orchard*, directed by Mr. Hugh Hunt of the Bristol company. ...

Next month will see Sir Laurence Olivier back at the New Theatre until June, along with Miss Vivien Leigh and an Old Vic Company fresh from Antipodean triumphs. Fame and fortune will smile again on the Old Vic, but the lesson has been learnt in his absence – that a great star should be an ornament to a national repertory company, but not the keystone of its arch.

Cyril Ray: *Spectator*
12 December 1948

... it is fruitless to suggest that, if such and such persons had been in charge, the Old Vic would not be in its present position, for who shall say they would not have made worse mistakes?

In its origin and upbringing, the Old Vic was essentially a community theatre, endowed by a remarkable personality with clear-cut ideals and precise economical ways of doing things; it held an honourable record in the service of these ideals. The accent was upon youth; and this was reflected not only in the quality of the performances, but also in the prices charged for the seats, and the salaries paid to the actors. On the other hand, the aims of the National Theatre Committee in those pre-war days were not less idealistic but decidedly less practical. They were inspired largely by the writings of Granville-Barker and by eager longings of enthusiasts who, gazing across the water at what had been accomplished in some of the capital cities of liberal Europe, desired to emulate those achievements at home. ... it is easy to see now the incompatibility that lay buried beneath the surface of this amalgam. And the emergence of two supremely good actors, both with screen reputations, and their ability to pack the New Theatre at all performances during the feverish conditions following the grand climacteric of the war only helped to confuse the picture and to delay the day of reckoning for those who sought to give the Old Vic the authority and status of a national theatre as it were overnight.

Basil Dean: *New Statesman*
1 January 1949

Sir, Peterborough's reference to the brighter prospects of the Old Vic winter season causes one to reflect with some anxiety, not for the first time, on the Old Vic's future and long-term policy. Sir Thomas Beecham's concern over the Arts Council's handling of the productions and affairs of Covent Garden by the Trustees is, in fact, paralleled by the handling of the Old Vic by its Governors.

Whatever may be the qualifications of those Trustees, there can be little doubt that the Governors of the Old Vic, with one or two exceptions, seem even less competent to run our most important theatrical enterprise. It is disturbing that people so little qualified should be so responsible for our highest artistic endeavours and be given so much of the taxpayers' money to play around with in an industry in which they have neither trained nor laboured. ...

Three years ago the Old Vic had reached a national position, due to the work of Sir Ralph Richardson and Sir Laurence Olivier. Accordingly, one would have supposed that the ardent co-operation and continuance of these two gentlemen as directors would have been a *sine qua non* of the Governors' policy.

It must accordingly cause some surprise that, at this vital moment in the life of the Old Vic, Sir Laurence Olivier who has just completed a great tour of Australia in which he did so much for British theatre there, and Sir Ralph Richardson, who absented himself from the Old Vic but for one season, have been summarily dropped – politely called resigning. In their places, and presumably to make up for them, have come £30,000 of public money and the bountiful and industrious secretary of the Arts Council. If Olivier and Richardson did wonders without that sum, what, it must surely occur to the theatre-goer, could they not have done with it?

(Letter to the *Daily Telegraph*, 18 January 1949, from Stephen Mitchell, Aldwych Theatre, WC2)

Sir, ... I do not propose to go fully into the many reasons which moved the governors of the Old Vic to make the recent changes which Mr. Mitchell condemns, but there is one point to which I must refer. If it were true, which it is not, that the new administrator of the Old Vic ever had control of the funds of the Arts Council, and could be bountiful to the extent of bringing with him £30,000 of public funds, £26,000 of that sum would be needed to cover the losses of the 1948 season.

It is possible that these losses, which follow upon losses made in the two previous seasons, may be diminished by the success of the Australia/New Zealand Old Vic Company during the next months, but not by more than a few hundred pounds. ...

Mr. Mitchell's general thesis shows that he shares with Sir Thomas Beecham a lamentable ignorance of how things are run in this country. The governors of the Old Vic, like the trustees of Covent Garden, are chosen of set purpose outside the profession. Indeed, the constitution of the Old Vic forbids the appointment as governor of anyone who derives profit from the theatre.

The English system of government has always been based on the principle that independent and intelligent minds, free from both profit and prejudice, should control public enterprise. But governors

so appointed never should, and indeed never do, interfere with
artistic direction. ...

(Letter to the *Daily Telegraph*, 24 January 1949, from Lord Esher,
Chairman, Old Vic Governors, London, WC2)

Love's Labours Lost

Shakespeare Memorial Theatre, Stratford
26 April 1946

While the Old Vic was at the height of its fame at the New Theatre,
Sir Barry Jackson was reviving the Shakespeare Memorial Theatre
seasons at Stratford-upon-Avon. Jackson was appointed Director in
1945, in his sixty-sixth year; and he was best known for his work in
establishing the Birmingham Repertory Theatre, which had become
the leading regional rep in the country. He also founded the Malvern
Festival in 1929; and he was a dedicated nurturer of young talent. In
1945, for example, he invited the twenty-year-old Peter Brook to
direct Shakespeare's *King John* (with the young Paul Scofield as the
Bastard); and following the success of this production, he asked
Brook to join him at Stratford. *Love's Labours Lost* began Brook's
long association with the Stratford company; and the reviews reflect
the mixture of delight, surprise and sometimes irritation which was
to accompany Brook's growing reputation during the 1950s and
1960s.

... a vaguely Watteauesque setting which would grace a de Musset
comedy graces equally well this play of Shakespeare's youth. The
revival is a feather in the festival's cap and something of a triumph
for Mr. Peter Brook, a producer who has not yet come of age. His
presentment of the play as a masque of youthful affectations shows a
remarkably complete grasp of its somewhat elusive values, and is,
from first to last, consistent with itself. He has given its movement on
the stage a puff-ball lightness, handled the shifting chiaroscuro with
delicate, imaginative expertness and once or twice succeeds in fading

out a scene in such a way that colour and grouping summarize and heighten its significance. ...

The Times
29 April 1946

Mr. Peter Brook is very young and very intelligent. Taking hold of this opportunity with both hands, he has very naturally produced the play to pieces. The fascination and poetry in this comedy can easily be buried if there are too many novelties. Too much is made of the various dressing-up episodes. Violent business does not make incomprehensible lines less boring. Above all, Mr. Brook should never have been allowed to play pantomime by dressing up Constable Dull to look like the funny policeman in *Old Mother Hubbard*, or by allowing his comics to make whimsy exits through the mouth of a telescope, or by allowing Costard to benumb us with modernisations of the text, altering 'he is o'erparted' into 'the part isn't right for him', and so on. The study of *Love's Labours Lost* brings this reward: that it helps us to see, budding beneath the damnable tortuosity of the cross-talk, the first fine gentle shoots of the true Shakespeare. If he had approached the play differently, Mr. Brook, who devises his curtains, his exits and his entrances like a master, could have fixed our attention not on the clowns, but on the poetry of Berowne and the magic of 'When Icicles hang by the wall'.

Stephen Potter: *New Statesman*
11 May 1946

A young, sage little person (in his middle twenties) established himself with this production amongst the new leaders of the English theatre, along with Peter Ustinov, Michael Benthall, and their like. The farce scenes came off badly: Costard was insensitively conceived and the pedants, who can be made hilariously funny, were caricatured out of life: I am sure Peter Brook's biggest gap is his lack of a wide sense of humour. But the rest was exquisite in the real sense of a freely traduced word. The play was set in Watteau costumes and groupings: the Princess was accompanied wherever she went by a mute, white-faced pierrot; and the whole stage had a wonderfully decadent *ancien régime* smell about it. The sudden change into the minor key at the end, when the tonic is replaced by a sudden diminished seventh on the entrance of Mercade with the news of the death of the Princess's father, came across as a superb dying fall, and left actors twilit, their laughter frozen on their lips. The master-performance was that of Paul Scofield as Don Armado. This was the first of Mr. Scofield's fine seasons at Stratford, and it followed a brilliant career at Birmingham Repertory Theatre. I do not think, at this stage, he had done better than Armado, which was played, not as a conventional blustering huffer-puffer, but as a fading grandee, tired and drooping, with a thin scurf of moustache curling down over his upper lip. He walked pensively, and a little rheumatically, tapping and describing slow circles with the head of a long swagger stick: Mr. Scofield, not yet twenty-five, suggested a most delicate senility, modulating the shrill honk of his usual juvenile voice to an urgent, breaking murmur. Only one flaw faulted the characterisation: it made the horseplay at the end, when Armado is baited by the rest of the court, seem unnecessary and unpleasant; even cruel.

Kenneth Tynan: *He That Plays The King*
(Longmans, 1950)

The Three Estates

Edinburgh International Festival: 24 August 1948
Assembly Hall of the Church of Scotland

The Edinburgh International Festival of Music and Drama was started in 1947; and quickly became established as the leading festival in Britain, to rank with other similar festivals abroad. The emphasis, from the beginning, was on music rather than drama; but its first seasons included visits from French companies, Jean-Louis Barrault's company among them, which influenced British theatre considerably. The event, however, which attracted most attention and proclaimed the Scottish flavour to the festival, was Tyrone Guthrie's production of Sir David Lindsay's sixteenth-century morality play, *Ane Satyre of the Thrie Estaits*, which was revived in 1949 and 1959 after its original production in 1948. Guthrie also took

the brave step of adapting the Assembly Hall of the Church of
Scotland, a large and apparently unwieldy debating chamber, for a
large open-stage production. His experiences there and his example
led eventually to the construction of an open-stage theatre at
Stratford, Ontario, which in turn was imitated at Chichester and
influenced the design of the Olivier Theatre at the National Theatre.

Scotland's own contribution to the drama of the Festival – a rough
and exceedingly lively 16th century satire on the Lords Spiritual, the
Lords Temporal and the Burgesses of the realm – is not perhaps for
export. It is a wine of the country, only to be rightly enjoyed in its
own place, on this occasion the Kirk Assembly Hall ...

Mr. Tyrone Guthrie makes a beautiful and exciting spectacle of the
old play. The stage projects itself into the midst of the audience and is
kept alive in part by the play's own natural vigour, but in part also
by the producer's adroit groupings. ...

The Times
26 August 1948

Tonight at the Assembly Hall here I have seen the most interesting as
well as the most appropriate dramatic performance yet staged at this
or the former festival. ...

W. A. Darlington: *Daily Telegraph*
25 August 1948

The Cocktail Party

Edinburgh International Festival: 22 August 1949
Lyceum Theatre

The Cocktail Party was T. S. Eliot's most successful attempt to
combine society drama with verse and religious allegory. Many
other writers of the period (Christopher Fry, Norman Nicholson and
Ronald Duncan among them) were attempting verse drama, usually
religious parables; but Eliot, disliking the blatantly poetical, adapted

a conventional theatre genre for his purpose. Eliot was the intellectual's dramatist, the one British writer whose name could be mentioned in the company of the French dramatists, Claudel, Sartre and Anouilh, whose works were becoming familiar to Edinburgh and London audiences. Unfortunately, society drama, with its social codes and conventions, was starting to sound old-fashioned even to British ears. Arthur Miller described the genre as 'hermetically sealed from life'. A new, raw and passionate theatre from the States was about to descend upon London, and shock it. After that invasion, society drama was increasingly thought to be pallid and somewhat precious. The intellectual triumph of *The Cocktail Party* was thus short-lived; but in its time, it represented the best of new British theatre writing. Its ambiguities irritated some critics, fascinated others; and its first production in Edinburgh with its fine cast offered a new high style which was hard to emulate. In subsequent years, the Edinburgh Festival, on its official level and latterly on the fringe, has had a good record in launching new plays. *The Cocktail Party* was the first major new play to be premiered at the festival.

In this brilliantly entertaining analysis of problems long since staled by conventional stage treatment, Mr. Eliot achieves a remarkable refinement of his dramatic style. His earlier plays have been successive moves towards simplicity; and now his thought, wholly undiluted, flows with certainty and a new sparkle of wit along present-day theatrical channels. The framework of ritual sat a little heavily on *Murder In The Cathedral*. Greek props gave an air of embarrassing artificiality to the narrative of *The Family Reunion*. These he has now dispensed with; and in lucid, unallusive verse which endows everyday speech with a delicate precision and a strictly occasional poetic intensity, he presents in the shape of a fashionable West End comedy a story highly ingenious in its construction, witty in its repartee and impregnated with Christian feeling.

The Times
23 August 1949

Several years ago Mr. T. S. Eliot wrote a successful play called *Murder In The Cathedral*. Were he a man of less delicate sensibilities, and of different convictions, he might have entitled his latest work, *Murder In The Consulting Room.*

It is certain that had Sir Henry Riley, in his Harley Street chambers, not placed before Celia Coplestone, as an alternative to a commonplace usefully happy life, the possibility of dedication to a high and perilous ideal, she would never have gone out into the wild places of the earth, and been crucified by fanatical natives, and devoured by ants. It is equally certain that when a doctor like Sir Henry, whose professional duty it is to know the character of those with whom he is dealing indicates a course of conduct that may lead to pain and death, he cannot acquit himself of responsibility for the consequences. And it is certain that Sir Henry had no desire to be acquitted of this responsibility.

It is fundamental to Mr. Eliot's purpose in this play that, had Sir Henry been able clearly to foresee the horror and the murder consequent on his advice, he would still, and with a clear conscience, not have altered that advice by one jot or tittle. For Mr. Eliot here, as in his drama about Becket, sees not murder but martyrdom.

It is important that this should be appreciated. Superficially, *The Cocktail Party*, with its lounge suite, its tinkling glasses, its gossip and its constant wit, is another of those trifling comedies about maladjusted people who solve their problems by unburdening themselves to a psychiatrist. ...

Harold Hobson: *Sunday Times*
28 August 1949

What was it all about? Well, there at a party is Alec Guinness as a Mystery Guest, who might be Devil or Saint and turns out to be a psychotherapist remarkable for taking no fees and keeping a Lady Sneerwell (Cathleen Nesbitt) as an eavesdropper in his anteroom. His business seems to be mending other people's marriages or lack of them. He tells a quarrelsome couple some stinging home truths, which apparently reconciles them, and sends a sad young woman to a death worse than fate in a way which struck me as purely sadistic. I have rarely disliked anybody so much as this icy healer of Mr. Eliot's: though he is a medico in mumbo-jumbo and incantations too, and is one of three self-elected 'Guardians' together with Sneerwell and a strangely unpleasant young man. If these be the forces of righteousness then 'evil be thou my good' was my reaction to the long vague sermon which commanded the distinguished

Alec guiness in [?]

services of Ursula Jeans, Robert Flemyng and Irene Worth, as well
as of Alec Guinness.

Ivor Brown: *Observer*
28 August 1949

The week after – as well as the morning after – I take it to be nothing but a finely acted piece of flapdoodle.

Alan Dent: *News Chronicle*
27 August 1949

A Streetcar Named Desire

Aldwych Theatre: 13 October 1949

A Streetcar Named Desire was Tennessee Williams's second play to reach London, the first being *The Glass Menagerie* in 1948. It created a minor sensation. Questions were asked about it in the Houses of Commons and Lords. Sir Laurence Olivier, surviving well his treatment at the hands of the Old Vic governors, and Vivien Leigh were surrounded by enthusiastic crowds on the first night. The press revealed a sharp division between those who regarded the play as lavatorial and indecent, and those who saluted it as frank and poetic. American drama, apart from musicals and plays by Arthur Miller, had long been regarded in Britain as brash and somewhat vulgar. But *A Streetcar Named Desire* could not be so easily dismissed, though some critics tried. With the new American drama, came the challenge of a new acting style, the Method, associated with Lee Strasberg and Elia Kazan at the Actors Studio in New York, founded in 1947. Olivier's production, though similar to the New York version, was not orientated towards the Method, and it revealed the adaptability of British acting techniques. Nevertheless, British actors, associated with a certain poise and well-bred behaviour, had to learn how to let themselves go, in order to cope with the emotional demands of Williams, the least reticent and restrained of dramatists. The production was expensive – Olivier calculated that it cost £10,000 which would then require 51 week of full houses to recoup – and the management turned itself into a non-profit-distributing registered charity in order to avoid paying Entertainments Tax. It was classified as a 'partly educational' play. This definition was challenged at the time, and eventually the old distinction between 'educational' theatre (exempt from certain taxes) and non-educational ones (which were not) was dropped.

FIRST NIGHTERS RUSH THEATRE DOORS (Headline in *Daily Express*)
A crowd of 100 people rushed the gallery doors at the Aldwych Theatre last night before the curtain went up on the London

premiere of the American stage hit, *A Streetcar Named Desire*. The police took over, turned about 70 out.

After the show 500 people waited nearly an hour for the star, Vivien Leigh, and her husband, Sir Laurence Olivier.

When they came out at last, there were cheers, and shouts of 'Well done, Viv' and 'Good old Larry'. Autograph hunters tapped the window of the car, but the two refused to sign. Said 51-year-old stage doorkeeper, Chick Garoghan: 'I've never known a night like it'.

Staff reporter: *Daily Express*
13 October 1949

All that an eager audience can gather from the first act is that the preposterous lady of leisure has been a loose woman. In the second act ... Mr. Williams develops the favourite illusion of nearly all dramatists: that hardened prostitutes are capable of a touching sentimental gesture. It is the third act – good strong 'theatre' – which comes nearest to justifying the extreme readiness of the audience to be pleased by this famous American play.

The Times
13 October 1949

The scene of Tennessee Williams's play is a sweaty New Orleans tenement; the heroine is a rabidly sexual woman of good but decayed family, who is raped by her brutal brother-in-law into madness; and at one point the curtain is lowered to permit her to be sick. Sir Laurence Olivier, as producer, however, has spared us the details of physical disgust, sometimes at the expense of credibility: the clothes, and especially the shirts, worn by the men in the play – the dregs of the 'white trash' of the South – are unbelievably clean. These poker players and workmen don't look, they only talk, like cesspools.

But Miss Vivien Leigh, more fatiguedly beautiful than ever, mitigates nothing of the horror and the evil terror of Blanche Dubois's moral and physical collapse. When she first enters, driven out of her home town by the scandal of her personal reputation, Miss Leigh's Blanche, wandering into her sister Stella's filthy home, may be thought already too restless, too distracted. That, however, is only because one is not expecting the overwhelming power of her final scene, when she loses her fragile hold on reason, and frantic fear gives way to a trust, even more frightening, in the asylum attendants

37

who lead her off the stage. This is an impressive performance, casting out pity with terror.

Harold Hobson: *Sunday Times*
16 October 1949

A Streetcar Named Desire (most cunning title) comes to us as a play, now on the crest of fashion on Broadway, that seeks follow-my-leader applause in the West End. Few dramas have had a bigger Puff Preliminary in recent years than this by an American dramatist, Tennessee Williams. Yet, at the Aldwych, when the night's tumult and shouting – much of it for Vivien Leigh – had died, at least one playgoer emerged puzzled by the reputation of a tedious and squalid anecdote. Blanche du Bois from a lost Southern mansion is a nymphomaniac in decline. Driven from one small town, she seeks refuge in a New Orleans slum tenement where her sister lives in surprising harmony with a primitive husky, who knocks his wife about when drunk and hugs her when he is sober. After two hours of tedium, the play crackles into a burst of violence. Now and then good writing glimmers, but little to explain the Broadway reputation and run.

J. C. Trewin: *Observer*
16 October 1949

Westminster's 60-minute quiz ended yesterday with *A Streetcar Named Desire* buffeting along its stormiest Parliamentary run to date. And MPs' main desire was to find out why the Streetcar was exempted from Entertainments Tax.

For the fourth time in three weeks, the Treasury was told that the exemption was unfair. But once again demands for a full enquiry were refused.

It was Financial Secretary Glenvil Hall's turn to face all-party criticism yesterday. He trotted out the government's familiar theme song: 'The company is non-profit-making ... partly educational, partly cultural.'

But even he had to laugh when Mr. A. Marlowe (Con. Brighton) added a line to his lyrics: 'The play is only educational to those who are ignorant of the facts of life.'

Parliamentary correspondent: *Daily Mail*
9 December 1949

Guys and Dolls

Coliseum Theatre: 28 May 1953

Despite the Method, and the plays of Miller and Tennessee Williams, the genre of American theatre which attracted the widest publicity and greatest popular support, was that of the musicals. Critics sometimes looked down on them; but in the late 1940s and 1950s, they were the great attractions of the West End. The songs, the spectacles, the well-drilled dance routines, the liveliness of the lyrics and the mixture of daring and politeness could not be matched by British musicals; and when I first started to go to the theatre regularly, in the early 1950s, an evening at an American musical was usually one of sheer delight, not unmixed with a sense of guilty awareness that I went to see Shakespeare or Eliot at the Old Vic in a spirit of dutiful respect. The great parade of American musicals in post-war years began with *Oklahoma* and *Annie Get Your Gun* in 1947, continued with such works as *Pal Joey*, *Kiss Me Kate* and *Call Me Madam* and, in 1952, London at last saw *Porgy and Bess*, Gershwin's folk opera which he wrote in 1935. But the musical which gave me the most intense pleasure, leaving so strong an impression that, years later, I could remember the words of the songs and the detailed staging of most scenes, was *Guys and Dolls*, with words and music by Frank Loesser, and a story based upon one by Damon Runyon. The language was as rich as the music, and a gift for Kenneth Tynan, who loved imitating and playing with words. I reproduce his *Evening Standard* review in its entirety, marvelling at his spontaneity of response and critical zest.

Guys and Dolls at which I am privileged to take a peek last evening, is a 100 percent American musical caper, cooked up out of a story called *The Idyll of Sarah Brown* by the late Damon Runyon, who is such a scribe as delights to give the English language a nice kick in the pants.

This particular fable takes place in and around Times Square in New York City, where many citizens do nothing but roll dice all night long, which is held by one and all, and especially the gendarmes, to be a great vice.

Among the parties hopping around in this neighbourhood is a guy by the name of Nathan Detroit, who operates a floating crap game, and Miss Adelaide, his ever-loving pretty, who is sored up at this Nathan because after 14 years engagement, they are still nothing but engaged.

Anyway, being short of ready scratch or dibs, Nathan lays a bet with a large gambler called Sky Masterson, the subject of the wager being whether The Sky can talk a certain Salvation Army doll into joining him on a trip to Havana.

Naturally, Nathan figures that a nice doll such as this will die sooner, but by and by she and The Sky get to looking back and forth at each other, and before you know it, she is his sweet-pea.

What happens next but The Sky gets bopped with religion and shoots crap with Nathan and the boys for their immortal souls. And where do the sinners wind up, with their chalk-striped suits and busted noses but at a prayer meeting in the doll's mission house, which hands me a very big laugh indeed. The actors who nab the jobs of playing these apes have me all tuckered out with clapping them.

Nathan Detroit is Sam Levene, who expostulates very good with his arms, which are as long as a monkey's. Stubby Kaye, who plays Nicely-Nicely Johnson, the well-known horse-player, is built on lines which are by no means dinky, for his poundage maybe runs into zillions, but he gives with a voice which is as couth as a choir-boy's or maybe couther.

He commences the evening by joining in a three-part comedy song about the nags. In fact it is a fugue, and I will give you plenty of eleven to five that it is the first fugue many patrons of the Coliseum ever hear.

Miss Vivien Blaine (Miss Adelaide) is a very choice blonde judy and she gets to sing a song which goes as follows: 'Take back your mink from whence it came' and which hits me slap-dab in the ear as being supernaturally funny. Myself, I prefer her to Miss Lizbeth Webb, who plays the mission doll, but naturally I do not mention such an idea out loud.

The Coliseum is no rabbit hutch, and maybe a show as quick and smart as this *Guys and Dolls* will go better in a medium-sized theatre as the Cambridge Theatre. Personally, I found myself laughing ha-ha last night more often than any guy in the critical dodge has any right to.

And I am ready to up and drop on my knees before Frank Loesser, who writes the music and lyrics. In fact, this Loesser is maybe the best light composer in the world. In fact, the chances are that *Guys and Dolls* is not only a young masterpiece, but the *Beggars Opera* of Broadway.

Kenneth Tynan: *Evening Standard*
29 May 1953

In the first and longer part of *Guys and Dolls* a trivial story prolongs itself interminably. I've hardly known anything in the theatre so wearisome as the dragged-out sequence of scenes which are required for the handsome gambler to get the pretty mission-lass tight, on doctored milk shake, nor anything so unrewarding. One reaches the interval, up to which this leads, bludgeoned with boredom. The second part is altogether more rewarding. What we had been expecting at last begins to arrive – the recreation of Damon Runyon's fabulous world peopled by prodigious characters who call themselves, Harry the Horse, Rusty Charlie, Angie the Ox, Liverlips Louie or Nicely Nicely Johnson. The magic touch of looney fantasy at last takes hold and finds its echo in the songs and dances, the Crap Game Ballet, Luck be a Lady, Sue Me, Sit Down You're Rocking the Boat. So it turns out not to be – as it looked like being in the first ninety minutes – a total loss. But it comes all too near, and what remains difficult to understand is the wild enthusiasm not only of Broadway, and of even its soberer critics, but of solid Englishmen who have seen it there too.

T. C. Worsley: *New Statesman*
6 June 1953

Guys and Dolls ... cannot indefinitely be avoided: and perhaps the moment for facing it has come. The root of the difficulty about this piece is that it has a vitality, a force, that would invigorate a hundred English musicals and yet leave enough energy over to drive an express from Paris to Madrid; it has a score by Frank Loesser of originality and verve; it has dances of swirling and controlled demonism; it is played by a company, many of whose members are American, who, in their crudity, naïvety and barbarism, resembling that of likeable morons, won their way into many hearts including my own; it has two excellent songs, 'Take Back Your Mink' and 'You're Rocking The Boat'; and it gave great pleasure to several judicious observers. Yet at the end of the evening, there was determined booing from the gallery, and in all parts of the house, the reception seemed to me the coolest given to any American musical since the disastrous failure of *Finian's Rainbow*.

Guys and Dolls may well recover from its unhappy start. It is, as I have said, full of incisive talent and ingratiating people. The aim of art is to produce desirable states of mind, and the state of mind from which *Guys and Dolls* proceeds can, if it is typical of America, cause only disquiet. Is America really peopled with brutalised half-wits, as this picturisation of Damon Runyon's stories implies? Is it really witty to bring a Salvation Army girl to the edge of fornication by the not very original trick of putting intoxicants into her milk shake? Is it clever to quote words of Jesus in the melancholy hope of raising a laugh? Let me make it clear that I am not protesting against either irreverence or impropriety as such. I only ask that they should attain a certain level of intelligence. I see no reason why religion should not be attacked or even traduced in the theatre. It is, I am sure, quite strong enough to defend itself. But let the attack have some rational intellectual basis. Otherwise it becomes a bore. That, alas, is what *Guys and Dolls* is, despite its numerous striking, incidental merits; an interminable, an overwhelming, and in the end intolerable bore.

Harold Hobson: *Sunday Times*
31 May 1953

William Archer, writing in 1882, felt obliged to say a word or so about the language of the theatre. He was worried by 'the vulgarity which seems to me such a prominent characteristic of the modern English drama'. Thus: 'The use of the word, "fellow", jars upon my ears so much that I unhesitatingly call it vulgar'. ...

I had been reading Archer on the day before hearing *Guys and Dolls* at the Coliseum. What the critic of 1882 would have felt about this piece I cannot begin to imagine: maybe it would have had to be inscribed (in the most genteel fashion) upon asbestos. First, he would have deemed the title incomprehensible; and he would hardly have dared to consider such a phrase as 'If a guy enters a restaurant, it looks nice if he has a doll behind him ...'

A new generation of playgoers is used to the line of fizzing American 'musicals'. It has been speaking the American language for years. It is versed in its Runyon. The use of the word 'fellow' would not jar upon its ears ...

This has taken time to reach the point, which is simply that *Guys and Dolls* shouting at us brassily, is a cheerful entertainment for anyone with a useful smattering of American, who is not bemused by the odd Runyon idiom, a kind of prim slang.

J. C. Trewin: *Illustrated London News*
20 June 1953

... the show remains fascinating in its exoticism, in its originality and in its verve. It is fascinating also in the success with which it keeps going through a really coherent story a recognizable reflection of the amused tenderness of Runyon's treatment of the seedy but vital creatures whose main purpose is to elude the police and start shooting crap. The charm of its satire is that it reduces the satirized to the harmless proportions of men and women fated in the end to succumb to respectability.

Some have questioned the propriety of a story which turns on a gambler taking a bet that he will carry off a pretty evangelist on a flying trip to Havana.

But the theme, whatever its passing dangers, moves to a highly moral end. The gambler finds himself beating the drum in the mission band. The most hopeless case among the bad guys is at last led away, the matrimonial captive of the lady who laments that for fourteen years she has been notorious as 'Adelaide the well-known fiancée'.

Anthony Cookman: *Tatler*
June 1953

Oyez! Oyez! The impossible has happened. The musical comedy that is a comedy with music has at last appeared. Some of us would even go so far as to say it is the best musical comedy we ever saw, but that is an expression of rapture, not criticism. The fact is that criticism may be for once what it would always prefer to be, a mere delighted appreciation. ...

To a plot that really holds together, the adaptors have added not only dialogue with the authentic Runyon raciness but songs the words of which are often unmistakably witty. Miss Vivien Blaine, for instance, who heads the 'doll' population, with their absurd tripping gait and their strong disposition towards domesticity of the conventional sort, has a song that purports to be extracts from a popular book on psychology and must be the cleverest thing of its kind since Mr. Cole Porter wrote 'The Physician'. But this is only one of a dozen, clever and catchy songs given to Miss Blaine, to Miss Lizbeth Webb, who is charmingly ridiculous as the evangelist who takes temporarily but only too well, to the wilder ways of Havana, to Mr. Jerry Wayne, as the gambler who shyly confeses to her that his real name is Obadiah – there is a touch of true sentiment for you – and to others of the strange personages, as well as to a first-rate chorus.

The piece is notable too, for the wit and pace of the dances, the elegance and inventiveness of the costumes, and the sheer fun of it all, from the bad men who gamble away their souls and are sheepishly marched away to the evangelist meeting, to the two women mentally resolving to make over their men, complete with inset visions of the future. *Pace* those who signified their disapproval in the usual way, it was a wonderful evening.

The Times
29 May 1953

Hamlet

Old Vic Company: Edinburgh International Festival: 24 August 1953
Old Vic Theatre: 14 September 1953

In 1953 the National Theatre project was no nearer fruition than in 1949; while the standards of the Old Vic company had been alarmingly erratic. After a time, the National Theatre enthusiasm had dwindled, despite the peripatetic foundation stone, laid, in what proved to be the wrong place, in 1951, during the Festival of Britain. In 1953 steps were taken to stabilise the Old Vic and to give it a stronger sense of purpose. Michael Benthall was appointed artistic director and he set himself a five-year programme to produce the 36 Shakespeare plays in the first folio. He immediately demonstrated his worth by directing a fine *Hamlet*, which was first seen under somewhat difficult conditions at the Assembly Hall in Edinburgh, then at the Old Vic and finally on tour, to Elsinore in Denmark. *Hamlet*, perhaps for symbolic reasons, is often used for inaugural productions. This one had Richard Burton in his first major classic role, although he had previously attracted attention at the Shakespeare Memorial Theatre, Stratford. The cast is studded with names: John Neville, Claire Bloom, Fay Compton, Robert Hardy, Laurence Hardy, Michael Hordern and William Squire. Benthall obviously knew how to pick good casts, the first hallmark of a director. His productions were straight-forward and vigorous, although they were sometimes considered to be unpoetic, lacking the attention to verse-speaking which characterised, say, Gielgud's Hamlet. They did, however, avoid the elocutionary sing-song which marred inferior imitators of the Gielgud style. These qualities stood him in good stead over the ensuing years, when the Old Vic's lack of money forced Benthall to take a heavy burden of work upon himself. The Shakespeare Memorial Theatre was better endowed and its productions during the mid-1950s displayed flair and inventiveness, which the Old Vic had difficulty in matching. But under Benthall, the Old Vic regained its reputation for good, reliable and highly theatrical productions, which attracted school and family audiences.

At the Assembly Hall, Edinburgh International Festival

The Assembly Hall offers the producer a platform stage surrounded on three sides by spectators. He is accordingly free to attempt something like an Elizabethan intimacy of playing. Mr. Michael Benthall takes up the challenge with likeable boldness. He is not deterred by the basely practical consideration that in a comparatively short while all his careful arrangements will have to be drastically altered to suit the requirements of the Old Vic's London stage. Nor is he deterred by the thought that the play to be exposed in these familiar conditions is *Hamlet*. He sets out to show Festival audiences just how much – and just how little – there is to be said for seeing this tragedy in the round; and the result is a most interesting evening.

Mr. Benthall plays the game fairly, dispensing with scenery, hanging the fourth side of the hall with looped curtains and a few scattered heraldic shields and trusting simply to a broad flight of stairs for his main entrance to the stage ... The play is projected as it were, into our midst, and we reflect that *Hamlet* abounds in 'incidents amounting to events' – ghosts walking, court

Hamlet (Old Vic)

entertainments, assassinations, insurrections, suicides, funeral pageants, sights, alarums and excursions, in short, a bustling, rapid, vivid action full of a certain kind of spectacular appeal. ...

The Times
25 August 1953

... the dramatic side of this year's Edinburgh Festival was inaugurated by a performance that I should like to describe prophetically as Richard Burton's first Hamlet. This well-graced and most promising young actor gave us a Hamlet full of fire and passion and instinct with intelligence, yet not fully moving. I attribute this failure in one at least of his audience to the speed with which the verse is delivered; and this, of course, may have been the doing of Michael Benthall, the director, rather than of Mr. Burton himself.

Time and again the great poetical passages were taken at a pace which prevented any emphasis from being laid on their musical quality, until it seemed as though the actor was deliberately playing down the well-known passages for fear they should sound like quotations.

The result was an exciting performance of freshness and vigour, but not one which made any attempt at greatness.

W. A. Darlington: *Daily Telegraph*
25 August 1953

Mr Benthall allowed his players to enter, as it were, by every gate and alley. They coursed (though not noticeably like quicksilver). If you sat at the end of a row, courtiers might brush past you, or Ophelia would dart out in her madness, or you would turn to find their Majesties of Denmark coming down behind the bier. There were moments too of dire peril. A distinguished drama critic beside me was all but impaled on a sword. As he observed, with some philosophy: 'I can begin by saying, "Last night I sat transfixed." '

J. C. Trewin: *Illustrated London News*
5 September 1953

At the Old Vic

The Old Vic has made a wonderfully good start with the opening plays of its repertory. And I am glad that I left myself a large loophole in my account of *Hamlet* when it was done at the Assembly Hall, Edinburgh. As I surmised there, the production comes into its own only now that we see it in the comparative intimacy of a proper theatre. But I admit that I had not expected Mr. Richard Burton's performance would transmute itself from a valiant attempt into a sure achievement. But it does. It may be argued that his interpretation is lacking in subtlety and even variety. But all other considerations are secondary, when passion and power combine to carry us out of ourselves into the living and suffering centre of poetic tragedy. Mr. Burton does this for us. We can hardly ask for more.

Two other performances 'come up' admirably. Miss Fay Compton's Queen now ranks for me among the very best. The closet scene has always struck me as excessively difficult for the actress, since it is so very largely a matter of 'backing up'. Miss Compton was supremely convincing in this, and in her report of Ophelia's drowning immensely moving. Then Mr. Michael Hordern's Polonius (so much of which was thrown away at Edinburgh) scales down here to a completely convincing portrait – freshly observed in its mannerisms and tricks of voice and amusing in a new way. Altogether this is a *Hamlet* of which the Old Vic may be justly proud.

T. C. Worsley: New Statesman
26 September 1952

Burton is a Rugger-playing Hamlet – an uncomplicated prince determined to revenge the murder of his father. He plays the part with dash, attack, and verve, not pausing to worry about psychology.

In a disjointed and often rowdy production (at times it was so noisy I thought it was going into competition with the rush-hour of the railway station over the road) Burton stands out.

The quality of his acting is matched by a delightful, prating Polonius, played by Michael Hordern. And Claire Bloom provides a most wistful, moving Ophelia.

But Fay Compton as the queen disappointed me. She appeared so drab that I thought her Queen Gertrude had come from a hard day's washing.

The Old Vic makes *Hamlet* brisk, lively drama. *Hamlet* for beginners almost. And Burton, who was once described by Jean Simmons as 'a curious cross between Groucho Marx and John

Hamlet (Old Vic)

Barrymore' adds a new dimension as an important Shakespearian actor.

David Lewin: Daily Express
15 September 1953

At Elsinore

I expected a dark, nightmare scene. Because this is the very spot where, said Shakespeare, the real history-book Prince Hamlet grimly plotted to kill the wretch who murdered his father.

Instead it is all as pretty as a fairy tale. On the sea outside, yachts bob as in a regatta. To add chic, the Kings and Queens of Denmark and Sweden are in the front row.

A trumpet blares and on to the stage struts Richard Burton as Hamlet. But he only looks like a film star with the sulks.

John Barber: Daily Express
19 June 1954

Shakespeare (why deny the possibility?) may have visited Elsinore with a troupe of actors. It was then that he would have heard of the story of Amleth, the pre-Viking Prince of Jutland, and picked up his local colour. The pity is that Shakespeare could hardly have been writing of the castle from memory nor have known its broad moat as we see it today in its 'lilac and syringa hood', for this Kronberg was built at about the time when he was busy immortalising the situation. But this awkward fact is handsomely offset in the mind of truly sympathetic pilgrims by the existence of Hamlet's garden and Hamlet's tomb. We ask to be deceived, and so richly have the Danish authorities played up to our romantic needs that almost we are deceived. And after all it is a valuable deception which thus enables peoples of two friendly nations to take a common pride in the most fascinating of tragic heroes.

The reality at the heart of this pleasant make-believe is the play itself; and this comes to the Danish audience in a performance which has been on the English stage long enough to ripen.

On the platform stage at Edinburgh, Mr. Richard Burton appeared to have selected from Hamlet's character all the most unsympathetic traits which he could find. His playing had power, but it was curiously without charm. He has since come by a charm which sits extremely well on youthful melancholy; and in gaining charm, the performance has lost none of its original power. The Danes, we hope, may regard the portrait as worthy to stand on the lines with those of Sir Laurence Olivier, Sir John Gielgud and Mr. Michael Redgrave, Mr. Burton's forerunners at Elsinore.

The Times
19 June 1954

Marching Song

St Martin's Theatre: 8 April 1954

Exciting, or even interesting, new plays during the early 1950s often seemed few and far between. The Editor of the *Stage Year Book* regretted that there were no particularly rewarding new plays for the Festival of Britain. There were many enjoyable farces and light comedies, a few poetic dramas and a worthy tradition (upheld particularly by Terence Rattigan) of middle-brow, middle-class domestic plays, the post-war equivalent of society drama. There were many competent playwrights. What was lacking was the kind of excitement which comes when good dramatists write with eloquence and conviction about matters which are of central importance. The theatre seemed irrelevant to the struggles of the day, without the power to disturb, persuade or assist their audiences to change their minds. *An Inspector Calls* and *The Cocktail Party* were, in their different ways, confident plays: Priestley and Eliot may have held opposite convictions, but they had no doubt as to the value of their views in the post-war world. But it was hard, during the early 1950s, to summon up similar coherent moral and political outlooks. The Cold War and the threat of nuclear warfare hung over us; and Britain was in the process of trying to disentangle herself from the colonial past and its empire. The collapse of the post-war Labour government, with its buoyant visions of the future, and the continuing economic crises caused a growing disillusion; and the better plays of the period were more content to ask questions than to answer them. In 1954, two years before the so-called revival of British theatre with the playwrights at the Royal Court, two plays were produced which revealed a serious determination to discuss the nagging questions of their time, *Marching Song* and *The Prisoner*. *Marching Song* is not necessarily John Whiting's best play – many would advance the claims of *Saint's Day* or *The Devils* instead – but it confronted audiences with several paradoxes. The hero was a war criminal, sustained in imprisonment by the sound of bawdy, country songs. His country is a defeated one, which needs a scapegoat for past failures. He is released to stand trial – which would be an act of expiation for the country; but the Chancellor invites him to commit suicide instead. Whiting was thus asking the audiences of a victorious country to appreciate the dilemmas of defeated ones; and he also raised the question that honourable men in war commit atrocities of which barbarians would be ashamed, thus anticipating Hochhuth's *Soldiers* which caused a stir in the 1960s.

With his new play, Mr. John Whiting confounds those of us who were too dense to recognise his talent in the famous Arts Theatre prize play, *Saint's Day*. The talent in *Marching Song* is indubitable and impressive. Whether or not we find the play sufficiently satisfying as a whole, we cannot help being aware of an original mind working with considerable originality of means. The original is always disconcerting, and in all branches of art has to create its own audience, partly by familiarising people with its idiom, partly by clarifying its own manner of communication. This may be a long business, and Mr. Whiting is only at the start of it.

There are two particularly disconcerting elements in *Marching Song*. First, the dialogue, which is exciting and taut, is also elliptical. A character will often respond not to what is said, but to what is implied, leaving the audience to jump the gap. This, of course, makes great demands on our concentration, at least before we have got the trick of it. Then, secondly, we are never absolutely certain on what plane the events developed are meant to be taken – or rather we have the uneasy feeling that a great deal more is going on than meets the eye or the ear. Of course this is true of any work of art of any complexity, but where the artist has been wholly successful, the duality doesn't worry us; we accept the more obvious meaning, and the overtones sing above and below it, deepening and opening out

JOHN
WHITING

the theme. In *Marching Song*, it is more as if we are looking through ill-adjusted binoculars and are seeing simultaneously two separate images neither of which is quite in focus. It may be that it is our sight that is weak, but it is the business of the artist to correct our vision.

The surface meaning of *Marching Song* anyhow offers no great difficulties. We are in the house of a rich woman, in the hills above a capital city. For nine years, Catherine de Troyes has been waiting for the return of her lover, a brilliant young general who failed at a decisive battle of the war, and has been in prison since. Meanwhile she has comforted herself in the vacuum with a set of hangers-on, a priest, a doctor and an American expatriate, a failure of a film producer who is no longer capable of making films but whom she enables by her money supply to prolong the fantasy that one day he will. On the day the play opens he has brought back to the house a girl he has picked up in a bar, ostensibly to use her in his picture. She is a totally detached young person, a sort of stray, clinging defiantly to her freedom and terrified of any involvement. Upstairs the general is sleeping on his first day of freedom, and Catherine comes down to dismiss her followers. She no longer needs them now *he* is back; the supply of money is to be cut off. But before they can go, there arrives from the city the Chancellor of the State, here to explain to the General why he has been suddenly released. The Opposition have demanded that he should be put on trial, and he, the Chancellor, is no longer able to resist the demand, although, more clear-headed than they, he sees that such a trial would be disastrous. The dirty linen of the State would be washed in public and all that he had done since the war to build up the reputation would be lost. So he brings with him a charming chased silver box, a solution for his dilemma – a quick and effective poison for the General to swallow. (The scene in which this present is handed over is quite admirably written.) The general is given 36 hours in which to dispose of himself, and then within the house and between the different kinds of people a drama of indecision is played out. The general after years of imprisonment is no longer in love with Catherine. His disposition – for we are dealing with dispositions more than with people – is the opposite of hers. She, like her protégé, the film producer, is a romantic, clinging to the past. He, realist and ruthlessly truthful, is, like the little stray urchin girl, a dealer only with the present. The mistake of his life – the mistake for which he paid with imprisonment – was to be trapped in a past moment, a moment from which he has not been able to break out since; it was an incident in the war which involved the murder of children, a sort of massacre of the innocents. His kinship now is with the untrapped girl, and this deflects him from the course the Chancellor persuaded him into, and ... the rest of the play is given to resolving the conflict on the basis of their different attitudes to freedom and personal dependence.

Mr. Whiting is not equally successful with all his people. The film producer and the Chancellor, both viewed only from the outside, are highly successful and such excellent actors as Mr. Hartley Power and Mr. Ernest Thesiger are easily able to give them a vivid life. Of the other three, the girl seems to me to come off best; here is a 'truly modern' character, who has made herself hard and ruthless, with a terror of chains of any kind, which is only cover for a terror of love. Miss Penelope Munday with her strange low voice and her suspicious self-possession caught her exactly. Miss Diana Wynyard brought all her skill to the job of making Catherine interesting, and if she was not entirely successful, it was not entirely her fault. Least successful as a character was the General with the atrophied powers of decision; he seemed to me to remain obstinately a conception rather than fully felt and realised. Mr. Robert Flemyng gave him a convincing mixture of hardness and self-condemnation; but his tricks of delivery make inevitably for a certain monotony. Indeed there seems to me in the writing to be much more variety than the actors found there; and this is my one quarrel with the very intelligent and sensitive production by Mr. Frith Banbury.

T. C. Worsley: *New Statesman*
17 April 1954

The general dies at dawn in John Whiting's new play – but, oh, the talk that goes on through the night before the death.

Talk about hope, talk about defeat, talk about love – and just talk.

David Lewin: *Daily Express*
9 April 1954

Its main feeling, that there is nothing in life to encourage us to keep a firm grip on it, comes out of Anouilh and the mood of the German films after the first world war. Mr. Whiting's Central European General, offered the choice, after his country's overthrow in battle of a disgraceful trial or of suicide, working out his resolution amidst the dark rectangles and twisted staircases of his mistress's rich and uncomfortable home, finding a momentary attraction in life through the magnetism of a disillusioned young slut, discovering that the song in a strange language which had upheld his spirit in years in prison had only been a tissue of obscenities, belongs to the psychology of a defeated nation.

He has a troubled and uneasy poetry whose shadowy tides never wash against the shores of our own land of cricket bats and football pools, of bells in the old school chapel, and the Welfare State. This, perhaps, is only another way of saying that the play extends the boundaries of English drama.

It has at least three outstanding scenes. The first is when Mr. Ernest Thesiger's old, anxious and thrusting Chancellor breaks to the General his mortal proposition; the second when the General recalls the crucial incident in which he lost the battle (Mr. Robert Flemyng tells this dreadful story of children murdered in the sunlight with a fine, cold, self-accusing and controlled fury); and the third is the General's discovery that the song he had judged to be an act of faith is just lechery. The first is a carefully sprung dramatic surprise, the second a set piece of rhetoric such as is rare in the modern London theatre; and the third is a slighter thing altogether, something marked only by Mr. Flemyng's sudden start; but it is a remarkable moment all the same.

Harold Hobson: *Sunday Times*
11 April 1954

The scene of John Whiting's *Marching Song* is 'a room of Catherine de Troyes's house' high over a European capital. This is a very odd place, with a huge mast up the middle. It seems to be a cross between a liner and one of those modern department stores that are a glazier's benefit. Yet, with all its modernism, it has no lift, only troublesome stairs. You feel at once that the whole place, with those gigantic windows and those stairs, is deeply symbolic – but of what? Miss de Troyes herself (Diana Wynyard) has an air of Britannia as she walks the top deck, but the lady is patently symbolic of something more elusive. There comes back to her an old lover, a tough general called Forster, first imprisoned by his nation's victorious enemy and now to be sacrificed to the new and free democracy as a war-blunderer. One gathers that his mistake was to be scrupulous; during an attack he butchered some children and then stopped to think about it and failed to press the attack home. Is Mr. Whiting emphasising the old and sage remark of Jonathan Wilde that many men fail in wickedness for want of going deeply enough in? And what exactly is the significance of the title, *Marching Song*? *Funeral March* would seem more accurate.

Ivor Brown: *Observer*
11 April 1954

The Prisoner

Globe Theatre: 14 April 1954

There were few critical doubts about Bridget Boland's *The Prisoner*, when it appeared, a week after *Marching Song*. Its subject was familiar through Arthur Koestler's novel *Darkness At Noon*, which may have influenced Boland's play; and also through the fate of Cardinal Mindszenty, the Hungarian prelate, who like the Cardinal in the play was forced to confess. The subject was brainwashing, using not torture but the techniques of psychoanalysis; and it expressed the current fears of totalitarian regimes, mainly communist, although Arthur Miller's *The Crucible* (partly directed against the McCarthyite witch-hunts against communists in America) received its first British production at Bristol in the same year.

It was a night such as a theatre-lover lives for. Alec Guinness gives the performance of the year in a play worthy of his remarkable art.

He is a Cardinal, thrown into prison in an Iron Curtain country and slowly 'persuaded' to recant in public. He is a national monument whom the State needs to deface.

The Cardinal rots in his cell. They starve him. They will not let him sleep. His visitors – a barber, a doctor – never speak.

He is tortured in the subtlest ways, until he begs to see his Inquisitor again.

With cunning, this man wins his friendship. In time, they sound like two sides of the same man, joking and suffering and agonising as one.

The Cardinal is trapped by a trick. A coffin is brought in and he is bidden to raise the lid. Inside is his mother. And then he breaks down: he admits he never loved her.

For she was evil. The whole of his career, he confesses, was self-glory. He only wanted to escape from her. He is not holy, but proud.

And he recants in court, falsely, to punish himself for his sins. Contemptuously, the State frees him.

Guinness's voice throughout has a dry precision as satisfying as the music of Bach. The wonder is to see him burn up before your eyes.

On the edge of hysteria, his muscles go lax. His eyelids drop. In time, he moves with the deliberation of an alcoholic.

Peter Gleville has directed the play with humour and terrible pity. There are only three speaking parts – Noel Willman, fine as the Inquisitor; Wilfred Lawson, grisly as the warder. And Guinness.

John Barber: *Daily Express*
15 April 1954

The subject is hatefully topical. In some country – perhaps Hungary? – a Roman Catholic cardinal, a national hero, has been arrested and is to be forced to confession by the slow breaking of his will under interrogation. Spirit of Torquemada come to judgement! But the irony of the inquisitor under inquisition is not the author's concern. Rather, in the manner of a BBC feature, it is to explain how a high courage and an iron will can be broken, without drugs or tortures other than long waking nights, simply by the application of a little artful psychiatry....

A big subject and one which seems to call for the dialectical skill of an Arthur Koestler, or the genius of the Dostoievsky of *Crime and Punishment*. Miss Boland had some notable successes; both in the cell, where Mr. Guinness gives a marvellous exhibition of a man staving off insanity, and in the interrogation room, where through the long nights priest and commissar fence and feint, each in deadly danger of becoming over the hours ensnared by affection for the mind he is trying to break and destroy. But it repeats itself; the interruptions at the psychological moments do not disguise the fact that the argument is not really advancing. So long as we do not know the cardinal's secret, and all is still unpredictable, the tension holds.

Once we stumble on it, a curious reaction of disbelief sets in. Instead of the inevitable march of events making strong theatre, it is all again unpredictable, even unimportant and – if that is possible with Mr. Guinness giving so moving a study of an unlovable man in defeat – dull.

The puritans were right in disliking the theatre exactly because what it tells in the theatre is not truth but the art of stage craft. A couple of really effective strokes of dramatic irony would have done more for the last two acts than all the explaining in the world.

Philip Hope-Wallace: *Manchester Guardian*
17 April 1954

The game is a prolonged and fearsome game of chess. We would not leave it without hearing the result.

Illustrated London News
1 May 1954

Miss Boland is, of course, closely tied to psychiatry. She does her best to relieve its severity by interpolating scenes in a prison cell where the prisoner is shown playing dangerous games with his reason with always a saving awareness of their danger. The severity is also relieved by the writing of three good parts. Mr. Alec Guinness gives the Cardinal the hardness which is part of the man and a sardonic humour which dies hard, and he takes great pains to make the character as unlovable as it is incapable of loving. Mr. Noel Willman, as the interrogator, has a no less rewarding part and he plays it brilliantly, laying unemphatic stress on perils that lie await for the eater of dreams. He may himself be eaten by them; and Mr. Willman, whether ostensibly friendly to his victim or laying the subtliest of traps for him, always keeps this peril clear in our minds.

The Times
17 April 1954

In *The Prisoner*, by Bridget Boland, we are given a conducted tour to one of the darkest spots of recent history, the interrogation as practised by Totalitarian authority on the enemy or the deviator. As in *Marching Song*, the scene is a European capital without a name – but probably possessing a curtain. The man in the cell is a Cardinal now exposed to the kind of Inquisition which his own Church once practised with such efficiency. He must be saved from his religion and for the people; he must be 'brain-washed' and broken and confess to treason. The old racks of medieval persecution are not employed against him: but the denial of sleep, the blinding light, and the ceaseless prod of the questioner are as severe as any physical torture. The Cardinal does collapse under remorseless investigation of his origins and his past. The interrogator gets his ludicrous confession of every possible sin against reason and the people. The audience gets two-and-a-half hours in the grill-room of the new 'psychology'.

Ivor Brown: *Observer*
18 April 1954

Separate Tables

St James's Theatre: 22 September 1954

Terence Rattigan was the theatrical craftsman of his time. His characters were convincing, his scenes worked theatrically, his dialogue was precise and telling. He could also build a play so that they proceeded with an even logic from beginning to end: and these skills attracted a wider audience than simply the Aunt Ednas for whom he was supposed to write. I prefer, on the whole, his one-act plays to his full-length ones, because his themes often seemed too slight to sustain interest over two and a half hours despite his technical control. Accordingly from his several successes of the early 1950s (*The Deep Blue Sea* among them), I have chosen *Separate Tables*, two one-act plays which share a common setting, a shabby genteel private hotel. The sympathy which Rattigan extends to the new middle-class poor contrasts with the later studies by John Mortimer and Giles Cooper, who are both more acid in their observations; while the skill with which Rattigan handles the different stories in the dining room anticipates Alan Ayckbourn, who was then a schoolboy.

Raffigan   Binky Beaumont

The high point reached by Mr. Rattigan as a serious dramatist in *The Deep Blue Sea* has been passed. In my opinion, he is now without question the master playwright of our day. His great strength is his strange, almost clinical gift of laying bare the hidden afflictions of the heart and the bad humours that cripple human behaviour.

Separate Tables is not one play but a duet of plays, the two parts running together in a splendid mathematical counterpoint. In both parts, *Table By The Window* and *Table No. 7*, the message is unmistakably the same: only the sick in heart, be they never so outwardly different, can heal each other.

Maurice Wiltshire: *Daily Mail*
23 September 1954

The two little pieces which make up *Separate Tables* are put together with such economy that either of them could make three acts. They gain by their compression.

They are interlocked securely by the fact that both depend for a climax on decisions taken by Miss Cooper, the breezily efficient manager of what looks like a fly-blown hotel in Bournemouth. In *Table By The Window*, she decides to encourage the man she loves to go back to his former wife. In *Table No. 7*, her decision is to invite a 'Major' Pollock to stay on at the hotel in the face of a petition by the other guests for his expulsion. Both problems are difficult, but Miss Cooper is emotionally involved in only one. She sends her man into the hands of the drug-dazed doll who will destroy him for certain. The 'Major' is a fake who had just been before the magistrates for 'insulting' behaviour to women in a cinema.

But if Miss Cooper, played deeply and downrightly by Beryl Measor, is the link in the construction of the plays, their real strength is that Margaret Leighton and Eric Portman take entirely different parts in each. Mr. Portman as the drunken, wife-beating, disgraced politician making a living by journalism has his dreary life transformed when Margaret Leighton floats back into it, looking like a fragile young dream not knowing that everybody will presently wake up and find her a fading 40.

With almost boastful ease, the two become entirely different characters after the interval, Miss Leighton changing herself into an hysterical, red-nosed, retarded daughter of a bullying mother, and

Mr. Portman into the lieutenant, RASC, transformed into major, Black Watch, entirely by his own imagination.

Gerard Fay: *Manchester Guardian*
24 September 1954

The general impression appears to be that the two plays which make up Mr. Terence Rattigan's double bill at the St. James's are of equal value. I believe this to be a mistake.

The first, *Table By The Window*, ... is an anecdote about a bitter but goodhearted Labour politician, ruined by drink and the personal power lust of his divorced wife, a woman pale, exotic and terrified of growing old. This is an excellent melodrama, but the second play, which takes place some time later in the same hotel, and deals with the unpromising topic of a bogus major who, in addition to being found guilty of improper behaviour in a cinema, is a liar, a coward and a snob, is much, much more. ...

If there is a defect in the second play ... it comes at the beginning, and it is not important. It is merely that the distressing class-consciousness of Mrs. Railton-Bell is re-established at too great a length. But after the unbelievably Public School major has been found out, and he admits, almost incidentally, and without fuss, to the sex-repressed girl whom Miss Leighton plays with such heroic disregard of her natural beauty, that he was educated not at Wellington, but at a council school, the play is without flaw. From this moment, Mr. Rattigan writes, and Mr. Portman acts, with a mastery which makes one proud of the English theatre.

Here, when all have given it over, the author and the actor do the unhappy major's manhood from death to life recover. Hitherto Mr. Portman has played the major with a relentless false heartiness, an unforgiving shiftiness of glance, an unmitigated refinement of accent. After this, the modification of Mr. Portman's performance is extraordinarily slight. The heartiness is a trifle subdued, a slight shame creeps into both the look and the voice. These things are so small that even to mention them is crudely to exaggerate them out of reality. And yet one is made aware that the man has discovered in himself a new and unexpected dignity as unmistakably as Saul was regenerated when struck down on the way to Damascus.

Harold Hobson: *Sunday Times*
26 September 1954

Sharply observed, beautifully written, both plays put middle-class loneliness under a microscope's eye.

But in both plays you see the exact point at which Rattigan stops telling the truth about his people. Suddenly he sees he is getting morbid. Violently then, he wrenches on the sentimental tap.

John Barber: *Daily Express*
23 September 1954

It can be held that Mr. Rattigan has scored by making us curious about the fate of his characters. Agreed: but one would not wish to pursue their future for long. It is rather as if one had put down a thoroughly well-made magazine story and mused, 'I'd like to know what happens next', with no intention of wanting more than a hint, a precis.

J. C. Trewin: *The Sketch*
22 September 1954

The scene is the dining room of a Kensington hotel, not unlike the Bournemouth hotel in which *Separate Tables* ... takes place. A Young Perfectionist is dining: beside him, Aunt Edna, whom Mr. Rattigan has described as 'the universal and immortal' middle-class playgoer.

Aunt Edna: Excuse me, young man, but have you seen Mr. Rattigan's latest?

Young Perfectionist: I have indeed.

A.E.   And what is it about?

Y.P.   It is two plays about four people, who are driven by loneliness into a state of desperation.

A.E.   (sighing): Is there not enough morbidity in this world...?

Y.P.   One of them is a drunken Left-wing journalist who has been imprisoned for wife-beating. Another is his ex-wife who takes to drugs to palliate the loss of her looks. She revives his masochistic love for her, and by curtain-fall they are gingerly reunited.

A.E.   (quailing): Does Mr. Rattigan analyse these creatures?

Y.P.   He does, in great detail.

A.E.   How very unwholesome! Pray go on.

Y.P.   In the second play the central character is a bogus major who has lately been convicted of assaulting women in a cinema.

A.E.   Ouf!

Y.P. His fellow-guests hold a conclave to decide whether he should be expelled from the hotel. Each contributes to a symposium on sexual deviation. ...

A.E. In pity's name, stop!

Y.P. The major reveals that his foible is the result of fear, which has made him a hermit, a liar and a pervert. This revelation kindles sympathy in the heart of the fourth misfit, a broken spinster, who befriends him in his despair.

A.E. (aghast): I *knew* I was wrong when I applauded *The Deep Blue Sea*. And what conclusion does Mr. Rattigan draw from these squalid anecdotes?

Y.P. From the first, that love unbridled is a destroyer. From the second that love bridled is a destroyer. You will enjoy yourself.

A.E. But I go to the theatre to be taken out of myself!

Y.P. Mr. Rattigan will take you into an intricately charted world of suspense. By withholding vital information, he will tantalise you; by disclosing it unexpectedly, he will astound you.

A.E. But what information! Sex and frustration!

Y.P. I agree that the principal characters, especially the journalist and the major, are original and disturbing creations. But there is also a tactful, omniscient *hoteliere*, beautifully played by Miss Beryl Measor. And what do you say to a comic Cockney maid?

A.E. Ah!

Y.P. Or to Mr. Aubrey Mather, as a whimsical dominie? Or to a pair of opinionated medical students? Or to a tyrannical matriarch – no less than Miss Phyllis Neilson-Terry?

A.E. *That* sounds more like it. You console me. ... Yet you sound a trifle peaky. Is something biting you?

Y.P. Since you ask, I regretted that the major's crime was not something more cathartic than mere cinema flirtation. Yet I suppose the play is as good a handling of sexual abnormality as English playgoers will tolerate.

A.E. For my part, I am glad it is no better. ...Clearly, there is something here for both of us.

Y.P. Yes. But not quite enough for either of us.

Kenneth Tynan: *Observer*
26 September 1954

I went to the most successful play in London last week, Terence Rattigan's *Separate Tables* and, apart from being fascinated from start to finish, I wondered how many women in the audience were aware of the fearful object lesson before their eyes.

Margaret Leighton, as you've no doubt read, plays two parts. A glamorous model and a pathetic drab of a young woman whose appearance alone is the very meaning of the word plain.

Now the whole point I want to make is that the lovely Miss Leighton does *not* use make-up to become that dismal depressing creature they call Sybil. ...

Why am I in such a lather? Surely it is easy to see. If *this* Sybil can look like Margaret Leighton; if *this* gawky sad-sack can look lovely to behold, then *why not all the others*?

Not nearly enough women realise the importance of how they hold themselves. Not nearly enough parents teach young girls the way to walk, to sit, to use their hands.

I have said it before and I howl it again – there is no such thing as a really unattractive woman if she can only learn how to present herself.

Iris Ashley: *Daily Mail*
15 November 1954

Waiting For Godot

Arts Theatre: 3 August 1955

In her biography of Samuel Beckett, Deidre Bair describes how Beckett wrote *En Attendant Godot* very quickly, between 9 October 1948 and 29 January 1949, as a relaxation from 'the wildness and rulelessness' of his novels. She also discusses the various interpretations of who Godot actually was, or what he signifies, quoting Beckett to dismiss the idea that he was God. It was first performed at the Théâtre de Babylone in 1953, and caused a *succes de scandale*, according to Martin Esslin (*New York Times*, 24 September 1967). 'Was it not an outrage that people could be asked to come and see a play that could not be anything but a hoax, a play in which nothing whatever happened!'

Waiting For Godot was Beckett's first – and became his most famous – play. No post-war play had a greater impact, in France, Britain or the States; but it was so original that managements and press alike handled it with caution when it first appeared. It seemed pointless and meaningless to those who did not realise that it was a play about waiting, not about something happening. Beckett distilled a feeling which underlies most of our lives, of time passing without purpose. Despite its Christian references, it is a deliberately agnostic play. Not knowing what will happen is as essential as not knowing whether anything will happen. Brecht, who disliked the play, thought that it typified Western decadence: he wanted to write a satirical version which would show how *Waiting For Godot* expressed the dead-end drifting of capitalistic societies. It may indeed, have caught a sense of political disillusion in the West, as it has done in the East; and it proved popular among prison audiences who knew nothing about the theatre, but everything about waiting. The two tramps, Vladimir and Estragon, and their music-hall crosstalk, influenced many British writers, from Johnny Speight to Harold Pinter; and tramps became almost a standard feature of television comedy series (such as the *Arthur Haynes Show*). Miss Bair points out that the language between them reflected the gentle, amusing chat between Beckett and Suzanne Deschevaux-Demesnil, when they were both escaping from Paris to the comparative safety of south-east France during the war; but she also points out that Beckett 'was the first postwar playwright to write dialogue in everyday ordinary spoken French.' 'The language Beckett used in *Godot* is the language any group of *clochards* sitting on a bench or in a café might say to each other.'

Waiting For Godot ...is another of those plays that tries to lift superficiality to significance through obscurity.

It should please those who prefer to have their clichés masquerading as epigrams. 'We always find something that gives us the impression that we exist', is Mr. Beckett's clumsy way of rehashing Descartes' old phrase, 'I think, therefore I am'.

Similarly his symbols are seldom more demanding than a nursery version of *Pilgrim's Progress*. If occasionally we get them wrong or

Samuel Beckett's WAITI

Godot

do not get them at all, we can safely assume they were not worth deciphering.

Two tramps are waiting by the roadside for a stranger called Godot. They pass the time away sniffing, grunting, whining, munching, scratching, quarrelling, snoozing, wondering.

In case the obviousness of the stranger's name – GODot – should escape us, we are assured in the final moments of the play that He wears a long, white beard.

Milton Shulman: *Evening Standard*
4 August 1955

Waiting For Godot has nothing at all to seduce the senses. Its drab bare scene is dominated by a withered tree and a garbage can, and for a large part of the evening, this lugubrious setting, which makes the worst of both town and country, is inhabited only by a couple of tramps, verminous and decayed, their hats broken and their clothes soiled, with sweaty feet, inconstant bladders and boils on the backside.

This is not all. In the course of the play, nothing happens. Such dramatic progress as there is, is not towards a climax, but towards a perpetual postponement. Vladimir and Estragon are waiting for Godot, but this gentleman's appearance (*if* he is a gentleman, and not something of another species) is not prepared for with any recognisable theatrical tension, for the audience know well enough from the beginning that Godot will never come. The dialogue is studded with words that have no meaning for normal ears; repeatedly the play announces that it will come to a stop, and will have to start again; never does it reconcile itself with reason....

Strange as this play is, and curious as are its processes of thought, it has a meaning; and this meaning is untrue. To attempt to put this meaning into a paragraph is like trying to catch Leviathan in a butterfly net, but nevertheless the effort must be made. The upshot of *Waiting For Godot* is that the two tramps are always waiting for the future, their ruinous consolation being that there is always tomorrow; they never realise that today is today. In this, says Mr. Beckett, they are like humanity, which dawdles and drivels its life away, postponing action, eschewing enjoyment, waiting only for some far-off, divine event, the millennium, the Day of Judgement.

Mr. Beckett has, of course, got it all wrong. Humanity worries very little over the Day of Judgement. ...But he has got it wrong in a tremendous way. There is no need at all for a dramatist to philosophise rightly; he can leave that to the philosophers. But it is essential that if he philosophises wrongly, he should do so with a swagger. Mr. Beckett has any amount of swagger. A dusty, coarse, irreverent, pessimistic, violent swagger? Possibly. But the genuine thing, the real McCoy.

Harold Hobson: *Sunday Times*
7 August 1955

... it might almost be a parody of Joyce. ...The one saving grace of this odd piece lies in the isolated moments when the author stops fooling and uses his subtle sense of language to convey the hopelessness of man's dilemma.

Ronald Barker: *Plays and Players*
September 1955

His work in two acts holds the stage most wittily, but is it a play? Its significance ... would seem to be that nothing is finally significant.

The Times
4 August 1955

Waiting For Godot ... is a play to send the rationalist out of his mind and induce tooth-gnashing among people who would take Lewis Carroll's Red Queen and Lear's nonsense exchanges with the fool as the easiest stuff in the world. The play, if about anything, is ostensibly about two tramps who spend the two acts, two evenings long, under a tree on a bit of waste land, 'waiting for Godot'.

Godot, it would seem, is quite possibly God, just as Charlot is Charles. Both tramps are dressed like the Chaplinesque zanies of the circus, and much of their futile cross-talk seems to bear some sort of resemblance to those music-hall exchanges we know so well: 'You know my sister?' 'Your sister?' 'Yes, my sister' and so on, ad lib. ...

The play bored some people acutely. Others found it a witty and poetic conundrum. There was general agreement that Peter Hall's production did fairly by a work which has won much applause already in many parts of the world and that Paul Daneman in particular, as the more thoughtful of the two tramps, gave a fine and rather touching performance ... It is good to find that plays at once dubbed 'incomprehensible and pretentious' can still get a staging. Where better than the Arts Theatre?

Philip Hope-Wallace: *Manchester Guardian*
5 August 1955

Waiting For Godot frankly jettisons everything by which we recognise theatre. It arrives at the custom-house, as it were, with no luggage, no passport, and nothing to declare; yet it gets through, as might a pilgrim from Mars. It does this, I believe, by appealing to a definition of drama much more fundamental than any in the books. A play, it asserts and proves, is basically a means of spending two hours in the dark without being bored. ...

Hastily labelling their disquiet disgust, many of the first-night audience found it pretentious. But what, exactly, are its pretensions? To state that mankind is waiting for a sign that is late in coming is a platitude which none but the illiterate would interpret as making claims to profundity. What vexed the play's enemies was, I suspect, the opposite: it was not pretentious enough to enable them to deride it. I care little for its enormous success in Europe over the past three years, but much for the way in which it pricked and stimulated my own nervous system. It summoned the music hall and the parable to present a view of life which banished the sentimentality of the music hall and the parable's fulsome uplift. It forced me to re-examine the rules which have hitherto governed the drama; and having done so, to pronounce them not elastic enough. It is validly new, and hence I declare myself, as the Spanish would say, *godotista*.

Kenneth Tynan: *Observer*
7 August 1955

Titus Andronicus

Shakespeare Memorial Theatre: 16 August 1955

1955 was a year of expansion for the Shakespeare Memorial Company at Stratford. Anthony Quayle and Glen Byam Shaw were co-directors, and they planned two companies, one touring and led by John Gielgud and Peggy Ashcroft, and the other resident in Stratford and led by Sir Laurence Olivier and Vivien Leigh. This was the first visit of the Oliviers to Stratford, with Sir Laurence playing Macbeth, King Lear and Titus Andronicus; and in the same season, Peter Hall also made his Stratford debut, directing *Love's Labours Lost*.

Before this Stratford production, *Titus Andronicus* was considered to be just a bloodthirsty relic, of dubious Shakespearian origin, from an age when horrors were fashionable. Peter Brook's production came as a revelation; and it also showed his extraordinary capacity to 'through-compose', for he designed the sets and costumes, composed the music and the sound effects, cut and adapted the text. *Titus Andronicus* was a superb example of what was later to be termed 'director's theatre', where the vision of a master *metteur en scène* reigns supreme. The supposed weakness of 'director's theatre' is that it reduces actors to puppets; but with Olivier as Titus and Quayle as Aaron, this was scarcely likely to happen. Olivier's performance ranked with his finest from the days of the Old Vic at the New; and the result was a rare blend of 'actor's' and 'director's' theatre, as well as combining mature craftsmanship with Brook's youthful inspiration.

Titus Andronicus also anticipated Brook's interest in the Theatre of Cruelty, a phrase associated with Antonin Artaud, the French actor, director and theorist, who died in 1948. Brook's blend of the theories of Artaud and Bertolt Brecht became most evident in his production of *The Marat/Sade* in 1964; but his cool, detached presentation of *Titus Andronicus* and its unsentimental treatment of horrors was a distinctive feature of his style even in 1955. In 1957, this production toured five European countries triumphantly, and established the Shakespeare Memorial Theatre as an international company, if not quite a national theatre.

The last professional London presentation of *Titus Andronicus* took the form of an anthology of the atrocities, included in a Grand Guignol programme at a theatre club. ...

If the horrors in *Titus Andronicus* are not merely horrific, they may as easily seem to be ludicrous. Mr. Peter Brook has sought to prevent us from finding them so by plunging the play into a Websterian world of nightmare. It is a prison, whose bars open only to admit their victims to deeper labyrinths of disaster. Mr. Brook designed the setting and composed the music, besides producing the play, and on the whole he has created an atmosphere in which the horrors can take hold of us.

That they do so, however, is mainly due to the magnificent performances of Titus and Aaron by Sir Laurence Olivier and Mr. Anthony Quayle. For the whole of the first half, the play grips us, as disaster rains down its thunderbolts on the grey head of the old Roman general. Sir Laurence Olivier acts him on the grand scale, and in the scene in which he severs his own hand in a vain effort to save two of his sons, he touched the heights. ...

Mr. Quayle ... gives Aaron the moor a volcanic vitality, which makes that monster of blackhearted wickedness alarmingly credible ...

The Times
17 August 1955

It is our English heresy to think of poetry as a gentle way of saying gentle things. *Titus* reminds us that it is also a harsh way of saying harsh things. Seneca's Stoicism, in which the play is drenched, is a cruel doctrine, but it can rise to moments of supernal majesty. Lear himself has nothing more splendid than:

> For now I stand as one upon a rock,
> Environ'd with a wilderness of sea ...

The parallel with Lear is sibling close, and Peter Brook cleverly strengthens it by having the fly-killing scene performed by a wanton boy. But when all its manifold excellences have been listed, the play still falls oddly short. One accepts the ethical code which forces Tamora to avenge herself on Titus, and then Titus to avenge himself on Tamora; it is the casualness of the killing that grows tiresome, as at a bad bullfight. With acknowledgements to Lady Bracknell, to lose one son may be accounted a misfortune; to lose twenty-four, as Titus does, looks like carelessness. ...

Much textual fiddling is required if we are to swallow the crudities, and in this respect Mr. Brook is as swift with the styptic pencil as his author was with the knife. He lets the blood, as it were, out of the bath. All visible gore is eliminated from the play, so that Lavinia, tongueless and handless, can no longer be likened to 'a conduit with three issuing spouts'. With similar tact, Mr. Brook cuts the last five words of Titus' unspeakable line, 'Why, there they are both, baked in that pie', as he serves to Tamora his cannibalistic speciality – *tête de fils en pâté (pour deux personnes)*.

Adorned by a vast, ribbed setting (the work of Mr. Brook, designer) and accompanied by an eerie throbbing of *musique concrete* (the work of Mr. Brook, composer), the play is now ready for the attentions of Mr. Brook, director. The result is the finest Shakespearian production since the same director tackled *Measure for Measure* five years ago. The vocal attack is such that even the basest lines shine, like Aaron the Moor, 'in pearly and gold'. Anthony Quayle plays the latter role with superbly corrupt flamboyance, and Maxine Audley is a glittering Tamora. As Lavinia, Vivien Leigh receives the news that she is about to be ravished on her husband's corpse with little more than the mild annoyance of one who would have preferred foam rubber. Otherwise, the minor parts are played to the hilt.

Sir Laurence's Titus, even with one hand gone, is a five-finger exercise transformed into an unforgettable concerto of grief. This is a performance which ushers us into the presence of one who is, pound for pound, the greatest actor alive. As usual, he raises one's hair with the risks he takes. Titus enters not as a beaming hero but as a battered veteran, stubborn and shambling, long past caring about the people's cheers. A hundred campaigns have tanned his heart to leather, and from the cracking of that heart, there issues a terrible music, not untinged with madness. One hears great cries, which, like all of this actor's best effects, seem to have been dredged up from an ocean-bed of fatigue. One recognized, though one had never heard it before, the noise made in its last extremity by the cornered human soul. We knew from his Hotspur and his Richard III that Sir Laurence could explode. Now we know that he can suffer as well. All the grand unplayable parts, after this, are open to him: Skelton's Magnificence, Ibsen's Brand, Goethe's Faust – anything, so long as we can see those lion eyes search for solace, that great jaw drop.

Kenneth Tynan: *Observer*
21 August 1955

Look Back in Anger

Royal Court Theatre: 8 May 1956

In the mid-1950s, there was not only a dearth of good new plays but also a shortage of places where new plays could be tried out, without the risks entailed in a full-scale commercial West End production. The little theatres of the early 1950s were dwindling away, with the Sunday night try-out productions of such companies as the Repertory Players. The English Stage Company, which took over the Royal Court in 1956, had been formed in 1955, specifically to produce new, interesting but possibly uncommercial plays; but, according to Irving Wardle's *The Theatres of George Devine* (1978), the immediate response to an advertised request for new plays was extremely disappointing, John Osborne's *Look Back in Anger* being the sole exception. 'Out of some 750 plays submitted to the Court after the *Stage* advertisement, Osborne's was the only script that was so much as considered by the two directors. The remainder, Richardson says, were either bottom-drawer pieces by playwrights in decline or "endless blank verse shit".' George Devine read *Look Back In Anger* first, and brought it to his younger co-director Tony Richardson, who directed the first production. Devine later wrote that he knew that 'this was the play we must do, even if it sank the enterprise'.

Look Back in Anger did not sink the English Stage Company, but saved it. After a fairly successful, but not triumphant, first run, it was brought back into the repertoire after a disastrous run of *The Good Woman of Setzuan*; and when an extract was briefly televised on 16 October, applications for tickets began arriving 'in sackfuls'. It found the young audiences who had shunned the established theatres; and its subsequent success as a film helped to finance the English Stage Company's future work, as well as taking away the threat of a premature bankruptcy. It established the new company's reputation for radicalism, as well as contributing to popular image of 'angry young men' writing 'kitchen-sink plays' for the new theatre of the 1950s.

More has been claimed for *Look Back in Anger* – that it was a significant political protest play and that it brought about a change in theatrical climate which allowed other would-be playwrights to develop and grow. Subsequent productions have cast doubt on the

great claims which came to be made about it; but it was certainly the right play at the right time, providing a basis on which Devine could build in future years. There were other signs in 1956 that British theatre was on the threshhold of a revival. Joan Littlewood's productions at the Theatre Workshop at Stratford-atte-Bowe, East London, were gaining in authority and distinction, with one notable production of Brendan Behan's *The Quare Fellow* in May 1956 occurring within days of *Look Back in Anger*.

John Osborne, however, was the dramatist who seized the public imagination; and *Look Back in Anger* provided a stark contrast not only to the restrained domestic plays of Rattigan and N. C. Hunter, but also to the stoical heroes of Eliot and Whiting. Jimmy Porter was a prototype anti-hero, whose shifting resentments expressed a dissatisfaction not only with specific failures of post-war Britain but with the establishment style, the bland paternalism of politicians who did not apparently appreciate the horrors of living in a dingy bed-sitter in a provincial town.

John Osborne is a 27-year-old actor who was out-of-work when he heard about this theatre's new repertory venture.

He submitted his play out of the blue. The management not only accepted it but offered him small parts in their next two productions.

They have not discovered a masterpiece, but they *have* discovered a dramatist of outstanding promise; a man who can write with seering passion, but happens in this case to have lavished it on the wrong play.

Its essential wrongness lies in its leading character, a young neurotic full of intellectual frustration who lives like a pig and furiously finds the whole world out of step except himself.

His bitterness produces a fine flow of savage talk, but is basically a bore because its reasons are never fully explained.

His virtual monologue of self-pity and unrighteous indignation leaves one gasping for spiritual breath.

The repetitiousness cries out for the knife. But, through all the author's overwriting and laborious shock tactics, we can perceive what a brilliant play this young man will write when he has got this one out of his system and let a little sunshine into his soul.

Cecil Wilson: *Daily Mail*
9 May 1956

Felicity Grein
BEVAN at THEATRE Royal Stratford - The Quar

[*Look Back in Anger*] is by no means a total success artistically, but it has enough tension, feeling and originality of theme and speech to make the choice understandable, and the evening must have given anyone who has ever wrestled with the mechanics of play-making an uneasy but not wasted jaunt, just as it must have woken echoes in anyone who has not forgotten the frustrations of youth.

Mr. Osborne's hero, a boor, a self-pitying, self-dramatising intellectual rebel who drives his wife away, takes a mistress and then drops her when, to his surprise, his wife comes crawling back, will not be thought an edifying example of chivalry. But those who have not lost the power to examine themselves will probably find something basically true in the prolix, shapeless study of a wretch, even if they do not get as far as extending much sympathy to him. But is the dilemma posed here in this ugly, cheerless Bohemia supposed to be typical?

The author and the actors too did not persuade us wholly that they really 'spoke for' a lost, maddened generation. There is the intention to be fair − even to the hated bourgeois parents of the cool and apparently unfeeling wife who is at length brought to heel by a miscarriage. The trouble seems to be in the overstatement of the hero's sense of grievance: like one of Strindberg's woman-haters, he ends in a kind of frenzied preaching in an empty conventicle. Neither we in the audience nor even the other Bohemians on the stage with him are really reacting to his anger. Numbness sets in.

Kenneth Haigh battled bravely with this awkward 'first-play' hero without being able to suggest much more than a spoilt and neurotic bore who badly needed the attention of an analyst. No sooner was sympathy quickened than it ebbed again. Mary Ure as the animal, patient wife, Helena Hughes as a friend who comes to stay and reign in the sordid attic and Alan Bates as a cosy young puppy, that third party who sometimes holds a cracking marriage together, were more easily brought to life. Tony Richardson's production and a good set by Alan Tagg help out this strongly felt but rather muddled first drama. But I believe they have got a potential playwright at last, all the same.

Philip Hope-Wallace: *Manchester Guardian*
10 May 1956

Nothing is so comfortable to the young as the opportunity to feel sorry for themselves. Every generation automatically assumes that it has the exclusive, authentic, gilt-edged, divine right to be described as 'lost'.

Look Back In Anger ... sets up a wailing wall for the latest post-war generation of under-thirties. It aims at being a despairing cry but achieves only the stature of a self-pitying snivel.

Milton Shulman: *Evening Standard*
9 May 1956

[*Look Back in Anger*] is intense, angry, feverish, undisciplined. It is even crazy. But it is young, young, young.

It is about a bitter man who has filched an upper class girl from her prim home.

He pours out a vitriolic tirade against the world. His wild and whirling words damn poverty, damn tenderness, damn pity.

His wife – lovely Mary Ure – listens in silence.

Why is he so angry? He is young, frustrated, unhappy.

In fact, he is like thousands of young Londoners today ...

John Barber: *Daily Express*
9 May 1956

One is sorry for his wretched little wife, pulverized by his verbal artillery (one began to feel bruised oneself); and delighted when she leaves him; but I could have smacked her for her final grovelling return, in hysterical renunciation of all the creeds black-listed by bed-sitter nihilism. Is this supposed to be a splendid gesture on behalf of the self-oppressed? In any case, it is no end to the play, for the whole silly cycle of torture and collapse will clearly begin again.

Eric Keown: *Punch*
16 May 1956

That the play needs changes I do not deny: it is twenty minutes too long, and not even Mr. Haigh's bravura could blind me to the painful whimsy of the final reconciliation. I agree that *Look Back In Anger* is likely to remain a minority taste. What matters, however, is the size of the minority. I estimate it at roughly 6,733,000, which is the number of people in this country between the ages of twenty and thirty. And this figure will doubless be swelled by refugees from other age-groups who are curious to know precisely what the contemporary young pup is thinking and feeling. I doubt if I could love anyone who did not wish to see *Look Back in Anger*. It is the best young play of its decade.

Kenneth Tynan: *Observer*
13 May 1956

John Osborne's play *Look Back In Anger*, which has been produced at the Moscow Arts Theatre as part of the Youth Festival, was praised in Moscow yesterday as a skilful mirror of contemporary life. 'One of the most attractive features of the work is its faith in everything that is good and radiant in the soul', the Tass dramatic critic wrote. – Reuter.

Daily Telegraph
5 August 1957

New York dramatic critics today gave high praise to the opening performance here last night of *Look Back In Anger*.

The *New York Times* critic, Mr Brooks Atkinson, said that Mr. John Osborne, the author, 'has written the most vivid British play of the decade', and Mr. Walter Kerr, of the *Herald Tribune*, said that Mr. Osborne 'is first of all a writer – a real one'. The *New York Daily News* critic, Mr. John Chapman, wrote that the drama was 'the most virile and exciting play to come out of London in a long, long time – something to set the wits tingling'. But Mr. Robert Coleman, of the *New York Daily Mirror*, was not so enthusiastic.

The Times
3 October 1957

[The New York Critics Circle chose *Look Back in Anger* as the best foreign play of the 1957/8 season. 8 April 1958.]

The Birthday Party

Lyric Theatre, Hammersmith: 19 May, 1958

If John Osborne's first experience of a London production was of a success, if a *succès de scandale*, that of another young actor-turned-playwright was of disaster. Harold Pinter's *The Birthday Party* lasted at the Lyric Theatre, Hammersmith, for less than a week, with box-office takings of only £260/11/5d. The one enthusiastic and perceptive review appeared after the show had folded; and I reproduce Harold Hobson's *Sunday Times* article fully, for, while critics can often rightly be blamed for their lack of perceptiveness, they are less frequently praised for their genuine insights. Hobson and the other London critics were facing, on this occasion, the reviewer's hardest but most rewarding task – the consideration of a new play by an unknown writer whose dramatic voice was highly individualistic, concentrated and intense. To appreciate some of Pinter's qualities at first hearing meant ridding the mind of preconceptions, of all the *ennui* of routine; while to assimilate and understand them sufficiently to write a coherent essay requires a certain flexibility of mind, as well as much professional skill. The other critics probably reflected more accurately the feelings of an ordinary London audience: they were doing their jobs as journalists. But there are occasions in most good critics' professional lives when they feel that they understood a production in a way which has eluded their colleagues. This was one of Hobson's moments; and from Pinter's point of view, it must almost have justified the *débâcle* of his first London run.

Disappointment was my lot at the Lyric, Hammersmith, last night.

As it chanced that *The Birthday Party* by Harold Pinter was sandwiched between two sets of visits to Sadler's Wells to see the Russians, I had looked forward to hearing some dialogue that I could understand.

But it turned out to be one of those plays in which an author wallows in symbols and revels in obscurity. Give me Russian every time.

The author never got down to earth long enough to explain what his play was about, so I can't tell you. But I can give you some sort of sketch of what happens, and to whom.

To begin with there is Meg (Beatrix Lehmann) who lets lodgings in a seaside town. She is mad. Thwarted maternity is (I think) her trouble and it makes her go soppy over her unsavoury lodger, Stanley (Richard Pearson).

He is mad too. He strangles people. And I think he must have strangled one person too many, because a couple of very sinister (and quite mad) characters arrive (John Slater and John Stratton) bent on – I suppose – vengeance.

There is also a mad girl (Wendy Hutchinson), nymphomania being her fancy.

The one sane character is Meg's husband (Willoughby Gray) but sanity does him no good. He is a deeply depressed little man, a deckchair attendant by profession.

Oh, well, I can give him one word of cheer. He might have been a dramatic critic, condemned to sit through plays like this.

W. A. Darlington: *Daily Telegraph*
20 May 1958

What all this means, only Mr. Pinter knows, for, as his characters speak in non sequiturs, half-gibberish and lunatic ravings, they are unable to explain their actions, thoughts or feelings. If the author can forget Beckett, Ionesco and Simpson, he may do much better next time.

M. W. W.: *Manchester Guardian*
21 May 1958

This essay in surrealistic drama at the Lyric, Hammersmith, gives the impression of deriving from an Ionesco play which M. Ionesco has not yet written. The first act sounds an off-beat note of madness; in the second, the note has risen to a kind of delirium; and the third act studiously refrains from the slightest hint of what the other two may have been about.

This sort of drama is all very well if the writer is able to create theatrical effects out of his symbolic dialogue. Mr. Harold Pinter's effects are neither comic nor terrifying: they are never more than puzzling, and after a while we tend to give the puzzle up in despair.

The Times
20 May 1958

One snag about being an understudy is that with all those hours to kill in the dressing room you are liable to write plays like *The Birthday Party*.

Harold Pinter is a 28-year-old actor who, under the stage name of David Baron, has lately been understudying at the Royal Court.

No doubt it was under its intellectual influence that he wrote this baffling mixture.

Cecil Wilson: *Daily Mail*
20 May 1958

... Mr. Pinter is a natural dramatist. He has a quick sense of the stage. He can write theatrically acute dialogue. The trouble is that he has been quite unable to clarify his play. He may hold that it does not need clarification; that it is the duty of an alert listener to catch every nuance, unravel every thread, accept every suggestion. If so, then I admit my dire failure. I was as baffled by the piece as by the play I saw in London years ago that began, if I remember rightly, in Tibet, and ended in Piccadilly Circus Tube Station, with nothing much to tell us what had chanced on the way.

J. C. Trewin: *Illustrated London News*
31 May 1958

Harold Pinter's *The Birthday Party* is about a fat, torrid young man who wants to be left alone, especially by his oppressively maternal landlady. A beaming Jew and a snickering Irishman visit him, nudge him into a game of blindman's-buff, break his spectacles and lead him off their captive. Ionesco and Nigel Dennis are the obvious influences: the theme is that of the individualist who is forced out of his shell to come to terms with the world at large, an experience which in all such plays is seen as castratingly tragic.

The writing contains some effective and even witty *non sequiturs*, which have led critics to compare Mr. Pinter with N. F. Simpson. The analogy breaks down in one vital respect. Mr. Simpson uses a surrealist technique to say something that could not be said in any other way. Mr. Pinter employs a similar technique to say something that could easily be said in many other ways; has, indeed, often been said in them; for the notion that society enslaves the individual can hardly be unfamiliar to any student of the cinema or the realistic theatre. That is why Mr. Pinter sounds frivolous, even when he is being serious; and why Mr. Simpson is serious, even when he is being frivolous.

Kenneth Tynan: *Observer*
25 May 1958

One of the actors in Harold Pinter's *The Birthday Party* at the Lyric,

Hammersmith, announces in the programme that he read History at Oxford, and took his degree with Fourth Class Honours.

Now I am well aware that Mr. Pinter's play received extremely bad notices last Tuesday morning. At the moment I write these lines it is uncertain even whether the play will still be in the bill by the time they appear, though it is probable it will be seen elsewhere. Deliberately, I am willing to risk whatever reputation I have as a judge of plays by saying that *The Birthday Party* is not a Fourth, not even a Second, but a First; and that Mr. Pinter, on the evidence of this work, possesses the most original, disturbing and arresting talent in theatrical London.

I am anxious, for the simple reason that the discovery and encouragement of new dramatists of quality is at present the most important task of the British theatre, to put this matter clearly and emphatically. The influence of unfavourable notices on the box office is enormous: but in lasting effect, it is nothing. *Look Back In Anger* and the work of Beckett both received poor notices the morning after production. But that has not prevented those two very different writers, Mr. Beckett and Mr. Osborne, from being regarded throughout the world as the most important dramatists who now use the English tongue. The early Shaw got bad notices; Ibsen got scandalously bad notices. Mr. Pinter is not merely in good company, he is in the very best company.

There is only one quality that is essential to a play. It is the quality that can be found both in *Hamlet* and in *Simple Spymen*. A play must entertain; it must give pleasure. Unless it does that, it is useless for stage purposes. No amount of intellect, of high moral intent or of beautiful writing is of the slightest avail, if a play is not in itself theatrically interesting.

Theatrically speaking, *The Birthday Party* is absorbing. It is witty. Its characters – the big oafish lodger in the slatternly seaside boarding house whose lethargy is subject to such strange bursts of alarm, the plain middle-aged woman who becomes girlishly gay, the two visitors, one so spruce and voluble, the other so mysteriously frightening – are fascinating. The plot, which consists with all kinds of verbal arabesques and echoing explorations of memory and fancy, of the springing of the trap, is first-rate. The whole play has the same atmosphere of delicious, impalpable and hair-raising terror which makes *The Turn Of The Screw* one of the best stories in the world.

Mr. Pinter has got hold of a primary fact of existence. We live on

85

the verge of disaster. One sunny afternoon, whilst Peter May is making a century at Lord's against Middlesex, and the shadows are creeping along the grass, and the old men are dozing in the Long Room, a hydrogen bomb may explode. That is one sort of threat. But Mr. Pinter's is of a subtler sort. It breathes in the air. It cannot be seen, but it enters the room every time the door is opened. There is something in your past – it does not matter what – which will catch up with you. Though you go to the uttermost parts of the earth, and hide yourself in the most obscure lodgings in the least popular of towns, one day there is a possibility that two men will appear. They will be looking for you and you cannot get away. And someone will be looking for *them* too. There is terror everywhere. Meanwhile, it is best to make jokes (Mr. Pinter's jokes are very good) and to play blind man's buff, and to bang on a toy drum, anything to forget the slow approach of doom. *The Birthday Party* is a Grand Guignol of the susceptibilities.

The fact that no one can say precisely what it is about, or give the address from which the intruding Goldberg and McCann come, or say precisely why it is that Stanley is so frightened of them, is, of course, one of its greatest merits. It is exactly in this vagueness that its spinechilling quality lies. If we knew just what Miles had done, *The Turn of the Screw* would fade away. As it is, Mr. Pinter has learned the lesson of the Master. Henry James would recognise him as an equal.

Peter Wood has directed the play with an absolute response to its most delicate nuances. It has six players, every one of them superb. Beatrix Lehmann is strangely funny and macabrely touching as the landlady. John Slater builds impeccably the façade of eloquence that hides Goldberg's secret quaking. John Stratton finely points McCann's nameless fears (his paper-tearing, with its horrible pause at the end, is unforgettable). Richard Pearson's Stanley, excellent throughout, is very moving in its hurt wonder when he is given the child's drum as a birthday present. Wendy Hutchinson's Lulu is an acceptable saucy young chit: this is a rarer achievement than one might think; and Willoughby Gray's husband is solid and believable. Mr. Pinter and *The Birthday Party* despite their experiences last week will be heard of again. Make a note of their names.

Harold Hobson: *Sunday Times*
25 May 1958

Brand

Lyric Theatre, Hammersmith: 8 April 1959

The old Lyric Theatre in Hammersmith, where *The Birthday Party* failed to find its audiences, had a chequered history. It was awkwardly situated in a Hammersmith sidestreet, beside a street market; and although its interior was originally finely decorated by Frank Matcham, in the 1950s that glory was looking very dim and dowdy. It was too far from the West End to attract casual theatre audiences, but a little too close to be a suburban try-out theatre. Managements used it for productions which they wanted to move into town but lacked the theatres or the finance to do so. Eventually, it was knocked down in a re-development scheme, and replaced by a smaller new theatre (though with a similar seating capacity). The old Lyric, however, had its days (and years) of triumph. It was particularly associated with Nigel Playfair's seasons during the 1920s; but after the war, the problems of sustaining a consistent programme became increasingly acute.

In 1959, however, the old Lyric was chosen for a remarkable repertory programme, staged by a newly formed company, led by the director Michael Elliott. For a few brief months, the '59 Company ranked with the best companies in Britain; and the selection of plays was particularly distinctive and ambitious, including *Danton's Death*, *Creditors* and *Brand*. Although it was financially impossible to sustain the company at that theatre, the success eventually led to the formation of the '69 Company operating in Manchester, at first in the University Theatre and then at the Royal Exchange, converted into a large arena theatre, placed like a 'space capsule' within the impressive surrounds of the old Exchange building.

Brand was a startling and unlikely success. Ibsen had written it as a long dramatic poem, to be read rather than staged; but Michael Meyer's adaptation, substantially cutting the original, brought out its theatrical qualities. Patrick McGoohan's Brand was a haunting performance, throwing aside normal heroic rhetoric in favour of an intense down-to-earth fervour, inspired but prosaic, a modern fanatic. His hero also captured the imagination of British audiences, exactly expressing the current fears that mesmeric leaders are also dangerous men.

It was exhilarating to hear the cheers which greeted the '59 Company's latest production at the Lyric, Hammersmith, for this group has not met the success its *Danton's Death* and *Creditors* deserved: and *Brand* is a fairly daunting theatrical peak to scale. Apart from a single production by W. G. Fay in 1912, this moral tragedy of the year previous to *Peer Gynt* seems never to have been professionally staged in London before. Read, it is puzzling and Sjoberg's production, which I saw in Stockholm, naturally left me darkling as I could not follow the language. But Michael Meyer's boldly reduced and prosaic version shows it clearly for what it is: a quintessentially Ibsenesque tragedy. ...

Pastor Brand is a Kierkegaardian 'Everyman' fiercely willing himself to be a 'tablet on which God may write'. To his uncompromising idealism everything and everyone must be sacrificed. The least welcome flock shall be his. His mother must be punished for her materialism. His child must be allowed to die rather than be taken to a warmer climate; his wife, Agnes, whom he has taken from 'the joy of life' to share his awful upward struggle, must even renounce the child's memories and part with its treasured baby clothes. 'Have you given all? Have you given willingly?' he asks. One cannot quite help thinking of *East Lynne*. Yet the searching wind of mid-nineteenth century morality is wonderfully stimulating. When at last, reviled, stoned, and shrugged off by the ignorant or worldly wise, Brand, alone save for the witch girl of the mountains, stands confronting the avalanche which kills him ('He dies who seeks Jehovah face to face'), we feel that a truly tragic assertion has been made, that a man's reach has 'exceeded his grasp'.

Philip Hope-Wallace: *Manchester Guardian*
10 April 1959

... Mr. Patrick McGoohan is magnificent throughout in a part which is pitched on a single note. As he passes from sermon to sermon, we can almost say with the adoring woman who is to suffer the awful fate of becoming his wife, 'as he spoke, he grew'. There are indeed times when the actor seems to grow visibly. Mr. McGoohan establishes what is basic in Brand's earnestness, strength and courage and leaves us in no doubt that his ruthless sacrifice of his mother, his child and his wife to the principle of willed renunciation costs him dear. He is no heartless monster, but an egoist with a pig-headed belief in the rightness of his sacred cause. ...

Mr. McGoohan retains even through these shocking doctrinaire excesses a measure of sympathy for the pastor, who, seeking an ever larger and larger church for his flock, leads them up the high mountain till the demands he makes on them break their spirit and they stone him.

It is at this point that the actor is more or less compelled to leave the rest of the play in the hands of his director. Mr. Elliott does not fail his principal, and the scenes of the egoist's recognition of his egoism – some carried through by the witch girl Gerd and some by subjective visions – come clearly and movingly over ...

The Times
9 April 1959

The '59 Company ... show glorious courage in their offering of *Brand*, the most bleakly austere of Ibsen's works, and Michael Elliott has directed it with imagination and a real understanding of its qualities. In this he is considerably aided by Richard Negri who, with bold simplicity and ingenuity, has evoked in a small space the ghostly splendours of mountain and fjord and of darkness and light.

The play, written a year or so before *Peer Gynt*, represents the genius of Ibsen, as I understand it, at its highest, and in this new translation by Michael Meyer, though one badly misses at times the more emotional rhythms of the Archer version, a great deal of the original stark majesty, as one may guess – for I have no Norwegian – is allowed to emerge.

Patrick McGoohan in the namepart is on the brink of an admirable performance, and comes at times so near to the Brand one dreams of that I could well wish he were less enamoured of the seemingly fashionable Morse-code delivery of speech. Why he does it – in order to thrust forward the image of the Spartan Calvinist – is completely understandable, but a richer and more trumpet-tongued delivery, a more nervous tempo, a greater authority of bearing would serve him better, and here I would even suggest that heavier clothes would help him, a more weighty aspect, a great-coat perhaps, dark as a thunder-cloud.

The Agnes of Dilys Hamlett, a young actress possessing a gravely dignified grace and distinction, has my total admiration. So, indeed, have Enid Lorrimer as the mother of Brand, Peter Sallis as the Doctor, and Harold Lang as the young painter Ejnar. All the parts are competently, and some of them, as in the case of Fulton McKay, Patrick Wymark and Robert Bernal, finely performed, and if I suggest that the superbly difficult role of the mountain girl, Gerd, played by Olive McFarland, would be aided considerably by letting her cast her spell over Brand crouching like a wild animal half-hidden by stones and boulders, or behind ridges of rock rather than allowing us to watch her as we might watch any young lady taking an eccentric stroll among the hills, it is not to say that I found her valiant shots at a well-nigh impossible target were inadequate.

The play, if not receiving its full measure of perfection in handling, is well served. Let no one say that *Brand* is an occasion for that epitaph bestowed by the evasive on the unknown as Highbrow. It is as overwhelmingly exciting as a thunderstorm.

Kenneth Tynan: *Observer*
12 April 1959

... Brand must have the glow that brings people to him. He cannot be just a theatrical fanatic: it is easy enough to set the jaw. Fifty Nine Theatre, which has had the courage to stage *Brand*, so long neglected in Britain, has found miraculously, the right actor: Patrick McGoohan. Here he has made one of the most exciting personal successes for a very long time.

The word 'brand' can mean both sword and fire. We have both in Mr. McGoohan. He is tall, governing of mien, craggily handsome. Throughout the play, the thunder sounds in his voice, and in his eyes we see the lightning. There can be no compromise. The actor cannot afford to compromise: he, too, must cry 'All or Nothing', and Mr. McGoohan's performance is an extraordinary reply to scholars who have claimed that the part is unactable, whatever it may appear to be in the study.

At Hammersmith, Pastor Brand seems always to be far larger than life-sized: he looms. He is one with the ice-peaks of the Northern land. Richard Negri, who has designed the sets – suggested with grand simplicity – secures the feeling of bleak and terrible beauty, and the actor of Brand is, or should be, the only player on the same scale. The sets appear almost to dwarf the other players in the mountains, and by the fjord, but Brand strides over all. At the end it is the mad Gerd's rifle-shot that brings down the destroying avalanche, but it might just as well have been the roll and flash of Mr. McGoohan's voice.

One can offer simply an impression of this uncanny night in the theatre. I am more anxious to convey something of its effect upon the playgoer than to go into the matter of Ibsen's influences and the writing of Kierkegaard. Brand must pull down the sky upon us: Mr. McGoohan does this. There are other things to recall: the suggestion – for it is no more – of the lashing waters of the fjord beyond the village quay; the hopeless yearning of Dilys Hamlett as, by the window of the bare candle-gleaming room, Brand's wife seeks to talk to her child in his lonely grave: the sense of height in the last scene when the villagers have followed the fanatic upwards towards the promised land. Peter Sallis and Patrick Wymark, practised players both, offer a certain relief to the play's grim single-mindedness; but when all is spoken, the night belongs to Mr. McGoohan, who seems likely now to climb into the high peaks of the British stage.

J. C. Trewin: *Illustrated London News*
25 April 1959

Roots

Royal Court Theatre: 30 June 1959

The Belgrade Theatre, Coventry, was the first new theatre to be built in Britain since the second world war; and it was a forerunner of the many regional reps constructed and opened in the 1960s. It was a model theatre (for its time) in a showplace town, for Coventry, largely destroyed during the war, had reconstructed the city centre, with such novelties as traffic-free precincts, mixed development schemes, and crowned its achievement with the building of a new cathedral, to which many of the best-known sculptors and painters of the period (Sutherland, Frinck) had contributed. The theatre was not to be just a visiting place for touring West End shows; but somewhere to generate new work in drama. The theatre had flats for the resident company built into its complex, a unique feature. The late Bryan Bailey, as artistic director, wanted above all to encourage new plays, preferably those with a regional flavour, not directed towards the West End or traditional middle-class audiences. Arnold Wesker, then twenty-seven, was his first discovery.

Roots was the second play in Wesker's trilogy, which began with *Chicken Soup with Barley* and ended with *I'm Talking About Jerusalem*. These plays are linked together, although they can be played separately, by the history of an East End Jewish family, the Kahns, whose strong socialist beliefs were reinforced during the 1930s by the presence of racist and fascist gangs in the streets where they lived. In *Roots*, however, this family is not seen, although their influence can be felt through the mainly liberating impact which Ronnie Kahn had on Beatie Bryant, the daughter of a working-class family in Norfolk.

It was still unusual, in the late 1950s, to find British plays of this skill and range set in working-class environments. The plays of D. H. Lawrence had not, at that time, been successfully revived; and, despite the so-called 'kitchen sink' drama at the Royal Court, the true parallels to Wesker's achievement came from America – from Miller, Odets and O'Neill – and from Ireland – O'Casey. Wesker's trilogy seemed fresh and original, partly for this reason. But when *Roots* transferred to the Royal Court, in its full Coventry production with Joan Plowright as Beatie and with John Dexter directing, it was as if many of the various elements constituting the new-wave in British theatre had been brought together for the first time – strong social concern, vigorous realistic acting, powerful directing. *Roots* later transferred to the Duke of York's, in the heart of the West End, illustrating that such plays were not just for *avant-garde* audiences or regional ones. The conquest of the West End by the new wave had begun, although perhaps it was never completed or seemed likely to be.

... One of the pleasures of this intelligent, stirring play, is to see the way in which Mr. Wesker has extended the social range of our drama – kitchen-sink and tea-table alike – by bringing alive these farm labourers and their fold as credible, actable people instead of

Arnold Wesker

the Mummerset grotesques with which most dramatists still populate the non-urban landscape. His scenes from provincial life lack the essential forward clash of drama, but they are stamped with authentic freshness of observation and compassionate insight.

Back from the city comes Beatie Bryant, trumpeting the virtues of her lover Ronnie – a Left-Wing intellectual who is the play's hidden standard-bearer of values, the built-in judgement on its people. With the eyes that Ronnie lends her, Beatie looks at the stubborn, insulated, inarticulate ways of her family – so different from that 'mystic communion with the soil' so dear to the hearts of old-fashioned metropolitans – and tries to convert them to a fuller life, as symbolised in classical music, love in the afternoon, opposition to the Bomb.

To this evangelism, Miss Joan Plowright, in a beautifully true and touching performance, gives an infectious gaiety and simplicity. The strength of Mr. Wesker's play lies, in fact, in its communication of the private realities in these grubby domestic interiors, and the underlying kinship between the militant Beatie and her passive relations.

Richard Findlater: *Financial Times*
1 July 1959

... [*Roots*] is exactly the kind of thing Shaftesbury Avenue never finds room for. It is original, entertaining, with a hard core of social criticism, well produced and acted admirably by the Coventry Company. It might easily have been Cold Comfort: it is in fact rural kitchen sink.

The action takes place in the cottages of Norfolk farm labourers. They have electric light, some of them; and some of them have the telly. They suffer from a mysterious complaint called gut-ache and seem not to have heard of the National Health Service. What Mr. Wesker is doing is quite simple: he is exposing the impoverishment of English working-class life, no longer necessarily economic impoverishment but, in the deepest sense, cultural – his title is an exercise in irony; beyond all this he is attacking his characters' own dumb acceptance of this condition, their very ignorance that they are impoverished.

The nature of the material sets Mr. Wesker obvious problems which he very nearly surmounts. The characters, all but one, are dumb oxen in Wyndham Lewis's sense of the word; moreover their vocabulary is so sparse as to make them almost inarticulate; and, it must be admitted, the Norfolk dialect is the slowest means of expression outside Texas. Nevertheless, Mr. Wesker triumphs, because of his own unsentimental sympathy, partly because of the character of the agent of light in the play.

This is Beatie Bryant, the one member of the family who has broken away. She has gone to London, become a waitress and has fallen in love with a young socialist intellectual, Ron, who has shown her a whole new world of experience. The action of the play consists in Beatie's and the Bryants' waiting for her Ron to arrive. He doesn't; as the family sits round the table set for high tea, his letter arrives instead: he is breaking off the engagement. It is a nice touch of Mr. Wesker's that we are made to realise that Ron himself is a phoney; but still, Beatie has to accept the fact of her own inadequacy, an inadequacy arising from the thinness of the soil in which her roots are set; and it gives her – and Mr. Wesker – the chance to launch out into an impassioned onslaught on the shallowness of her environment.

Beatie is beautifully played by Miss Joan Plowright. She attacks her part with a gusto that is always under control, and she quite splendidly renders Beatie's bewildered uncomprehending love for her Expresso-bar Romeo and her numbed realisation, in the end, both that she has failed him and that he has betrayed her. But she is admirably supported by the other players, and especially by Miss Gwen Nelson as her mother. This is by far the best and most faithful play about British working-class life that has appeared for a long time.

Walter Allen: *New Statesman*
11 July 1959

In its genre of the kitchen-sink-propaganda play, *Roots* is a major achievement. Perhaps it could never have been written without the precedence of *Look Back In Anger*, but Mr. Wesker is a better writer than John Osborne.

When Jimmy Porter rants and raves in *Look Back In Anger*, we know he is pleading a special case – Mr. Osborne's case. But Mr. Wesker's simple country girl is angry for all of us and at all of us who will die rather than think for ourselves.

Robert Wraight: *Star*
1 July 1959

... After the Angry Young Man, the Royal Court Theatre now gives us the Perplexed Young Woman.

In her own way, Beatie Bryant ... may prove as much a prototype as Jimmy Porter. She speaks with all the frustrated longings, all the dimly-perceived stirrings in the damp souls of a million unfulfilled girls.

Every waitress who, while she tells you the chocolate mould is off, as she is wondering how she can live up to the pretensions of her boy friend, is poor perplexed Beatie.

Mr. Wesker shows her returning to the Norfolk farm where her young roots found such thin soil. She's been three years away in London living with a voluble young Socialist who has pulled back a few inches for her the curtain on life.

She rails against the rustic turnip tops, and drives her mother and the rest of the family nearly mad with her talk of the wonderful 'Ron' and what 'Ron' says and does and thinks.

Ron ditches her, but out of immediate sadness, self-realisation emerges. As the final curtain falls, she cries aloud that she has found a voice of her own at last. One hears the door of a new Doll's House slam.

There is not enough room in an ink-thirsty newspaper to do real justice to this very interesting play, or its excellent production by John Dexter ... but Joan Plowright gives the performance of her career as Beatie, in her way a modern proletarian version of Nora Helmer ...

> Felix Barker: *Evening News*
> 1 July 1959

The setting is a farm labourer's kitchen − scruffily cosy, meagrely cluttered, with hand-me-down furniture, zigzag linoleum, gaudy wallpaper, a clock and a radio both designed like jerry-built Greek temples and (of course) the over-stuffed sink. Mother, with cottage-loaf figure and Yorkshire-pudding face, is taking a purely token sit-down on the edge of her chair. Daughter, in a housecoat and bathing hat, is trying to explain the appeal of good music. As the gramophone spins out the two interlocking themes of the farandole from *L'Arlesienne*, the daughter begins to prance around in her bare feet, eyes closed, fingertips widespread, in a parody of the ballet. Mother jogs her old bones and mutters indulgently, 'She's like a young lamb'. Curtain to second act of *Roots*.

I should have thought that such a scene would have spread prickles of embarrassment through the audience such as the Royal Court has not felt since that bear-and-squirrel romp in *Look Back In Anger*. Can this really be the high peak so far from one of our most talented young actresses? I don't know what reply you were expecting but it is a resounding 'Yes'.

That scene is somehow the most touching and true incident I have seen on the stage in eighteen-months relentless theatre-going. Somehow – but how? Joan Plowright is half the answer. In the daughter, Beatie, she has a role which fits her like her own skin. In her previous plays, her technique has always been showing an inch or two beneath the hem of costume. That rosebud pout of mouth, those wide ragdoll eyes, that surprised, reproachful, breathy pipsqueak voice, all have usually seemed too consciously manipulated with a ventriloquial ingenuity. But she is Beatie without make-up or make-believe – the country girl who returns home only to find that her roots end in bare rock. A warm-blooded three-dimensional human being, she begins by feeling a happy superiority to the tepid, torpid, farm animals who constitute her family.

She sets them moral problems to solve over tea. She rolls up her sleeves and sets about tidying up the muddles both inside and outside them. Prettily, funnily, movingly, she prods them out of their life-long hibernation. But in forcing them to examine their own hidebound callouses, she painfully strips the dead skin from her own sunburn. She discovers that in the country of the blind, the one-eyed woman is outcast. Her dance at the end of the second act is a premature victory celebration, an audaciously conceived and dazzlingly executed solo expressing the triumph of living over existing. It is balanced by the final curtain of the third act when the family chorus, grunting and snuffling, jostle round the trough, happily transformed to beasts again. While Beatie, alone and amazed and defeated, recognises that she is at least partly human.

Alan Brien: *Spectator*
10 July 1959

Oliver!

New Theatre: 30 June 1960

During the 1950s, British musicals made a sad showing beside the zest and professionalism of the American ones. Although many were delighted by Sandy Wilson's *The Boy Friend* (1954) and *Valmouth* (1958) or by Julian Slade's *Salad Days* (1954), the sheer scale of the British musicals contrasted unfavourably, deriving from intimate revues and university pastiches. They lacked the American drive and energy, as well as skill.

They were also rather genteel, and it was the gentility, rather than any other factor, which inhibited them. The growing reputation of Joan Littlewood's company at Stratford-atte-Bowe during the late 1950s was based upon an earthy directness, liveliness and a working-class attack – qualities which enlivened British theatre generally, but also had a rejuvenating effect on musicals. Littlewood loved songs and dances, which she incorporated even into apparently naturalistic studies of life in Liverpool and the East End of London. Lionel Bart, who wrote *Oliver!*, was one of many writers, composers and actors who were encouraged by Littlewood; and in 1960, he saw the first production of Littlewood's London answer to *Guys and Dolls*, *Fings Aint Wot They Used T'be*, for which he wrote the music and lyrics. Bart had previously written the lyrics for the hit British musical which opened the Mermaid Theatre, *Lock Up Your Daughters*; but *Oliver* was his first direct entry into the West End.

Its staging was splendid, with a rambling, complicated set by Sean Kenny, the architect-turned-set designer, whose inventiveness fired the imagination of other designers and contributed to a revival of *mise-en-scène* productions during the 1960s. The songs were catchy, the direction highly professional and the actors plainly enjoyed what they were doing. *Oliver!* was an old-fashioned show-business hit, and recognised as such by most critics. It also signalled a new virility in commercial theatre, demonstrating that managers and producers were prepared to gamble for higher stakes than usual and looked for higher rewards. Future Bart gambles (*Maggie May*, 1964, and *Twang*, 1965) were sadly less successful.

Oliver! at the New may do for Dickens what *My Fair Lady* did for Shaw. It could stimulate an avalanche of Dickens musicals with titles like *The Pickwick Capers* or *Miss Haversham Misses A Wedding*.

The flamboyant theatricality of Dickens fits in admirably with the florid and melodramatic techniques of the musical.

Oliver Twist with its simple story of virtue triumphant, its thieves' kitchen atmosphere, its blatantly false characters, its uninhibited violence, its nose-sniffing sentimentality, cannot lose any credibility by having music added to it. It is already incredible enough.

By stripping this, in Graham Greene's phrase, magnificent juvenilia down to a simple story line – Oliver sold by Mr. Bumble to an undertaker, Oliver falling in with Fagin and the Artful Dodger, Oliver rescued by Mr. Brownlow and recaptured by Bill Sykes, Nancy murdered by Sykes and Oliver restored to his wealthy family – the atmospheric essence remains, even if Dickens' fanatics will miss some of the book's characters.

Much of the triumph of *Oliver!* can be attributed to the ingenious, timbered sets of Sean Kenny, which were manipulated like some gigantic jig-saw puzzle and could wondrously conjure up for us the cavernous depths of the workhouse, the rollicking gaiety of a Cockney dive, the claustrophobia of Fagin's den and the eerie loneliness of London Bridge at night.

Lionel Bart's music is a zestful and unabashed blending of Tin Pan Alley, Yiddish folk melodies and the rhythms of Old Kent Road. They not only buttonhole you; they practically slug you.

Bart's lyrics are less vitamin-packed than his music, but he has written a very amusing number – *Reviewing The Situation* – which should go a long way to converting Fagin into a loveable character on the level of the Crazy Gang.

Ron Moody's Fagin, a slippery rascal rather than an unctuous villain, threatened to stop the show two or three times with his skilful and comic cavorting.

Georgia Brown, as Nancy, possesses that rare feminine quality of abandon and she threw it about the stage last night with gusto. A pile-driver could not have punched home her songs with more enthusiasm.

To find an Oliver Twist with as cherubic a face as Keith Hamshere's and who has a nice soprano voice that can carry a tune is an astonishing piece of good luck and casting.

Peter Coe's busy, but disciplined, direction has also made splendid use of young boys who all appear to be aspiring to become Al Jolsons.

My only reservation about *Oliver!* is that there is only a suggestion of dancing and with the exciting opportunities available, it is a pity so little was attempted.

But this should by no means deter you from rushing to the New Theatre immediately to see this imaginative, virile, pulsating and melodic British musical.

Milton Shulman: *Evening Standard*
1 July 1960

It was one of those big old-fashioned nights of fermenting enthusiasm at the New Theatre when the gallery goes mad with joy, and the cast at the end is forced to sing reprise after reprise of the hit numbers.

The applause had real heart to it. Palms smarted with clapping. And rightly gratitude centred on Lionel Bart, the writer of book, music and lyrics, whose only words when he took a curtain call were: 'May the good Dickens forgive us!'

'You've done a wonderful job', came a shout from the gallery, and about this there is no shadow of doubt. For a year, Mr. Bart has wrestled with the task of bringing *Oliver Twist* to the stage as a musical and this is the result.

The first half of *Oliver!* is superlatively good. From the opening scenes in the workhouse with the pathetic waifs hungrily singing 'Food, Glorious Food', through Oliver's initiation as a pickpocket under Fagin, until his arrest, this show stampedes its way to success.

The action is condensed but never hurried, and the songs – each a winner – emerge naturally from the situation.

Sean Kenny has devised an ingenious set which, with a turn, gives us workhouse, undertakers, thieves kitchen, and an early Victorian street scene which might be a tinted engraving by Cruikshank.

Above all, to give the famous characters life, there is an angelic Oliver in Keith Hamshere, a benign, eye-rolling, iip-licking Fagin in Ron Moody, and a cocky little Artful Dodger in Martin Horsey.

After the interval, the promise of the first half is not quite sustained. There is too much shouting and Peter Coe's previously well-disciplined direction becomes a little woolly.

Somehow Bill Sykes and Nancy (though admirably played by Danny Sewell and Georgia Brown) don't integrate with the story and the music and songs do not carry us forward to a crescendo.

We lose Oliver. From being the centre of interest, he is swept away in a tide of melodrama, and I think he needs a solo song to reassert himself and to tell us his feelings when, after being adopted by the rich Mr. Brownlow, he is recaptured by Fagin's gang.

But these reservations must not blur the fact that, all in all *Oliver!* is a piping success, a hit to fill the New Theatre for many months.

Perhaps here at last is that British musical for which we have been waiting with Messianic patience for so long.

Felix Barker: *Evening News*
1 July 1960

If the rigours of the end are understandably softened – to execute Ron Moody's Fagin would be unthinkable – it is the tough side of Dickens rather than the sentimental that Lionel Bart brings out in *Oliver!*. ... Fagin slips away, and could well look after himself, but Bill Sykes is shot on Waterloo Bridge in one of the most exciting scenes I remembered in a musical – exciting not so much because of the man-hunt, but because Sean Kenny's set of massive timbers, John Wyckham's lighting that marvellously suggests the river by night (as elsewhere he hits off, for a pub scene, the exact quality of Hogarth's light) and Peter Coe's stirring handling of a London crowd marry into one of those rare and complete illusions.

Mr. Bart is a one-man band that will not be asked, I think, to move into the next street ...

Eric Keown: *Punch*
6 July 1960

There are several reasons why *Oliver Twist* should be a good bet as the material for a musical. First, children in a cast are always a great popular asset (*cf. The King and I*), especially if they are pathetic. Second, good adult singers are often fat, and Dickens' period allows an amplitude that is generally frowned on now; weight for weight, the chorus in *Oliver!* must go half as much again as the chorus in, say, *Guys and Dolls*. Third, wrapped snugly in the knowledge of free milk and the Welfare State, nobody today is going to be upset by what little social comment is left in Dickens' work when the musicalising process has gone to work on it. Fourth, the ambience of *Oliver Twist* is not only the London that Britain loves best, thereby tapping a possible audience of fifty million, but also the London that the British Holidays and Travel Association loves best, which ropes in the whole of America.

Fifth and foremost, though, *Oliver!* succeeds because the author is Lionel Bart and the designer Sean Kenny, who are respectively now confirmed as the best writer of musicals and the best stage designer that we have. ...

The chief glory of a generally infectious evening is Sean Kenny's set, a charred-looking timber silhouette that somehow evokes a treadmill and makes the stage of the New Theatre look as big as the Bolshoi: like Orson Welles' filing-cabinet scene in *Rhinoceros*, it unearths distances in a theatre that we had forgotten all about.

Penelope Gilliatt: *Queen*
20 July 1960

The Devils

Shakespeare Memorial Theatre Company, Aldwych Theatre, London: 20 February 1961

On 1 January 1960, Peter Hall succeeded Glen Byam Shaw as the director of the Shakespeare Memorial Company. Since the war, the Stratford seasons had grown in size, scale and variety; and the company was comparatively wealthy, from the proceeds of foreign tours, the growing tourism to Stratford and the careful investment and endowment policies of the Stratford governors. From this position of strength, Hall, enthusiastically supported by Sir Fordham Flower, chairman of the governors, undertook a major gamble. He wanted to transform what was a seasonal company into something equivalent to a continental repertory theatre, with a large, basically permanent group of actors, who would work together over a period of years to establish a company style. Productions would be held together in the repertoire over the seasons and not simply forgotten at the end of the year. To encourage actors to stay with the company, he sought a second theatre in London, eventually choosing the Aldwych. The London theatre provided the company with three great advantages. It enabled Stratford productions to transfer easily, without any elaborate negotiations with commercial managements. It allowed the company to tackle new plays and modern revivals, whereas the policy at Stratford had always been – and remains – centred upon Shakespeare and the Jacobeans; and it allowed actors and directors, who might otherwise have been alarmed to spend their creative lives in Stratford, away from London and the major metropolitan theatre circuit, to have the opportunity of being seen in a central, rather than regional, theatre.

'The plan', wrote Peter Brook in the RSC's Annual Report (1968), 'was radical and creative ... before the structure was ready, he opened his grand project: suddenly, the vast company, the immense repertoire, the constant output, the excitement, the disasters, the strain all came into existence.' Britain had never had a company quite like it before, not even in the great days of the Old Vic or at the time when Sir Barry Jackson ran five companies from his base at the Birmingham Rep. But it was a gamble. It meant diving into the financial reserves of the Shakespeare Memorial Company and, later, demanding adequate funds from the Arts Council.

Much depended upon the success of the opening London season; and on Whiting's new play, *The Devils*, in particular. It was the first new play performed by the Shakespeare Memorial Theatre in the eighty-two years of its existence, specially commissioned by Peter Hall from John Whiting, who, despite his critical reputation, was neither an established nor a successful dramatist. Since *Marching Song*, Whiting had been concentrating on translations and adaptations. *The Devils* was also the kind of play which no other management was at all likely to tackle – requiring a large cast, a fluid and distinctive use of the stage – with acting areas rather than formally built sets, ambitious both in its handling of themes and language, comparable with certain Jacobean dramas rather than with modern plays. 'How many other English playwrights,' asked Whiting rhetorically, in an interview with Richard Findlater (published in *The Art of the Dramatist*, 1970), '... have been given the kind of opportunity that Peter Hall gave me?'

The success of Hall's first years with the Shakespeare Memorial Company at Stratford and in London led to a change of company name, to the Royal Shakespeare Company, and of status, as a truly national theatre. Hall demonstrated beyond doubt, the value of such a company to British theatre; and his success with commissioning

"THE DEVILS" by John Whiting

The Devils spurred other managements to take major chances,
including the National Theatre itself, when it was formed in 1963.

This is a play about religion, true and perverted. It is a high bid. John Whiting, whose talent for treating the enigmatic and doom-laden will not be doubted by those who saw his *Marching Song* or *Saint's Day*, could have made a play on the level of *A Man for all Seasons*. Or treated an historical story with a dramatist's simple surgery, as Miller did in *The Crucible* (with a slightly similar, but much easier, theme, easier dramatically). If his play turns out only a flawed masterpiece, at least it is not because he hasn't tried but because his hero in truth does not yield to the stuff of tragedy. The paradox is that if the author had left his hero enigmatic (as the hapless man is left in history), he might have pulled off a more impressive play. It is in trying to explain him and in making him justify himself that a most absorbing play, in my opinion, goes fatally awry.

The hero (see Aldous Huxley, Michelet, Alfred de Vigny) is Father Urbain Grandier, the curé of Loudun who was burned at the stake in 1634, not for his venery and wenching but for having, they said, been the instrument whereby the Ursuline nuns of the local convent were possessed of the devil. The trouble was started by the prioress, a hunchback without a vocation who, inflamed by stories of the libertine priest (whom she had only seen if at all in vision) develops acute sexual (or diabolic) hysteria and names him as the culprit to the witch hunters.

Mr. Whiting lays out the premise with theatrical imagination and an atmospheric power which a beautiful production by Peter Wood intensifies. The setting of the drama is masterly, if sometimes prolix or wilfully obscurantist. But one is here unquestionably in the climate of a 'great' play: but then levity breaks in. Max Adrian, for some reason, plays the part of chief witch hunter in the manner of a petulant Shavian 'villain' (e.g. Cauchon in *St. Joan*) and collects fatal laughs in quite the wrong way. Dorothy Tutin, however, is extremely effective as the possessed Sister Jeanne, torn between bestial ecstasy and sober horror; and Richard Johnson is splendid as the soulful sensualist.

But it seems as if Mr. Whiting, two-thirds of the way through his play, has doubts about his hero. If we, the audience, are to be able to endure and to be moved by Grandier's end, ought we not to get (so Mr. Whiting may have thought) a fuller insight into that soul? Grandier, who discusses himself first with a sewage man, then with an old priest, becomes now (to my mind) someone out of quite a different century and climate. He becomes a sort of Tennysonian or Wagnerian hero, who seeks to find God through the senses, who invents a god of his own from elements which Wordsworth might have laid under contribution and reconciles himself with that god in a manner which is pathetic certainly, but not by any means convincing. Perhaps Mr. Whiting means us to feel that the true horror of the thing is that Grandier is not himself convinced by this new 'projection' of God and feels that his faith is slipping, and will not stand the final strain. He is tortured, admits his lechery but will not admit to witchcraft. But 'we' are not 'with' him. The horror leaves me, at least, quite unmoved. Nor is the remorse of the nun any more moving. I think it is that this piece of history, for all Mr. Whiting's skill and elevation of thought, refuses to bend into a dramatic shape. Many small parts, lighting effects, sounds and *coups de théâtre* could be praised in detail. But some people may find it compelling, even if its power finally misfires.

Philip Hope-Wallace: *Guardian*
22 February 1961

The material supplied by Mr. Aldous Huxley in *The Devils of Loudun* is abundant and threatens to be well-nigh overwhelming for stage purposes. Mr. John Whiting disengages a story which enables him in a succession of short scenes which naturally vary a good deal in their dramatic impact to put together a play which is rich in ironic implications and has a fascination of its own. It wastes itself in the end in scenes of torture which are merely painful to witness. ...

Mr. Richard Johnson gives a most satisfying performance as the priest, suggesting at once his considerable intellectual capacity, his self-conceit verging upon arrogance and his physical attraction. And he rises in accordance with the story Mr. Whiting has to tell, to a curious state of mind in which the hope of coming to God by way of married happiness he goes through the form of marriage with the pupil he has seduced. He rises no less successfully to the long soliloquy in which the priest claims to have created God out of all the worldly phenomena that he can grasp imaginatively, to have given himself to him, and to have been received by him. Mr. Johnson even gets what theatrical effect is to be got by the prolonged scenes of torture. ...

The Times
21 February 1961

What one expects from John Whiting is intellect. He has himself warned us what to look out for. Some time ago, Mr. Whiting declared that what bothered him about the new school of social drama was its tiny, tiny brain. A dramatist who makes a remark like that has either a big brain himself or no brain at all.

Now the showing of intellect on the stage is not a simple matter. The conditions of the playhouse necessarily restrict the drama, in its social and philosophical criticism, to a rather low level. All the more gratifying then that in *The Devils* Mr. Whiting does succeed, even in this recalcitrant medium, in vindicating his intellect, and in proving that, whatever may be wrong with the brains of the Royal Court, his own are in sound working order.

It is true that in doing this he has received great assistance. He has been helped by Aldous Huxley's original account of the demoniac possession of Loudun; by Peter Wood's superbly flowing production; by Sean Kenny's miraculously adaptable setting; and by the Stratford-on-Avon company's able performance. But the main credit is his.

His is the mind that has conceived the wonderfully complex method by which the tale of lust and hysteria and salvation is unfolded in a narrative that, in spite of constant changes of character and setting, preserves an absolutely uninterrupted progression from beginning to end. Out of a multiplicity of brief scenes, he has conjured an unbroken unity. *The Devils* is a marvel of organisation, a mosaic so finely put together that it has the effect of a living picture.

His reading, too, of the character of Grandier, the lecherous priest whose downfall was brought about by lay jealousy, ecclesiastical superstition and feminine sexual obsession is a remarkable feat of dramatic intelligence. The man's search for God, first through lust, then through human affection, then through martyrdom, and finally through disciplined thought, takes us on a journey which, in its essential dramatic ascetism, is rare in the theatre.

Harold Hobson: *Sunday Times*
26 February 1961

Mr. John Whiting in *The Devils*, presented by the Stratford-on-Avon company at the Aldwych, makes a bold attempt on the big, fine play which it seems in the natural order of things he should some day write. But for one reason and another, this study of religion, true and false, in 17th century France, though holding the attention for some three hours, finally misfires.

One reason is the misplaced levity with which the witch-hunting cleric is treated. Another is the long closing scene of torture on the rack that is merely painful to watch. And the most important reason of all is that the spiritual progress of the womanizing priest who pathetically invents a god willing to receive him despite the sins of the flesh, is never wholly convincing ...

Anthony Cookman: *Tatler*
8 March 1961

Much was expected; more was fulfilled. From Aldous Huxley's *The Devils of Loudun*, John Whiting (a new play at last!) has fashioned a powerful dramatic spectacle, a play of depth, force, terror, and beauty.

With consummate craftsmanship, he has distilled the essence of Huxley's detailed and relentless reconstruction of one of history's more ghastly moments: the mass 'possession' of a group of nuns in a 17th century priory.

The effect is of a Jacobean dramatist writing a contemporary tragedy (for which he would surely himself have been put to death as a devil) equipped with a miraculous foreknowledge of Freud.

We see the whole phantasmagorical procession pass before our eyes: the local priest, Urbain Grandier, exciting the jealousy of the townsfolk with his worldly charm and male seductiveness; the deformed Prioress Jeanne succumbing to sexual hysteria, infecting other nuns with her obsession; the priests and governors exploiting the women's erotic exhibitionism to their own ends; the downfall, torture and death at the stake of the priest, struggling not only against the fanatical and primitive superstitiousness around him, but also against his threatening loss of faith.

Perhaps for some tastes, we see too much. Mr. Whiting spares us nothing, the obscene exorcisms, the hideous self-intoxication of the nuns, the priest's lusts, and his jailer's instruments of torture will shock – as they are meant to do.

But for those with adequate stomachs, this production can hardly be overpraised. The playwright has chosen a bold epic form, and within it, he carries us from climax to climax.

To recreate the period he has chosen an almost classical mode of speech, which avoids 'period' mannerisms almost as brilliantly as Arthur Miller avoided them in *The Crucible*, which *The Devils* resembles in stature and content.

The production by Peter Wood is of a visual splendour rarely encountered in a modern play, and he has been aided by the magnificently bold settings of Sean Kenny. ...

The Devils was commissioned by Peter Hall for the first Aldwych season of the Stratford company. And if it represents the type of New Drama we are going to see at this theatre, Mr. Hall's policy will have been triumphantly vindicated.

Robert Muller: Daily Mail
21 February 1961

Oh, What a Lovely War

Theatre Royal, Stratford, E15: 19 March 1963

Joan Littlewood's original vision of a community theatre in the East End of London was a victim of its own success. During the late 1950s, so many of her productions transferred to the West End, that she found it difficult to keep a stable company together. After the transfers of Shelagh Delaney's *A Taste of Honey* (1958) and *Fings Aint Wot They Used T'be*, her sense of frustration grew and, in 1960, she left the Theatre Workshop company to pursue her dream elsewhere. In 1963, however, she returned and her first production was a musical documentary on the First World War.

I was lucky enough to be at Stratford on the first night of *Oh, What a Lovely War*; and I shall never forget the waves of anguish and nostalgia which seemed to sweep over the audience as the old war songs were sung, *Good-byee, Tipperary* and so many others. The Pierrot Show setting, the awful casualty figures flashed on the screen and Charles Chilton's sketches all combined to offer a devastatingly ironic attack on past heroic follies. The pace and assurance of the production were also remarkable, so much matter packed into so short a time, and to such effect. Littlewood drove Chilton to provide more and more material; and her decision to present the documentary as a Pierrot Show was taken almost at the last minute. It was a tribute to the flexibility of her outlook, and the hardworking loyalty of her company, that such drastic changes could be made like that; and the performances retained a freshness and vitality of outlook, long after the inevitable transfer to the West End.

She's back! For far too long Miss Joan Littlewood, the Mother Courage of Theatre Workshop, has been away from home.

At last, surrounded by a fine Theatre Workshop cast (it includes Murray Melvin, Brian Murphy, Griffith Davies and Victor Spinetti), she has returned in triumph with her first production for more than three years.

The entertainment is stamped firmly with her trade-marks. It is a devastating musical satire on World War 1, with the carnage played out amid the merry songs of the day ('We don't want to lose you, but we think you ought to go' may stand as an archetype), with a running band of lights upstage spelling out the casualties: 'Passchendale: British loss 135,000 in the first day. Gain: 100 yards.'

The result is, of course, lop-sided. (Miss Littlewood's faults are as much in evidence as her virtues). The war was only fought because of the profiteers and only the other ranks were any good. (She would do well to remember that Wilfrid Owen and Siegfried Sassoon were both officers.)

Still, the point about such lopsidedness about World War 1 is that the lop is on the right side.

The villain of the piece, for instance, squarely and without reservations, is Haig. We are not allowed to forget that for a Haig there was a Ludendorff and for both a Pétain: but it is on Haig that the author's sights, and Miss Littlewood's, are set, and right in the middle they get him, yapping eternally about the one big push that will see the Army through the enemy line, as the casualties mount from the thousands to the hundreds of thousands and the hundreds of thousands to the millions.

'Battle of the Somme: British loss 65,000 in three hours. Gain nil.'

It is not as grim as that, in truth, Miss Littlewood's touch is light, and the humour is uppermost, even in the savage parody of a field service, with the men singing, to the tune of *Onward, Christian Soldiers,*

Forward, Joe Soap's Army,
Forward without fear,
With our brave commanders

Safely in the rear.

But be not deceived: even in the safe purlieus of Theatre Workshop, there were uneasy stirrings in the house at some of the things that were being done with the Union Jack, and when the inevitable transfer to the West End takes place, this may well be the first satire to score what we are told is the satirist's bull's eye: to make the audience walk out.

Bernard Levin: *Daily Mail*
20 March 1963

[The field service was one of two scenes which the Theatre Workshop feared – or hoped? – might drive Harold Hobson 'howling from the theatre'. 'Alas,' he wrote, however, 'I enjoyed it'.]

The effect of both scenes may be considered blasphemous by the excessively sensitive; but in each case, the music's throbbing rhythms are so irresistible, and the singing is so good, that it would be absurd to protest.

More questionable is Theatre Workshop's generosity of nature which, in some ways, knows no limits. Theatre Workshop despises British generals; sneers at English royalty; finds it impossible to forgive Sir Winston Churchill. But in *Oh, What a Lovely War*, it shows the Kaiser as a dignified and peace-loving figure. British officers it sees as cowards and fools; German officers, however, have good sense and compassion. Theatre Workshop obeys to the letter the injunction to love its enemies. What it apparently cannot manage to do is to love its friends.

These, of course, are West End managements, West End audiences, bourgeois critics, Old Etonians, diplomats, gentlemen farmers – almost anyone, in fact, except those working people whom Miss Littlewood outrageously represents as being pushed to death and misery by the behaviour of the very classes upon whom Theatre Workshop depends for support. You would think, from *Oh, What a Lovely War* that no officer was ever in danger in the 1914–18 war. But despite its injustice – or perhaps because of the sincerity of Miss Littlewood's belief in this injustice – the piece is stamped with originality, with entertainment and pathos, with the true life of the theatre.

Harold Hobson: *Sunday Times*
20 March 1963

113

The presentation of the battles and slaughter of 1914–18 in the guise of a pierrot entertainment is one of an irony not matched anywhere else in the London theatre. Miraculously, the precisely judged casualness of this conception rises unfalteringly to the height of its great argument. ...

Joan Littlewood's satire is of the highest kind: it admits and presents the grandeur of Haig (superbly played by George Sewell) and of the Church at the same time that it excoriates them. I had not expected to be so moved, so entertained, so excited.

Harold Hobson: *Sunday Times*
11 July 1963

The so-called entertainment has now graduated to the West End to Wyndham's and in spite of slight alterations, once again makes an overwhelming effect. The notion is so simple. The execution so unerringly sure. Noël Coward first did the same thing (and briefly) in *Cavalcade*: the Great War was 'potted' in terms of three or four recruiting songs, sung as a start with enthusiasm, then in fading light, with growing unease, while a platoon of gassed soldiers trudged over a ramp of duck boards at the back of the stage.

The idea is here extended and brilliantly so. The barrack-room lawyers, the rumour-scared wives and the generals are there, touting their pious hopes. Tendentious in the way things of the theatre always must be is the whole leftish slant of the piece, but those who fear that 'their conscience' may not be able to stand it as the advertisement seems to hope, may like to know that though the piece is as unfair as any powerful cartoon, it is only anti-war and only, incidentally, anti-national, and then as much anti-French or anti-German as anti-British. ...

It could be over-praised; but if the idea catches you, as it did me, between wind and water, you may easily come out of it calling it the most brilliantly imagined political comment of our theatre in all the years since the *second* war.

Philip Hope-Wallace: *Guardian*
21 June 1963

As a theatrical experience, it moves one in many ways, to feelings strangely mixed.

It moves one to rage that humanity should have been capable of making a fool of itself on such a scale, and to horror lest it should prove capable of doing so again on an even greater scale.

And yet, mingled with that, there comes a strange exhilaration and a nostalgia. For those who fought in that war and were lucky enough to survive it, the show conjures up memories that are not all painful.

To hear the songs we sang – even though the younger generation doesn't always know how to sing them – is to catch again a whiff of that wry, disillusioned, humorous resignation with which our armies faced trench life.

W. A. Darlington: *Daily Telegraph*
21 June 1963

Thanks to our General Sherman and a couple of others, we are aware that war is hell, but Miss Littlewood and her colleagues in the Theatre Workshop Group Production, who put this musical entertainment together, point up the fact that war isn't only satanic but horrendously silly. Before the curtain went up on *Oh, What a Lovely War*, I was beguiled by this note in the programme: 'In 1960, an American Military Research Team fed all the facts of World War One into the computers they use to play World War III. They reached the conclusion that the 1914–18 war was impossible and couldn't have happened. There could not have been so many blunders or so many casualties.' Miss Littlewood, however, who knows a fact when she sees it, insists that there *was* a First World War ... Dressed in Pierrot and Pierrette costumes, the cast performs in front of a kind of Times Building news tape that recounts such things as the fact that thirteen thousand casualties were incurred to gain a hundred yards. (This, presumably, is when the computers turned in their suits.) You may be sure that the usual inept military set – Sir John French, Sir Douglas Haig, the Kaiser, Moltke and that popular Irish target, Sir Henry Wilson – are given their lumps here, but the show by no means consists entirely of kicking dead dogs. It is full of the songs and absurdities of the First World War (which, of course, persisted into the Second World War), and it has on hand a cast that cannot be faulted. ... In a cast drilled with enormous precision, Victor Spinetti stands out as a sort of military master of ceremonies (one of his turns involves a magnificent bit of double-talk) and then there is Valerie Walsh who is miraculously configured, and then there is Barbara Windsor – But why go on? These are all fine people.

John McCarten: *New Yorker*
10 October 1964

Alfie

Mermaid Theatre: 19 June 1963

Bill Naughton was a magazine writer and radio dramatist before he turned to the theatre in the early 1960s. He was at least twenty years older than the other new playwrights of the period – Osborne, Pinter, Orton and Bond – and his plays were less dashing and outrageous, not technically innovative or particularly angry. His three best-known plays for the Mermaid Theatre – *All In Good Time*, *Alfie* and *Spring and Port Wine* – were thoughtful, mature and compassionate works; and they helped to establish Bernard Miles's Mermaid as another pioneering theatre, outside the West End, which for a time ranked with the Royal Court and the Theatre Workshop, Stratford. Miles's policy was not politically radical, like the writers congregating around Devine in Sloane Square, nor community-based, like Joan Littlewood's; but it represented a kind of earthy commonsense, warm and unpretentious.

These were also Naughton's qualities; but in Alfie, he created a character who was not only a leading example of the amoral and swinging sixties, but a warning. Alfie was not a rebel without a cause. He was not a rebel and he knew what he wanted, money and birds, with a talent for getting both without hard work. But his rootlessness brought with it a nemesis, which Naughton under- rather than over-states. Alfie simply reaches a point where life doesn't seem to be worth living, although he is not the kind of person to contemplate suicide. He was a proletarian Don Juan, turned not to stone by the statue of an avenging father, but to plastic and polystyrene.

John Neville, previously associated with classic Shakespearian roles at Stratford and the Old Vic, whose elegant appearance and beautiful voice encouraged certain critics to compare him with the young Gielgud, transformed his image for Alfie, from juvenile lead to juvenile delinquent. It was a time for such anti-heroic transformations. Olivier played the seedy music hall comedian, Archie Rice, in Osborne's *The Entertainer*, as well as Fred Midway in David Turner's *Semi-Detached*. Heroism and even stage glamour was out of fashion; and in its place, came that sixties determination not to be fooled by life, but to enjoy it while one can, unsentimentally and uninhibitedly.

Alfie was an unsentimental play, and certain scenes in it, such as the abortion, shocked audiences of the time. But unlike *Entertaining Mr. Sloane* or *Saved*, it was not a *succès de scandale*. Within a few years, indeed, *Alfie* came to be considered as a standard middle-brow play, almost suitable for family audiences, which indicated the remarkable swing in tastes which had occurred since the early 1950s.

The new, refreshed summer of the Mermaid Theatre continues apace, with the West End strewn with its transfers, here comes another to join them very soon.

What is more it is by the author of *All In Good Time*, which left the Mermaid only a couple of months ago for a long stay at the Phoenix.

What is more still, it is, in its way, as good a play as the other. Alfie is a sharp Cockney lad whose various amours the play chronicles – chronicles them, I may say, with an overwhelmingly refreshing absence of prudery on the one hand or self-consciousness about its frankness on the other.

His technique is the old one: catch 'em young, treat 'em rough, tell 'em nothing. But with one difference that finally destroys him: Alfie is a real human being.

He may say (indeed, he does say): 'The average bloke knows in 'is 'eart what a rotten bleeder 'e 'is; 'e don't want to keep being reminded of it with somebody good around.' But the truth beneath the banter is that Alfie is fleeing the Hound of Heaven, the voice which tells him the truth about his treatment of his birds, his callousness and selfishness, his fornicating and his adultery.

At one point, the voice is made audible to him; at the end of a scene of hideous power, recounting the progress of an abortion he has arranged for one of his passing fancies, the wailing of an unborn child sounds in his ears, horribly echoing the cries of the live bastard child he has fathered earlier.

At last, Alfie comes face to face with his nature and with the cul-de-sac at the end of which lies the Nemesis of his own conscience. ...

There are the splendid set-pieces, like his distracted interview with the doctor who is trying to tell him his lungs are touched, while he is intent only on recounting his amorous stream-of-consciousness.

All this, and much more, goes to make up a play of richness and high purpose, of wit and bubbling humour, of perception and understanding, and finally of uncompromising truth.

... the evening is above all Mr. Neville's. Mr. Neville must have been waiting all his life to play this part. His cockney is effortlessly perfect, his stance and walk and nervous, flicking movements, likewise.

But these are only the externals; inside Mr. Neville has got the reality of Alfie to the last detail, the last twist of his mind and heart, the last desperate defence against his own good nature.

Bernard Levin: *Daily Mail*
20 June 1963

The chief character of Bill Naughton's new comedy (originally a radio play, Third Programme no less) is an immoral young man but at least he does not seem to be a security risk, so perhaps it is all right. He tells the story of his birds without owing anything to Aristophanes. He is sharply dressed ... with an insatiable appetite for birds, married or single (preferably married, because if you can make them laugh you're half-way there), and for light ale (Whitbread's). He is handsome, charming and slim – in fact he has to get rid of one bird, snared in a trunk road caff, because she feeds him too much Lancashire hot-pot and steak-and-kidney pie. Another, snatched from under the nose of her husband in hospital, has to be put aside after an abortion – and the abortionist is the only one in the play who strikes any kind of moral attitude. The best scene of all is where the bird in question is a doctor and Alfie carries on his monologue to the audience while she is diagnosing his infected lung.

The doctor is the only bird he does not make a pass at, and all his passes are uninhibited. Alfie is John Neville, so well played that you might sometimes fall into the error of thinking that John Neville is Alfie. There is not a weak performance among the fairly big cast, though Glenda Jackson, Audine Leith, Alan Townsend and Margaret Courtenay (respectively a bird, the doctor, a truck driver and a rich bird with a Zodiac automatic and three hairdressing shops) are particularly strong. The only trouble with the play is that it sags very dangerously in the middle of Act 2, having reached the first interval at a cracking pace ...

Gerard Fay: *Guardian*
20 June 1963

... I thought the beginning of his *All In Good Time* disgusting and nearly walked out. But this judgement was premature; *All In Good*

Time is one of the healthiest, one of the most touching and brave plays in London. It says things about friendship between men – true and moving things – that no other play dares even glance at.

I have had the same experience with *Alfie*. Alfie, a spry Cockney seducer with no grammar, but with a jaunty, confident walk, assertive clothes, and a tolerant taste in girls, talked so incessantly about 'a bleeding this' and 'a bleeding that' that I sat horrified, distressed and angry. Perhaps this was my fault. Perhaps the reason I hate the adjective is not, as I think, aesthetic, but psychologically disreputable. Disreputable or not, misery rose up inside me. I had no professional duty that required me to stay in the theatre, for *Alfie* has already been reviewed here. Nevertheless, stay I did, for I remembered *All In Good Time*; and I was rewarded.

Alfie will, no doubt, attract a large number of people who want their drama to consist of sexual aphrodisiacs. Alfie is always thinking about girls, and when he does think about them, it is not their intellectual qualifications that springs to his mind. There is, it is true, only one scene in the play in which he paws them with any freedom; but he gets two of them with child, and in one of them he brings an abortionist, played by Norman Wynne with an obscene rectitude which is both revolting and artistically right.

Alfie is not an unkindly man, but he has no intention of allowing the feeble dictates of his heart to interfere with his fun. He genuinely enjoys buying a teddy bear for his bastard son, but he would not dream of marrying the child's mother. He is shaken by the mechanics of the abortion, but not by the principle of it, nor the sordidness. He is ruled by convenience and physical pleasure. It is not that he despises right or justice or honour, no-one has ever told him that these things exist; or if they did, he was not listening at the time.

Some of the scenes are melodramatic. ... Many episodes, however, are remarkably good. The best two are Alfie's official medical examination and the preparation for and the aftermath of the abortion. The first is extraordinarily funny. The woman doctor's astonishing but matter-of-fact questions, absolutely in line with what happens at this sort of thing – do you sweat at nights? are you growing increasingly ill-tempered? and so on – impinge more and more on Alfie's pre-occupied mind so that, though he begins the interview in the highest possible spirits, he ends up in a dead faint.

It would seem improbable that an abortion scene should be

dramatic, terrible and beautiful. This one is all three. Here only does Alfie, in a disjointed, uninhibited and profoundly moving and disturbing speech, see right down into himself. This speech, John Neville, spotlit in a world of darkness, delivers less with self-disgust than with a kind of awed wonder at the unexpectedness of his feelings. It is the high point of the play and of Mr. Neville's performance, just as the whole evening is the high point of Mr. Neville's career. For a decade, Mr. Neville has concealed himself in costume, and subdued his voice to talking posh. *Alfie* is his moment of revelation. It shows him to be one of our first actors, touching, sincere and very, very comic.

Harold Hobson: *Sunday Times*
4 August 1963

We leave Alfie as we have found him. A morsel of human debris floating on the scum of society whose lust for life and passion for survival is both lovable and damnable.

Milton Shulman: *Evening Standard*
20 June 1963

... the interesting and important thing about Alfie is that he is at heart a decent fellow, meaning no harm to anyone. He even betrays glimmerings of paternal pride, hastily suppressed. There is a scene in a hospital, where he is recovering from TB in which he shows himself genuinely concerned for the welfare of his wife-loving room-mate − but concerned lest the poor fellow should be hurt by indulging his sincerity by not being able to be cynical. 'Even your thoughts have a proper place'. The moment Alfie *thinks*, he will be finished ...

Gerald Barry: *Punch*
3 July 1963

Everything which Bill Naughton writes has the quality which perhaps John Whiting lacked in his work, and which Pirandello and O'Neill could, I suppose, afford to ignore: a quality of simple warmth, a kindness towards people. Therefore everything he writes gives pleasure − up to a point.

Harold Hobson: *Sunday Times*
23 June 1963

A Severed Head

Criterion Theatre: 27 June 1963

In the same month that *Alfie* opened at the Mermaid, Iris Murdoch's
and J. B. Priestley's *A Severed Head* transferred from the Bristol Old
Vic. Of the two, *A Severed Head* had the worse notices, but ran for
longer, into 1966. Both, in their different ways, contributed to a
certain sexual libertarianism of the 1960s, which moralists
sometimes dubbed as amoral. On one level, there was growing
opposition to the British censorship system for the theatre, abolished
in 1968; and on another, a proliferation of strip clubs. In between the
political and the sleazy, there were many comedies whose views
were as strongly against marriage and bourgeois domesticity as
1950s comedies had been for marriage. In 1962, Ann Jellicoe's *The
Knack*, presenting a more flattering view of Alfies, was produced at
the Royal Court; while in 1964, Frank Marcus's *The Formation
Dancers* was a slightly less complicated version of the sexual dances
celebrated in *A Severed Head*.

Marcus was influenced by the Austrian dramatist, Arthur
Schnitzler, whose *La Ronde* (*Reigen*) he had translated and adapted.
Behind such plays as *A Severed Head* and *The Formation Dancers*,
there was a kind of longing to provide London with the
sophisticated, cosmopolitan, sexual comedies previously associated
with Vienna and Paris. London which had once the reputation of
being, in Wedekind's phrase, 'a grey city', was determined not to be
grey and stuffy any longer; and so, side by side with many satires on
bourgeois life, such as Giles Cooper's *Anything In The Garden*, were
comedies ostentatiously displaying an adult broad-mindedness.

Murdoch's novel, *A Severed Head*, was published in 1961; and
with its strong formal structure and unlikely couplings of seven
characters, each of whom have some kind of sexual relationship with
each other, it immediately presented itself as a likely candidate for a
stage adaptation, although Priestley, in his sixty-ninth year, was an
unlikely adaptor. The milieu of the wealthy middle class, a world of
analysts, wine merchants and afternoon sessions, may not have
reflected Hampstead or Kensington societies any more accurately
than Restoration comedy reflected the intrigues of Restoration

London; but it did reflect an elegant desire to be rid, once and for all, of a shifty, twilight world where marital respectability had to be preserved at all costs. Nor were plays like *A Severed Head* entirely without other dimensions, for Britain had seen several minor, sexual-political scandals in previous years – involving cabinet ministers and call-girls – whose consequences in political terms were far more serious than the original lapses, if indeed they could be called that. *A Severed Head* was part of a much broader appeal for maturity and tolerance; and it also delivered glancing blows against the palliatives which keep respectability going, the theorising of the analysts, the heated confessions and the cold calculations.

... it is literary in the best sense: there is no trace of the stylistic vanities which are the usual mark of the novelist-turned-playwright. All the effects – the laughs, shocks and ironies with which the play abounds – are expertly placed, and the timing of the episodes shows an exact understanding of the relationship between duration and impact. It is a dazzling piece of entertainment.

Miss Murdoch's subject is the sexual behaviour of a society that has thrown out sexual morality. Martin, the central character, is a leisured young wine merchant happily equipped with a wife and an adoring young mistress.

His contentment receives its first shock when his wife embarks on an affair with her analyst, and the frantic exchange of partners that ensues reduces him to a quivering wreck. Besides the opening triangle, the action also includes Martin's brother and the analyst's sister, and the play ends with a pairing-off of the most unlikely characters as partners – a strong suggestion that their relationships are as transient as all the others are.

However, one cannot safely attribute any comment to Miss Murdoch for her attitude is one of cryptic detachment. Her play occupies a mid-zone between high comedy and farce, never committing itself to more than demonstrating how the characters behave. One cannot fairly complain about this: Miss Murdoch is writing about a morally lawless society, and she treats it on its own terms, refusing to falsify the subject by injecting moral comment of her own. What she does brilliantly convey is the idea that freedom is merely a hunt for the next servitude.

Martin, for instance, submits to the authority of the analyst who has cuckolded him – a moral authority who avoids the language of morality: and there are some deliciously funny scenes in which the adulterous pair quiz Martin in the tones of aggrieved Victorian parents.

Heather Chasen, as the imperturbably frail wife, and Paul Eddington, who plays the analyst with a marvellous combination of furtive suspicion, plummy authority and physical smugness extract every comic nuance from these scenes.

Martin deserts his leader when he discovers him in the act of incest, and transfers his loyalty to the analyst's sister – a sinister anthropologist with a belief in violence and the dark gods. Perhaps she is intended to be his salvation – a means of regaining contact with the basic human impulses from which, as a 'severed head' in the earlier scenes, he had been cut off. But it is just as likely that she represents merely the next attachment which will be tried out and discarded. In either case, the writing remains as poised and dangerous as a waiting cobra.

The Times
28 June 1963

It is a long time since I have been so acutely disappointed and confused by a play as I was last night by *A Severed Head* ...

Having admired Miss Iris Murdoch's ironic novel about sex among the intelligentsia, I was completely unprepared for this glib and cheap version of it, adapted, oddly enough, by Miss Murdoch herself and J. B. Priestley.

No one, of course, could take the romantic adventures of the hero, Martin Lynch-Gibbon, too seriously. This is probably because a woman author will never really understand what motivates a man in love.

When Lynch-Gibbon discovers that his wife is leaving him for her psychiatrist, he is shocked in spite of the fact that he has a mistress of his own. Trying to behave decently, because he is still in love with both his wife and her psychiatrist (only a woman novelist would make this assumption), he is sucked into a morass of steaming and ludicrous passionate relationships.

... Eventually everything is straightened out by a highly unlikely game of musical beds, in which arbitrary couples are sorted out on arbitrary mattresses.

But underlying the fantastic nature of this highly articulate sexual fable was a deep sympathy and understanding of their problems. These edgy, sensitive, civilised characters may have behaved ludicrously, but their plight was touching and meaningful.

At the Criterion, the whole business is sent up as if it were some revue, starring Hermione Gingold. ... This is not black comedy, but black-and-white comedy, striped in much the same way as those humbugs one used to suck at school and with just as much nutritious and sticky content.

Milton Shulman: *Evening Standard*
28 June 1963

The confused pretentiousness of Iris Murdoch's 'urbane?' novel − half straight woman's magazine fantasy, half dons' joke − has been in one way removed from this dramatic version (on which J. B. Priestley has collaborated). This has been done by turning it into unequivocal farce. Martin Lynch-Gibbon the attitudinising wine-merchant is now nothing else but that; his wife Antonia is now Maudie Littlehampton; and Palmer, the analyst, is also a caricature − 'an imitation human being' quite literally. And in one way this is all most honest and satisfactory. ... But is it really funny enough just to have these awful phoney people exposed to us as awful and phoney? And is that really all Miss Murdoch ever meant? She may have succeeded better with the play by trying to make it *only* entertaining but at the cost of also making it utterly meaningless, and whatever else she may have meant by the book she certainly didn't mean that.

Robert Kee: *Queen*
17 July 1963

The twinkle in Miss Murdoch's eye is very merry, but her warning is serious: Englishmen would be more dignified (and Governments might last longer) if they kept their marriage vows. We are not at the present moment, in a position to say that in affairs of gallantry she does us an injustice.

But the fatuous and unresourceful absurdity of Anglo-Saxons in this kind of affair is only superficially Miss Murdoch's subject. Behind, running through, and underneath the headlong transfers of affection between Miss Murdoch's wine merchant, her psychiatrist, her artist and her fashionable wife are three serious themes: freedom, sincerity and peril. ...

Freedom preoccupies Miss Murdoch, particularly that freedom

which fulfils itself in service. Is the sun free, which controls the planets: or do the planets hold the sun prisoner? Is not freedom itself another bondage? In high Keatsian manner, she deals with these questions in her latest novel, *The Unicorn*, which has been read in America but not yet here. The freedom discussed in *A Severed Head* is of a less exalted kind. When all the rules are broken, the breakage of the rules still rules us. Miss Murdoch's three principal fools are emancipated; but they are not free. ...

The sincerity is less well-handled. The husband's mistress wanders from lover to lover like the rest, but she is the only character in whom there is a vein of true feeling. It is never tapped, and she is genuinely bruised and broken. This permanent reminder that there is value in human nature is not, I am afraid, convincingly or touchingly presented by Monica Evans, who is too shrill, even too peevish to affect us much.

But Sheila Burrell as Honor Klein infuses the play with an inscrutable suggestion of a surrounding and underlying threat of savagery – the indestructible Mau Mau at the end of the suburban garden – completely successfully. It is Miss Burrell's task every time she appears to still the laughter and to make the air shiver. I do not think that she fails once.

Harold Hobson: *Sunday Times*
30 June 1963

Decades ago, at school, I took a piece of work I had just completed in carpentry class to the teacher. He held it for a long time in silence, turning it this way and that, his face cold and hard.

Then he spoke. 'Is this a joke?' he asked. Falteringly, I replied it was not. 'Ah,' he replied, 'I think I would have been less upset if it had been.'

I own to much the same reaction to this play ... Indeed, I confess that I fled, intellectually speaking, from it in the greatest disorder, barely managing to burn my papers and blow up my ammunition as I ran. If it is a joke, it is not a good one. If it is not. ...

... The whole thing is written in a kind of prose that is not so much stilted as paralysed from the waist down, like some huge, mad parody of infidelity and its consequences.

Maybe it is a parody, a prolonged joke on the attitudinising and rationalism of modern people caught in a basically emotional situation.

But it can hardly be; for if it were it would not only have to be a good deal funnier, but it would also have to omit the passages and scenes (and they are many) in which the authors are clearly taking the whole thing in deadly seriousness.

Often, it is true, it is impossible to tell whether one is in a funny scene or a serious one. As witness: the husband finally punches the analyst in the eye, the latter staggers out, clutching a handkerchief to the shiner.

At the door, he pauses, turns and glaring downstage out of his one good eye, intones – to the husband – 'Come and see me soon'. Is that a joke? If so, at whose or what's expense?

The feeling, grimly, grows that the joke is on the audience.

'... Is this a joke? Oh sir, please sir, no sir. I think I would have been less upset if it had been.'

Bernard Levin: *Daily Mail*
28 June 1963

The Wars of the Roses

Shakespeare Memorial Theatre, Stratford-upon-Avon: 17 July 1963

The three parts of *Henry VI* remain among the least well-known of Shakespeare's plays; and it was not until 1977 that I saw a production of them (at Stratford) in anything like their original versions. But my awareness of at least part of their dramatic power came in 1963 with a remarkable, simplified and adapted account, in which John Barton and Peter Hall compressed the three plays into two, *Henry VI* and *Edward IV*; and presented them with *Richard III* under the collective title of *The Wars of the Roses*.

It was a typically bold adaptation, from a management confident of its intentions and of the virtues of audacity. It unfolded as an epic of power politics, clearly establishing its relationship to modern struggles and Shakespeare as our contemporary. Its relevance to the modern world was perhaps the most startling feature of the series; and it heralded many other Stratford productions, such as the Hall/ Warner *Hamlet* or Barton's *King John*, in which Shakespeare's plays were given a distinctly contemporary gloss. Ten years later, this particular determination to find relevance started to look old-fashioned; and was superseded by an attempt to present the plays straightforwardly, without slants or interpretations. The value, however, of the marginally over-interpreted Shakespeares was that they encouraged young audiences to look at the texts again with heightened interest, not dismissing them as just an elaborate form of costume drama. On this basis, they may have developed a taste for the unadulterated product. That at least was a theory often expressed; although it could be argued that simplified Shakespeare coarsens the taste for the original.

Whatever the merits of simplified or unsimplified Shakespeare, *The Wars of the Roses* was a magnificent spectacle; and displayed the Stratford company in the prime of its recently won status as the Royal Shakespeare Company. With such productions, the RSC established itself as the leading national company for the production of Shakespeare and the Jacobeans, although the National Theatre itself was in the process of formation at the Old Vic and would open its doors later in the year.

There has been much cutting, most of it (though not all) of dead wood, and a good deal of re-writing by Mr. Hall and his resident scholar, Mr. John Barton, some of which is downright unforgiveable.

No matter: such a project could not have been mounted without flaws, and this, and the other flaws, are no more than blemishes on what is already (and we have still to see the *Richard III*) a production of epic, majestic grandeur, a landmark and beacon in the post-war English theatre, and a triumphant vindication of Mr. Hall's policy, as well as of his power as a producer.

His policy? To fashion a 'company that can play together', to and with each other, with the occasional use of stars with ready-made reputations.

To strip away the romantic, false accretions of centuries from Shakespeare, and let him shine forth, wearing nothing but his own genius.

And to this triumphantly realised end, he has bent his talents as a director.

In settings of breathtaking splendour by Mr. John Bury – great slabs and gates of iron and copper, bars and joists of wood and steel, all the solidity and roughness of an English oak and English history – he has marshalled his players for the greatest show on earth: the pageant of the kings of England, and their rise and fall.

The first play opens with the body of Henry V in his coffin: the second ends with crookback Gloucester (a magnificent, malignant spider by Mr. Ian Holm) plotting the ruin of the new-crowned king.

In between, we have seen the warring factions of York and Lancaster moved about the stage, in and out of each other's trust and party, like the pieces of some effortless, shining machine.

Yet these are no doom-driven puppets. On the contrary, what gives this production its marvellously exciting quality is its constant insistence that whatever distant historical ends these Kings and nobles may be carrying out, it is their individual actions that are determining the sway of the struggle.

Bernard Levin: Daily Mail
18 July 1963

How much Shakespeare actually did to these old plays is a question for textual experts. The chief point about them that the dramatic critic notices is that because so much of them consists of bustling action they do act a great deal better than they read.

Yet even so, the early part of the trilogy, consisting as it does of continual French battles in which almost the only interest is an attempt to keep track of the contestants, is of a dullness that cannot be denied.

The Joan of Arc scenes with their travesty of the Maid as history has come to know her is a relief theatrically but not spiritually.

Then suddenly with the entry of Queen Margaret, the play begins to take real hold. The intriguing nobles at Henry's court and Henry himself – good irresolute man and hopelessly ineffective ruler – begin to take shape and to emerge as individuals.

The treacherous execution of Gloucester the honourable Protector, Margaret's love for Suffolk and his murder, the naked ambition of York now have colour and force.

By the time the curtain falls on the first part of the new division – which it does soon after Henry and Margaret have been driven apart by his anger over Gloucester and hers over Suffolk – there is no doubt the audience is being thoroughly and firmly held.

With the second play, as the Wars of the Roses develop to their full peak of horror, the characters seem to lose some of their individuality and sink back once more into their background of promiscuous slaughter.

Henry, the only man in the whole pack with anything like a conscience, continues to waffle feebly while all about him heads are rolling and corpses are being cleared away, as Englishmen kill Englishmen, sons their fathers and fathers their sons and hatred runs riot.

With Margaret growing more and more into a monster the human interest is difficult to maintain. One's feeling when the carnage is over is relief rather than dramatic satisfaction.

W. A. Darlington: *Daily Telegraph*
18 July 1979

The victory of Mr. Hall and Mr. Barton is not evident from the outset. They have cut, transposed, interpolated and changed much of Shakespeare's text, finally reducing the three Shakespearian plays into two of their own, *Henry VI* and *Edward IV*. They begin by seeming to share the common anti-Lancastrian feeling of our day. It is fashionable to scorn Henry V living, and Mr. Barton and Mr. Hall start their chronicles with a speech (his own, it must be admitted) designed to show him unappetising dead.

This prejudice soon vanishes. But the unease remains. Some of it is due to the director, Mr. Hall, and some of it to Shakespeare. It is Shakespeare's fault that we surprise Joan of Arc in bed with the Dauphin. Tossed in as a malicious sop to nationalistic prejudice, this may be spicy but it is neither drama, chivalry nor history. But it can hardly be Shakespeare's mistake that the valiant Talbots are so ludicrously miscast that we seek for some Brechtian jeer at physical courage. The interminable battles seem meaningless, and even I (who love that city) grew actually bored with Orleans. Yet in the rare, unfamiliar felicities of speech – 'the dusky torch of Mortimer', 'the pale and angry' rose of York – there were compensations from the very beginning.

But when we reached the half-way mark of the first play such doubts as existed about the issue vanished, and never afterwards returned. On all sides of Henry, the ice began to crack, and that saintly, patient, exasperating man moved at terrifying speed with beatific and anxious smile down the bursting river towards destruction.

It is a spectacle full of awe and fear, centred on the superb performance of David Warner. He and Mr. Hall between them discover in Henry one of Shakespeare's greatest parts. The discovery is the more exciting for being improbable, since drama gives its principal opportunities – itself an action – to active men. Henry is never active, and he would – with some reason, seeing what action was in the fifteenth century – that none else were active either. He suffers only, and endures, never resisting, never striking back. There is no obvious beauty about him, for, tall as he is, he walks with the slouching gait of a clumsy scholar or farm-hand. Yet his sad, distressed face beneath his fair hair, meeting each new misfortune with an absolute absence of protest or indignation spreads over the darkest waters of the play a quiet and persistent golden glory.

Harold Hobson: *Sunday Times*
21 July 1963

... After the extensive re-working of the Henry plays, one might have supposed that *Richard III* – one of the most popular and actor-proof of plays – would have enabled the company to romp home easily with a triumphant finale. But as it happens, Peter Hall's production is one of the least satisfactory that has appeared so far this season ...

A virtue of two previous productions in the cycle was that sense of accumulating history. But in the new production the slate is wiped clean. The same visible properties remain – the iron conference table, the towering throne, and the vast metallic walls; but they have lost their old associations and fail to generate any fresh ones.

The play itself is partly responsible for imposing this role on them: but it is unusual to find characters as sizeable as Buckingham and Catesby reduced to the insignificance of Tom Fleming's and Ian McCulloch's performances. The one notable exception is Charles Kay's Clarence; here there is a strong link with the past, and in the brief scenes before his murder, the production regains some of its lost momentum. Peggy Ashcroft too, as the half-crazed Margaret, raises the cursing scenes into something genuinely portentous.

What other original touches there are often seemed misguided. Susan Engel as the bereaved Elizabeth responds to the news of her children's death with a display of moon-struck charm, adopted presumably out of a misplaced trust in playing against the lines; and the novel characterisations of Tyrrel and the other murderers seem equally remote from the text.

Any production of *Richard III* stands or falls by the central performance, and it is here that this version is at its most disappointing. The emergence of Ian Holm's Crookback in the Henry plays was auspicious: in its combination of boyish spontaneity and psychotic violence, it promised to be the first performance since the 1940s to escape from the shadow of Olivier. The full-scale portrait retains the original qualities. But it adds nothing else. Mr. Holm still presents Gloucester as a likeable juvenile, open-faced and friendly in spite of his hump and surgical boot.

Mr. Holm's reading is acceptable in the opening of the production – particularly in his heartfelt wooing of Lady Anne over the blood-drenched corpse. But it fails totally to develop into Satanic magnitude. Instead of the boar, the bottle spider or the hunchbacked toad, Mr. Holm remains a high-spirited minor; he exhausts his lung-power in the later scenes, but finishes up on Bosworth Field, loaded down with an armoury of medieval weapons, crooning to himself like a baby inside his visor.

The Times
21 August 1963

Richard's soldiers are shown as storm troopers, his slaughterhouse at Pontefract as something out of a nightmare concentration camp, his battles as fantasies full of mist and clangour. Visually it is hard to think of a way in which the difficulties – or even impossibilities – of the play could be better solved. But, of course, as any production must, it comes down to the words in the end and almost all of them, even when they seem unfamiliar, are spoken or declaimed nearly to perfection.

Ian Holm's reading has more self-mockery in it than we are used to but it hangs together and finishes in a fine frenzy. Each of the 'big scenes' – the strange wooing of Lady Anne, Margaret's cursing, the plotting after the coronation, the haunting in the king's tent – is as big as it can be made but never at the expense of the wandering theme. In the resounding roll call of the House of York it is the Duke of Buckingham, by Tom Fleming, who turns out the completely dominating character, outdoing even his gangster master in cynicism and brutal intent.

As a self-contained production, without reference to the other parts of the trilogy (which I have not seen), this is the most integrated and memorable *Richard III* for a very long time.

Gerard Fay: *Guardian*
21 August 1963

The Recruiting Officer

National Theatre at the Old Vic: 10 December 1963

After 120 years of intermittent campaigning and six months of frantic preparation, the National Theatre eventually began its career at the Old Vic on 22 October 1963. The opening production was of *Hamlet* with Peter O'Toole, competent but not triumphant; while the subsequent two – of *St. Joan* and *Uncle Vanya* – had already been seen at Chichester. The fourth production, however, did much to establish the National Theatre's identity. *The Recruiting Officer* was directed by William Gaskill, a young director previously associated with George Devine at the Royal Court, whom Sir Laurence Olivier had invited to join the National Theatre.

Gaskill was particularly concerned to build up the company as a team, not as just a collection of individual stars. He introduced improvisation into the rehearsals, whose purpose was 'to establish the sequence of emotions in the actors' minds'. Some leading actors in the company, including Max Adrian and Olivier himself, were at first sceptical of his methods, which included asking certain social and even political questions, such as 'who owns whom'. Gaskill approached *The Recruiting Officer* with the experience of having seen Brecht's adaptation of the play, *Trumpets and Drums*, which had been performed by the Berliner Ensemble in London seven years before. Gaskill had been much influenced by Brecht; and he also disliked the somewhat affected, over-stylised playing of Restoration comedy, with its emphasis upon heavy gallantry, distorted vowels ('obleeged' for 'obliged') and elaborate bows. He wanted to present Farquhar's play as a clear account of what life was like in a provincial town, Shrewsbury, in the early eighteenth century, stressing its realism and the analysis, perhaps unwitting, of the structures of power.

There were various ways in which Gaskill's production seized the imagination. He encouraged other directors to explore the content, rather than the surface style, of Restoration comedies; and as a result, antique foppery went out of fashion. He demonstrated that the National Theatre company was composed of fine young actors, like Colin Blakely, Robert Stephens and Maggie Smith, as well as of established stars, like Olivier, who on this occasion played a subordinate character part of Captain Brazen. Above all, it was the confident clarity of his *The Recruiting Officer* which was impressive. Gaskill amended the text to assist the smooth story-telling, transposing scenes 5 and 6 in the last act and omitting some minor passages. The result was the re-discovery of *The Recruiting Officer* as a lively comedy and a fascinating social document, exactly the kind of work for which the National Theatre had been established.

The Recruiting Officer is not a typical Restoration piece. Its provincial setting, its breadth of social characterisation, its sexual realism all set the play apart from the charmed circle of fops and wits which dominates the work of Farquhar's contemporaries. In many ways this virile portrait of a Shrewsbury recruiting campaign for Marlborough's army is closer to Jonson than to Congreve – except that Farquhar has no indignation. Brecht, who rewrote the play with an American Civil War setting, gave it a strong element of social protest. But Farquhar, himself a former recruiting officer, saw the corruption and cruelty of the trade, and used it as comic material without advancing any moral conclusions.

Technically the play's originality springs from the brilliant stroke of fertilizing conventional eighteenth-century comedy with the military theme. The recruiting scenes are dovetailed in a formal love intrigue complete with a jealous father and a female travesty part – the two elements complement each other beautifully – on one side it is natural for the gallants to pursue their girls as if conducting a military campaign, and on the other it is equally natural for them to ensnare their recruits with the tactics of seduction.

In a programme note Mr. Gaskill rightly points out that the play's main point of contact with the modern world is its portrayal of the 'systematic deception of the ignorant'. Certainly the most concentrated scene in the production is one showing the capture of two reluctant volunteers. The illiterate pair see through the trickery of the sergeant, but then fall into the hands of Captain Plume, whose maxim is 'those who know the least obey the best', and who conjures up such a glowing vision of the soldiers' life that they capitulate – only to have their ambitions dashed by the point of the sergeant's halberd.

This scene – which reaches its climax when the two dupes are drawn, mesmerized, towards Plume's outstretched hand – takes one far beyond the regions of comedy. And to that extent, it is untypical of the remainder of the production which is, first and foremost, riotously funny.

From the moment in the first scene when a weather vane drops from the flies and settles on the church with an audible bump, it is plain that the comic spirit has descended on the stage. Rich performances are abundant. Colin Blakely as the wily sergeant, whose villainous past life has ideally prepared him for his present trade, gives a superbly resourceful performance of a military front office man – liberally garnishing his delivery with dropped aitches and genteel vowels. Max Adrian as Justice Balance puts across the character's foxy motives and warmth of heart with copious double-takes and beautifully timed asides; and Maggie Smith, as his outspoken daughter, capitalizes to the full on her possession of free speech in an artificial society. There is also Laurence Olivier as the egregious Captain Brazen – an irrepressible pockmarked vulgarian seen characteristically in a dialogue with a lady during which his gaze travels down from her face until he is addressing his compliments vertically into her bosom.

Robert Stephens as the protagonist Plume is saddled with an awkward part which undergoes steady moral improvement throughout the play, strait-jacketed to the formal framework of the comedy. (In general, the second half, in which the conventional idiom gains the upper hand, is much less rewarding than the first.) But he handles it with a bravado and directness which almost makes it appear consistent.

The Times
11 December 1963

Events culminate in a comic trial which in the playing proved the one dull moment in the present delightful production. I believe that the producer William Gaskill was here trying for some sort of solemn satire of 'justice' perhaps in honoured memory of the adaptation of this play which the Berliner Ensemble brought us some years back – in itself rather less good than the Alec Clunes production of 1943, though you'd have a job persuading anybody of *that*.

Philip Hope-Wallace: *Guardian*
11 December 1963

George Farquhar's *The Recruiting Officer* is a lusty, uninhibited comedy deriding the methods used to coerce, wheedle, bribe, bully or kidnap recruits in Marlborough's army.

At the National Theatre, it is done with the pace and gusto it needs to make contemporary audiences ask why it has taken 20 years since this delicious play was last seen in the West End.

The answer probably lies in the fact that it is only a National Theatre that can supply the wealth of acting talent that a comedy of this kind requires.

There is, for example, the recruiting sergeant himself who has to embody the toughness, the cynicism, the loyalty and ruthlessness of the English NCO who was proud of his ability for 'pimping, bullying, swearing, whoring and drinking'. The abrasive, impudent performance of Colin Blakely hits it off just right.

Then there is Captain Plume, constantly torn between his loyalty to the army and his passion for women. Robert Stephens plays him with the unheroic leering quality of a car salesman on the make, which is preferable to the dashing romantic the part could become.

Then there is the outsize comic role of Captain Brazen. With flowing moustache and shoulder-length wig, Laurence Olivier becomes the essence of every doltish, bravura, self-important officer that ever wore uniform. This is a real delight.

Then there is Sylvia, a girl 200 years ahead of her time. For Sylvia dresses up like a man because she wants to experience the freedom and abandon of behaving like a man. And Maggie Smith is beautifully comic as she squirms with delight watching the discomfiture of men in the sex war.

Milton Shulman: *Evening Standard*
11 December 1963

If it were an ordinary playhouse my opening paragraph would be a footnote. But this is our National Theatre subsidised to the tune of £130,000 a year, and by the time I arrived (five minutes before curtain-up), it was not even a question of one programme between two; there were none at all.

By the nine Muses, the seven Arts and the three Graces, I will shame the London theatre out of this swinish meanness if it is the last thing I do.

Through the good offices of the ladies of the Press department I was provided with a programme at the interval.

Mind you, when I got it, I found that it contained, along with much interesting and useful information, most handsomely presented, an essay by Mr. William Gaskill, the director, of such chilling fatuity that I am almost glad I didn't have it to spoil the first act.

Just listen to this: 'No classic is timeless ... For the '30s *Richard II* was another *Vortex* ... , and for us today Falstaff's questioning of honour in *Henry IV* is the same as Joan Littlewood's in *Oh, What A Lovely War* ... It would be false to impose on Farquhar Brecht's statement of the social situation but we cannot ignore in Farquhar those elements which excited Brecht to make his version ...

'What is the particular compulsion for us today of the image of a group of soldiers arriving in a country town...? I think what we recognise from our experience is the systematic deception of the ignorant to a pointless end by the use of heroic images of the past.'...

And so on, and so forth. The clue is, of course, 'Brecht', and, yes, there are the old whore's own words next to William Gaskill's, full of the old, sweaty rubbish about a 'declining middle-class theatre' and the play's 'ideological meaning' and 'petty-bourgeois concept of classicism' and so forth and so further.

What is going on down there? Are we going to have more of our classics forced through these Marxist imbecilities?

It was the late Ian Mackay who memorably described the whole fumble-bumble as caused by fools who got it out of 'a big, bad book on Victorian economics written by an old man with a beard in Tufnell Park', and he might have added that none of them have actually read it.

It started coldly, and a lack of audience response set off a downward inter-reaction that nearly sank the ship. But with the arrival on the horizon of Sir Laurence Olivier the upswing started and I laughed myself thereafter into a bad attack of bronchitis.

The plot (a fine time to get to the plot, I must say) is composed of most of the usual elements of Restoration comedy, with gallants and ladies at amatory cross-purposes, sexual mistaken identities and venerous misunderstandings.

Withal, there is a bitterly funny satire on the impressment of men for Marlborough's wars – Farquhar himself took part in such recruiting drives – and an immense amount of witty bawdry, much of it in the form of elaborate double-meanings.

Bernard Levin: *Daily Mail*
11 December 1963

The difference between *The Recruiting Officer* and most other Restoration comedies is that the participants in its formal patterns of love and seduction care as much for their work as for their play; and what is more, it contains an element of social criticism that is no less evident because the wrong side; or what we would now consider the wrong side, is allowed to win. This makes it a peculiarly suitable choice for the National Theatre's first essay in comedy; and the National Theatre has certainly done it proud. ...

... William Gaskill's production is elegant beyond words, and Rene Allio's sets, that shift before our eyes from one street to another, from a market square to a drawing room to a court of law, dropping from the flies or turning to reveal some unlooked-for metamorphosis at the back of a flat, are not only beguiling to the eye but amusing in themselves. All in all, this is a marvellously successful evening.

B. A. Young: *Punch*
18 December 1963

Othello

National Theatre at the Old Vic: 21 April 1964

With *The Recruiting Officer*, the National Theatre quickly established a reputation for high comedy, which persisted over the following years; but one production from its remarkable first season became almost legendary. Sir Laurence Olivier had never previously played Othello, although before the war he had acted Iago to Ralph Richardson's Othello. It was his last remaining challenge from the canon of Shakespearian tragic heroes. Orson Welles thought that Othello was one role beyond Olivier's scope. 'Larry's a natural tenor,' he confided to Kenneth Tynan, 'and Othello's a natural baritone'. Olivier needed some persuasion to tackle the part at all, but after he had decided to do so, he went into rigorous training, partly to extend his vocal range and partly to cope with the physical demands of a role which, he became convinced, Shakespeare had written to prove that no actor could play it, from Burbage onwards. One emotional crisis succeeded another with such rapidity that it is almost impossible for actors to conserve their energies for the final scenes.

Olivier was fifty-seven, and he conceived the part as one for a younger man, athletic, rhythmic and deeply black. Although he was famous for his physical transformations, Olivier had taken on what seemed an almost impossible task, at a time too when, as first Director of the National Theatre, there were many other pressures on his attention. From his first appearance on the stage, prowling barefoot, carrying a rose, it was apparent that here was a characterisation which would haunt the minds of a generation of actors, as Olivier's Richard III and Titus Andronicus had done. The news of his triumph spread quickly. *Othello* broke box office records at the Old Vic, with queues stretching down The Cut: touts were rumoured to be offering places in the queue for £5 each.

Othello toured Britain and a film was made which carefully preserved the stage version without trying to change it into something more suitable for cinemas. It was also chosen to represent British theatre in a cultural agreement with Russia, which symbolised a stage in the thaw of the Cold War. Olivier's reception in Moscow was tumultuous; and for the British public, this triumph represented the value of having a National Theatre which could act as a cultural ambassador.

... Before the war, Sir Laurence appeared as Iago to the Othello of Ralph Richardson. It was a memorable performance, alive with a sophistication unusual in those innocent days when the name of Wolfendon had not yet been heard in the land. Its excess of super-subtlety was such that it may be doubted whether Sir Ralph ever cottoned on to what his mercurial colleague was up to.

The only trace lingering of this interpretation of the play at the Old Vic is a scene in which, when Iago pours poison into Othello's ear, the two men, the African and the European, sway together in a sickening rhythm that suggests a bond uniting them closer than marriage. For the rest, Frank Finlay's convincing and powerful Iago is bluff, provincial, noisy and professionally jealous, sometimes goading himself into hysterical fury, less a Machiavelli than one of those amoeba-minded Southern Senators who still foam at the mouth at the thought of a black man and a white woman getting into bed together.

This is in keeping with John Dexter's direction and Sir Laurence Olivier's sensational performance. Sensational it is: who would have believed that Sir Laurence could make his voice so deep and dark? Who could guess, when in the final scene Othello with one hand clasps Desdemona tightly to him, by what mighty feat of prestidigitation with the other Sir Laurence is going to stab himself, no knife being anywhere in sight? This last is only a decoration to the play, albeit an exciting one. It is one of many touches which show that Mr. Dexter, when with Sir Laurence he has settled the strategy of the production, still has plenty of invention left to make its tactics vigorous and unexpected.

This strategy demands that Iago should be thick-headed. The dominating social and political fact of today, as Arnold Toynbee has pointed out, is that everywhere there is a revolt against the ideals and the faith of the white races. This dynamic schism of our times is recognised in Mr. Dexter's production of *Othello*; in the light of this circumstance, *and the theatre being what it is*, it would be unrealistic to expect that Iago, the persecutor of the blacks, should be shown as a man of high, even if malicious intelligence. ...

There is here a concern with the relations between the black and the white races which gives to this production a contemporary urgency lacking in its predecessors. With a curl of the lips, a catlike movement of the body, a roll of staring eyes, an uncomfortable mixture of arrogance and inferiority, Sir Laurence makes this *Othello* a world-drama as well as a tale of individual poignancy and betrayal.

There is little comfort, but much beauty, in Mr. Dexter's

interpretation of the play. Before the evil and the cruelty and the unscrupulousness of the white man, the civilization of Othello is stripped off. In Galsworthy's despairing phrase, it can't stand fire. In one of the tremendous climaxes of which Sir Laurence builds up an astounding series, flinging himself into the theatre of ritual which today commands the best part of our stage, this Othello tears the crucifix from his neck, and on his knees bows his head to the ancient gods of magic, barbarism and human sacrifice.

The power, passion, verisimilitude and pathos of Sir Laurence's performance are things which will be spoken of with wonder for a long time to come. Sir Laurence speaks the line 'Not a jot' with a casual pain that is extremely moving; there is a tropical storm of energy in his 'Othello's occupation's gone'; with Emilia he is extraordinarily savage and intense; and to Maggie Smith's candid and rousing Desdemona tender and tormented.

Harold Hobson: Sunday Times
26 April 1964

There is a kind of bad acting of which only a great actor is capable. I find Sir Laurence Olivier's Othello the most prodigious and perverse example of this in a decade ... Sir Laurence is elaborately at ease, graceful and suave, more like a seducer than a cuckold. But as the jealousy is transfused into his blood, the white man shows through more obviously. He begins to double and treble his vowels, to stretch his consonants, to stagger and shake, even to vomit, near the frontiers of self-parody. His hips oscillate, his palms rotate, his voice skids and slides so that the Othello music takes on a Beatle beat.

Alan Brien: Sunday Telegraph
26 April 1964

At first consideration, Olivier may not seem ideal casting for Othello. His emanations are not Moorish to put it mildly. His timbre tends to lightness, his grey eyes are rather for the poetry of Macbeth. And yet, what of the evidence of that Coriolanus, that Lear, that Titus Andronicus above all, with all the gravitas of stark tragedy and where at the height of an unremitting role he cut his hand off before our eyes and then for an eternity of seconds withheld his howl of pain?

In great tragic acting there is always a strong element of surprise. Othello, on the rack last night, was agonising in the sheer vehemence of his anguish, but it was the inventiveness of it above all, the sheer variety and range of the actor's art which made it an experience in the theatre altogether unforgettable by anyone who saw it. True it was the noble, wounded professional thrown out of kilter rather than the lumbering bull in Othello that was uppermost: the general self-broken, self-cashiered. 'Othello's occupation's gone'. We saw it go.

The initial surprise, however, is that it is exactly at first sight that this Othello compels you to accept him, not merely as a coloured man, but as a Negro, with a negroid speech and easy, generous, frank and easily articulated gait and physically imposed authority. It is the breaking down of these and the passing into the torment which is so magnificently taken; slow at first, almost to a point of losing rhythm and momentum (it was one hour fifty minutes to 'Now by yon marble heaven'), slow, but immensely powerful in building, this Othello caught us, most in the scenes of the second half, overwhelmingly pathetic in the epilepsy, fearful in his scorn ('I took you for the cunning whore of Venice') and at the end cradling his dead wife in his arms, Olivier struck deeper chords than I have ever heard from him: a marvellous assumption of the part which I could write about till morning and after.

Philip Hope-Wallace: *Guardian*
22 April 1964

A clue to the interpretation is given in the programme, which quotes F. R. Leavis's assessment of Iago as 'not much more than a necessary piece of dramatic mechanism'; less a character in himself than the embodiment of a concealed element in Othello's own nature. This role is certainly contained in the part; but to erect it into the whole truth amounts almost to mutilation. Iago is not merely on the level of a tempter in a miracle play: the part plainly exists in its own right, enigmatic perhaps, but freed with a personal vitality which keeps the riddle of his villainy a permanently open question.

The penalties of translating the Leavis theory into action are graphically displayed in Frank Finlay's performance. Instead of the alert ensign, the resourceful actor who is all things to all men and who shapes his plot with the delight of an artist, we are confronted by a lumpish figure. The approach has some advantages. When all Othello's resistance has gone, Iago clings about his neck — almost with the embrace of a succubus — pouring poison into his ear in tones of satanic lullaby.

The physical attachment between him and the Moor – present from the first scene together with Othello playfully brushing his ancient's face with a bunch of flowers – often yields powerful effects. (Olivier is always at his best when he is in close tactile contact with an opponent.) But when Iago is left to play on lesser victims or to commune with himself, the part loses its coherence. Speed, changeable resourcefulness, nimble invention – all the qualities one expects are replaced by a plodding sameness, occasionally varied by arbitrary grotesqueness, and an unhappy attempt to humanize the character by introducing a whimpering note into the soliloquies.

The lack of a fully realized Iago seriously impoverishes the production – even in the Othello scenes, where Mr. Finlay's reading makes most sense. Othello needs an adversary, not an accomplice. As it is, Olivier's Othello stands as a heroic solo performance which is more remarkable for its technical mastery than for its power to move. Physically he departs from the image of the old soldier descended 'into the vale of years'. He presents a graceful, sensual figure to whom the duties of a bridegroom seem as familiar as those of the battlefield. His voice (a factor that has held him back from the part in the past) has acquired a measured deliberation and a new lower resonance: and – perhaps most striking of all – he has evolved a range of movements organically related to the part: a stance with feet apart and trunk thrown forward, and a use of oblique arm gestures and flattened palms of the hand.

Beautifully controlled at the beginning, where his modest playing suggests Salvini's 'sleeping volcano', its underlying savagery becomes increasingly pronounced until – in the oath scene – he tears the cross from his neck and bows to the floor in atavistic obeisance to a barbaric god.

The Times
22 April 1964

As the curtain fell on the tragic figures of Desdemona and the Moor entwined in death's agony on the bed, the audience from the back of the theatre swept down the central gangway in a great human tide. They stood three-deep in the front of the stage, hurling flowers and clapping, many with their hands above their heads.

But two rows in front of me, I saw a woman in black – sitting while all around her were on their feet, crying 'Bravo'. What was the matter? Was she anti-Shakespeare, anti-British? A Russian critic perhaps? Then she turned slightly and I saw. Tears were running down her cheeks. She was too overwhelmed to get up.

Three hours before I had been stopped in the Red Square by young Russian girl students begging for a ticket. Only fear of the police, I suspect, prevented them from offering black market prices. I had watched the extraordinary enthusiasm of an audience who, even with tickets, fought and shoved their way through the single entrance as if their lives depended on being seated to hear Roderigo's first line.

> Felix Barker: *Evening News*
> 8 September 1965
> (reporting on *Othello*'s reception in Moscow)

The Royal Hunt of the Sun

National Theatre at the Chichester Festival Theatre, 7 July 1964, and at the Old Vic, 8 December 1964

The Royal Hunt of the Sun by Peter Shaffer was the first new play staged by the National Theatre. Shaffer had offered it to many other London managements, who thought it too costly and ambitious to stage, since it required a large cast and, from the script descriptions, many changes of set. Nor was Shaffer then a well-known dramatist: his previous play in the West End, *Five-Finger Exercise*, had received a respectable run without winning much critical acclaim. John Dexter, the director, was first attracted to *The Royal Hunt of the Sun* by one laconic stage direction which caught his eye while leafing through the script – 'They cross the Andes'.

Dexter's imagination immediately started to picture how this effect could be achieved by mime alone, for obviously the Andes could not be built on stage. Dexter, one of three resident National Theatre directors, excelled in the choreography of productions: he had directed a successful British musical, *Half A Sixpence*, and his brilliant staging of Arnold Wesker's *The Kitchen* included among its delights the frantically co-ordinated preparation of restaurant meals, a kind of *ballet trouvé*. Shaffer's new play was one which suited his talents; and it also gave him the opportunity to improve the physical and vocal training of the National Theatre actors, so that they could work as a co-ordinated team.

British acting, in general, had always been associated with a somewhat cerebral approach to the art – very good on the spoken delivery of lines, able to convey nuances of words and precise in its naturalism, but not athletic or physical. Two productions from 1964, *The Royal Hunt of the Sun* and Peter Brook's *The Marat / Sade*, helped to change this reputation, so that for the next ten years, there were many British productions which explored the visual and tactile qualities of the stage. Dexter, like Brook, was a splendid *metteur en scène*; and *The Royal Hunt of the Sun* with its comparatively simple set but constant variety of effects brought a spectacular dimension to the National Theatre's work which it had previously lacked. Some critics even complained that it was too spectacular, too lavish, not realising that Michael Annals, the set designer, had constructed the brilliantly glowing stage sun from beaten out bottle tops.

The National Theatre had taken a risk on an ambitious play which nobody else had wanted to tackle; and its success was well-deserved, although the play's merits, those of a gripping adventure story, may have been over-rated at the time. Shaffer wrote other plays for the National Theatre, including *Black Comedy* and *Equus*, which Dexter also directed; and he was the first dramatist to become unofficially associated with the National Theatre's work, although he continued to write for the West End. The company experience gained from this play started to be seen in other National Theatre productions, including John Arden's *Armstrong's Last Goodnight*. *The Royal Hunt of the Sun* set the seal on the National Theatre's triumphant first year of its existence: no British company ever had a better start.

This giant drama, seen earlier this year at Chichester, has now moved into the National Theatre's London home, and a third seeing confirms and strengthens my belief that no greater play has been written and produced in our language in my lifetime.

That is a large statement; and it is a large play that calls it forth. It is large in every way, from every angle, in every sense.

Its theme is large, to begin with; it tells the almost incredible (yet true) story of the conquest of the mighty Inca Empire of Peru by a tiny handful of Spaniards under Pizarro in the 16th century. The Incas had peace, stability and gold. The Spaniards had courage, avarice and guns.

And Christ. For it was in the name of their Redeemer that the expedition of 167 men conquered a nation of ten million, and took their gold, their social order, their freedom, their lives and their history.

Mr. Shaffer's indictment of the conquistadores who beat men's brains out with the Cross seems even more savage now, yet no more answerable. The two religions, like the two nations, met high in the frozen Andes and, unable to understand each other, fought. Once again, God was on the side of the big battalions.

Yet this is not a pessimistic play, which is another of the large things about it. It is a humanistic hymn, an agnostic affirmation.

Its theme is not 'Lord, I believe; help thou my unbelief', but 'Lord, I disbelieve; you look after yourself'. For it is man's honour that conquers, not God's; it is Pizarro's own religion that he is rejecting when the murdered Inca King does not rise again the third day, though he has suffered under a newer and more terrible Pontius Pilate.

And Mr. Shaffer's faith – that it is in man that such goodness, truth and beauty as the world affords is to be found – is expressed in language that clothes his theme in majesty.

The Inca kingdom was founded in gold, and Mr. Shaffer's language is golden, bright, with metaphor and insight, ringing clear with the brilliant speech that is soft and malleable as gold in his master hands.

A large story; a large theme; and a large nobility of language. There remains the large audacity of a playwright who has blown open the cramped introspection of most of our best post-war plays (including his own) and dared to write on a scale, and for a spectacle, that we had long thought dead.

With a designer (Mr. Michael Annals) and a producer (Mr. John Dexter) who are fully seized of his genius and indeed partake of it, the result is finally a play which is breathtaking to look at, in its use of mime, dance, ritual, masks, gesture, colour, costume – all playing their large part in providing a suitable frame for this tremendous, this admirable, this profound, this enduring play.

Bernard Levin: *Daily Mail*
9 December 1964

The great pictorial set pieces, like the opening of the golden rose to reveal the figure of the painted god, the irruption upon the stage of the feathered Incas, the slow, painful climbing of the Andes by the rapacious and stunningly courageous Spanish invaders continue to amaze and delight. They are, in a sense, overwhelming; but at the Old Vic they do not, as they tended to do at Chichester, overwhelm the text. At the National Theatre, the muscular and compassionate quality of Mr. Shaffer's thought is what one mainly remembers; that, and Robert Stephens's presentation of the god Atahualpa: an electrifying, an almost incredible performance: unhuman, inhuman, superhuman.

Mr. Shaffer meets and accepts St. Paul's crucial challenge. His mind is influenced by what I should call the eighteenth century fallacy. Rousseau's myth of the Noble Savage; and by the Platonic fallacy, that man's perfect condition is one of poetic and benevolent communism. The gorgeously coloured Incas are good and gentle men; and Mr. Shaffer gives a superb description of their state of idyllic servitude, in which a happy working life is followed by more than adequate retirement pensions. He also, through the mouth of the Franciscan Fray, Marcos de Nizza (played by Kenneth Mackintosh with convincing intellectuality), exposes the weakness of this attractive social system: it necessarily excludes the element of choice. But it seems to me (not so much in London, I admit, as in the country) that the exposure has less fervour than the exposition. This is not a thing to complain of, when it results in so accomplished and warm a picture as Atahualpa paints of the glowing Inca life. These men move in perpetual sunshine through a rich field of standing corn, like one of Dufy's strong and beautiful horses; and, remembering how much better a job the socialistic Benevolent Despots made of human happiness than our democracies have achieved, one surrenders the picture and conforms to the friar's strenuous assertion of liberty only with regret. But here again is not the heart of the play.

Colin Blakely's rugged Pizarro is not in search of organised human bliss. He is not even, though in the first instance he thinks he is, in search of gold. The gold he found: the value of the gold and silver extracted from the Inca mines finally reached the total of 4,851,156,000 Spanish dollars. But the gold corroded in his pockets, as the sublime Atahualpa showed him, by the mere assertion of divinity, what he really desired. The force that drove on Pizarro with a contemptible handful of followers into a presumably hostile land with millions of soldiers in it, was the hope that he would come again to believe, as he had believed in his poverty-stricken youth in Spain, that a man could die and on the third day rise again.

That is why he came in the end to sacrifice to the hatred of his men the god-king Atahualpa. The struggle with himself is finely presented by Mr. Shaffer. Pizarro, though a vulgar fellow, had a soldier's instincts of humour and recoiled from the thought of killing a captured enemy. But this enemy's unsinkable, seraphic confidence in his resurrection gradually moved him from his notions of justice, gradually in fact lit in him a great, irrational hope: if Atahualpa could rise from the grave, then why not Christ?

There is no doubt that Mr. Shaffer links the two cases intimately together, though probably putting it the other way round from Pizarro: if Christ may rise, why not Atahualpa? Orthodox Christians, battle-scarred from Transubstantiation, Free Will, and Grace, would attempt to confound Mr. Shaffer with an appeal to the doctrine of the Trinity: Christ – the argument would presumably run – was God, and Atahualpa was not God, whatever he may have thought. I fancy that Mr. Shaffer would not be perturbed by this; nevertheless, logically, I cannot follow him. It is one thing to say, if Andrew Carnegie could become a millionaire, then why not me; but quite another to assert, as Mr. Shaffer seems to come close to doing, I am not a millionaire, therefore Andrew Carnegie wasn't either. In other words, however dead Atahualpa remained, Christ could still have risen; though Pizarro was right in thinking that if Atahualpa rose the possibility of resurrection was proved.

Mr. Shaffer takes a different view from me; or at any rate his Pizarro does. I do not think that he offers his denial of immortality with any appearance of unseemly rejoicing. I got the impression at Chichester and may have expressed it in print that this play was designed to give Christians a hearty crack on the jaw. At that time I was even inclined to regard as blasphemous Atahualpa's jeering remark that Christians make their God into a biscuit and eat him. I have since been convinced that I was wrong on this point; the observation is hardly different from Belloc's talk about 'bottling God the Father in a flask'.

Harold Hobson: *Sunday Times*
13 December 1964

... This epic theatre, with all the ingredients thrown in will come as a special surprise, perhaps, to those who do not keep pace with the lyrical or dance theatre or accept the stylisation of the Asian drama. It is compelling to watch and nearly always carries conviction in a bold way.

As for the content of the play and the dilemma which is built towards its end, I find less profundity than I had expected, but in the way in which Barrault's production of Claudel's *Christopher Columbus* finally whirled one into acceptance (of a wholly different point of view I need hardly add – for Mr. Shaffer's is anti-clerical and almost Wordsworthianly humanist) the closing stages of the drama, where Pizarro himself dying cannot bring himself to kill the trusting Inca Son of the Sun who has paid his gold ransom to be free, held the audience very firmly.

Philip Hope-Wallace: *Guardian*
9 December 1964

The Persecution and Assassination of Marat Performed by the Inmates of the Asylum of Charenton under the Direction of the Marquis de Sade

Aldwych Theatre: 20 August 1964

Peter Brook's production of Peter Weiss's *The Marat/Sade* sought to combine the influences of the two most pervasive dramatic theorists of the time, Antonin Artaud (the French actor, director and writer, who died in 1948) and Bertolt Brecht (the dramatist and director, who died in 1956). On one level, these influences seemed incompatible. Artaud, who wrote *The Theatre of Cruelty* in 1932, despised rational theatre, either on the bourgeois 'well-made-play' level or of the politically didactic variety, which sought to persuade and convert audiences to a particular point of view. He aspired towards a new theatre of ritual, involving masks, movement, magic and, above all, shock. He believed that 'the theatre will never find itself again ... except by furnishing the spectator with the truthful precipitates of dreams, in which his taste for crime, his erotic obsessions, his savagery, his chimeras, his utopian sense of life and matter, even his cannibalism, pour out on a level not counterfeit and illusory, but interior.'

Before tackling *The Marat/Sade*, Brook with Charles Marowitz had launched a Theatre of Cruelty season at LAMDA, whose sessions, though essentially part of a rehearsal process, were open to the public. At this season, Brook and Marowitz concentrated on violent, irrational and sometimes shocking sketches, which included Artaud's own short play, *A Spurt of Blood*, containing such images as a prostitute beneath whose skirts lies a nest of scorpions and a man who bites the arm of God to fill the stage with a torrent of blood.

Brecht, on the other hand, was committed to reason rather than sensationalism, with using the theatre to explain and illustrate a certain political point of view. Shock and irrationality were justified only as means to an end. Whereas Artaud sought to involve the audience in the overall ritual of theatre, Brecht wanted the spectator to maintain a certain critical detachment towards the events on the stage.

Brook, however, did not see these two views as being essentially incompatible; and in Peter Weiss's play he saw a work which alternated from the emotional, sometimes insane shock of Artaud to the cold, sometimes pontificating rationalising of Brecht. He explained how the two influences could combine in his introduction to the text of *The Marat/Sade*: 'Everything about his [Weiss's] play is designed to crack the spectator on the jaw, then douse him with ice-cold water, then force him intelligently to assess what has happened to him, then give him a kick in the balls, then bring him to his senses again.'

The Marat/Sade had an immediate appeal for London's more adventurous theatre-goers; and Brook's production, with the preceding Theatre of Cruelty season, influenced the development of the fringe theatre movement during the 1960s profoundly. Marowitz went on to establish the Open Space theatre in Tottenham Court Road, which with the Traverse Theatre in Edinburgh, led the way for many other experimental theatre clubs. They had to be clubs to avoid theatre censorship; and if *The Marat/Sade* attracted young and adventurous audiences, it also alienated some of the older ones. Emile Littler, a governor of the Royal Shakespeare Company and a member of its executive committee, publicly attacked Peter Hall, the

RSC's director, for allowing the company to put on 'dirty plays'. The row made headlines in the papers and filled the correspondence columns of *The Times*. It was a time when the theatre really did seem to have seized the centre of public debate, dividing left from right, young from old, the libertarians from the conservatives; and many practical issues too were at stake, such as the role of the censor and the power of theatre boards over theatre directors. Hall won the backing of his board, led by Sir Fordham Flower, and of the majority of London's critics; and I was one of many theatre-lovers at that moment who felt that this cause had to be won, in the interests of the theatre as a whole and indeed of freedom of speech.

The surrounding controversy sometimes seemed to be on the point of obscuring the merits of Brook's remarkable production, a *tour de force* and, to my mind, the most memorable of his career. Its control was as striking as its originality; and Brook forced and cajoled performances from comparatively unknown actors which were totally unexpected, powerful, commanding and obsessively brilliant. *The Marat/Sade* demonstrated how dramatically the theatre in Britain had changed over ten years: it was a major achievement from an aspiring age.

What happens is this: we are taken into the asylum to witness one of the therapeutic theatrical performances which de Sade produced under the free-minded, long pre-Freudian supervision of de Coulmier who ran the Charenton Bedlam. The play deals with the stabbing to death of Marat, in his bath, by Charlotte Corday. It is a bloodbath, violently attacking the emotions and sensibilities of any audience. It will send Aunt Edna round the bend but cannot fail to conquer anyone who has the slightest trace of compassion in him.

The story is acted out in a deadly insane charade which as it approaches moments of meaninglessness becomes the most emphatically true and moving. There seem to be, to begin with, many false notes but they all ring true in the end, even in the music which is anything but incidental. The acting? Nobody is merely a player, the smallest incidents are done with complete conviction but Clive Revill as Marat, Glenda Jackson as Corday, Ian Richardson as the Herald and Patrick Magee as de Sade all achieve performances which it would be grudging to call merely memorable.

The whole evening was a triumphant victory by Peter Brook and his cast over a subject which nobody in his right senses would have tried to put on the stage. But then hardly anybody on this particular stage is in his right senses.

Gerard Fay: *Guardian*
21 August 1964

Basically the content of the play represents the merging of political and psychological action which derives from Europe's experience of the Nazi death camps. And as such, it is less about the mechanics of revolution than about regimes which lead countries into the equivalent of a pornographic dream. 'The world', says Sade, 'is made of bodies', and his own status as a political thinker is that, in a criminal society, he dug the criminal out of himself.

From scene to scene, however, the play is shaped so as to prevent one from advancing much farther than that. Its Chinese box construction is one cause of this. Marat on one level is presented as a pure politician, whose idealism is not disqualified by the degeneration of the Revolution after his death. But as Sade is supposed to have written his lines, presumably his attacks on Marat, condemning a machine-like society in favour of a world of passionate individuals, are intended to carry the argument.

Discussions of the multiple references of the play could be indefinitely prolonged. And on a first showing one is far less impressed by the intellectual line of the play than its impact on the visceral level which, in Peter Brook's production, is tremendous. The use of music (by Richard Peaslee) mirrors the grotesque figures of the actors with harsh bell and organ sonorities, and sets bloodthirsty events in the idiom of Lully. Surrounding Marat's bath (a Beckett image straight from history) the Goya-like performers – the anonymous white crowd, a trio of deranged *commedia dell'arte* singers, and a narrator in a cocked hat (superbly played by Ian Richardson) – play with mounting ritual frenzy up to the final murder.

Patrick Magee as Sade, a gross physical bulk with the face of a debauched saint, maintains a tortured delicacy which conveys the quality of a mind exclusively inhabiting extreme situations. And Glenda Jackson's Charlotte Corday, a shivering and inviolably private figure – part sacrificial virgin and part mechanical doll – is a performance to haunt the memory.

The Times
21 August 1964

... another product – latest and best – of the Theatre of the Absurd rather than the Theatre of Cruelty. What Peter Weiss has produced is an image which, true to Martin Esslin's definition, revolves and unfurls itself, throwing off glints of possible meaning from different aspects, without reaching any fixed premise or conclusion. The image is superbly powerful, a living Géricault: a dungeon of bleached, fantastic ghosts of sanity mopping and mowing round the waxy tableau of death in cold water. Peter Brook's production captures not only the ashen hues of the painter but his spirit: the loving science which gazed steadily into dim, reddened eyes, on stiffening grey flesh, attempting to embrace all extremes life includes, the negation of life descends to, with its human vision. As everyone has agreed, this is Brook's finest work: a compelling, completely unified theatrical *tour de force*. De Sade's great cry in the play, 'This is a world of bodies', gives him the licence to indulge his strongest gift, the building of stage-pictures out of massed, writhing limbs.

All the same, as the image turns like a carousel, one or two recurring hobby-horses begin to predominate. Their riders are Marat and Sade: the 18th-century fanatic of reason (Clive Revill plays him as a fox hunted by his own mind) grating out in the dry voice of desperation the need for a dictatorship of the proletariat to yoke the passionate mob, as he subdues the agonized itchings of his body; and the Romantic anarch, singing in high musical accents of madness (Patrick Magee croons his vowels and smacks at his labials lasciviously) his determination to unseat mind, like all other despotisms, from its monarchy over instinct. Their debate is loaded, of course, for 'Marat', like all the other lunatic players, is simply another voice of De Sade: the voice of the young disciple of Rousseau who, watching the guillotining of 1,000 people from his cell window at Picpus, realised that the master of creation was a mad animal. The old pessimist presents his younger self as the Friend of the People whose egalitarian logic led to massacre, and gently lays the knife in Charlotte Corday's hand. The revolutionary who thought he could harness man's violence will be destroyed by it.

And the epilogue is not Weiss's last word. As the enlightened director of the asylum complacently thanks the audience for their interest in this experiment in group-therapy, the lunatics huddled upstage start singing and surging down behind him. Lurching, flailing, they battle their warders, shouting out their demands for freedom now. Violence – the tumultuous mob of voices De Sade discovered inside himself – takes the final bow; and as the audience starts to applaud, ironically applauds them back. Why not, concludes Weiss. We are they, they are ourselves.

It's a stunning stroke of theatre. All the same, it ends the play, not on some lofty, ambiguous plane of art, but well within the 'Filthy plays' debate which has been raging, since its first night, in our silly-season press. Violence and cruelty, it asserts with De Sade, are natural: they can no more be legislated out of existence than sex can. Although I've no axe to grind on behalf of box-office tycoons who worry lest good plays about vice drive out the bad plays about in-laws, it seems time someone knocked this fashionable bit of nonsense on the head.

Violence *isn't* equatable with sex. The only evidence we can have that an instinct's general is statistics. Statistics show that the enormous majority of human beings copulate in some way or other. Only a tiny minority of them – fewer, probably, than the number whose kink happens to be chastity – commit violent crimes. There's no reason why people shouldn't write and stage plays about this minority; but when the Theatre of Cruelty boys argue that they're performing a liberating service by exploiting the roots of algolagnia in all of us, they're flying in the face of the science De Sade invoked.

The fact that our age has been blackened by history's greatest cruelties since the Terror doesn't make cruelty a universal problem of human psychology. The problem, now as then, is how to contain it. The only solution still seems to be that the majority should legislate firmly against the minority, sit as juries in judgement over them and confine them if they can't be cured or dissuaded. Endeavouring to persuade the majority that we're all as guilty, really, as the minority, and therefore can't judge, seems unhelpful. Weiss has written a brilliant play; not what I'd call an intelligent one.

Ronald Bryden: *New Statesman*
4 September 1964

It is without doubt one of the half-dozen most amazing achievements in *mise-en-scène* that the English Theatre has seen in my lifetime.

Its breadth, its totality, its breathtakingly rapid and varied use of every imaginable technique, dramatic device, stage-picture, form of movement, speech and song, make it as close as this imperfect world is ever likely to get to the *Gesamthunstwerk* of which Richard

Wagner dreamed, in which every element, every force that the theatre could provide would fuse in one overwhelming experience.

Bernard Levin: *Daily Mail*
21 August 1964

As a theatre man for 42 years, Mr. Littler was fiercely critical of the 'theatre of cruelty' and bestiality.

'This London season is a disgrace', he said to me. 'As a governor of the Royal Shakespeare Company and a member of the executive I have dissociated myself from this programme of dirt plays at the Aldwych.

'These plays do not belong, or should not, to the Royal Shakespeare. They are entirely out of keeping with our public image and with having the Queen as our Patron.'

Extract from an interview with Emile Littler
Daily Telegraph: 25 August 1964

What a week for the theatre! Headlines every day, blow-by-blow accounts of the latest development in the Dirty Play Controversy, and frenzied demands by Picture Editors for head and shoulders studies of 'someone called Michael Codron'. You'd have thought for all the world that he was a fifteen-year-old goalkeeper readying himself for the Big Kick-Off, or perhaps even a clothes designer for the latest pop group. But no – he was a serious theatrical producer.*

And the row raged on. The *Evening News* got telegrams from Penelope Gilliatt and Ken Tynan. What a terrible moral struggle they must have had. Which is more important – to support Peter Hall or to disguise the fact that we actually read the *Evening News*?

In the end it took the full force of the Lord Chamberlain's Office and a leak in Princess Margaret's yacht off the coast of Sardinia to put the theatre back in its place, away on the critics' pages.

David Frost: *Punch*
2 September 1964

---

* (Michael Codron resigned from the executive committee of the Society of West End Theatre Managers, in protest against Emile Littler's remarks in attacking both *The Marat/Sade* and Orton's *Entertaining Mr. Sloane*, which Codron had produced.)

The Homecoming

Aldwych Theatre: 3 June 1965

By 1965, Harold Hobson's prophecy, made in 1958 after the disastrous reception given to *The Birthday Party*, that time would reveal Harold Pinter's 'original, disturbing and arresting talent', had been proved correct. Pinter's *The Caretaker* at the Arts Theatre had demonstrated his ability to write haunting full-length plays; while such short pieces as *A Slight Ache* and his revue sketches had acquired a vogue reputation. The word, pinteresque, had already been coined to denote those elliptical, half-sinister, half-humorous stretches of dialogue which could be found in the work of many dramatists of the period, other than Pinter himself.

That was, however, only half the story, for in the mid-1960s, Pinter was lucky enough to become associated with the director whose productions of his works were, for the next ten years, regarded as definitive. Peter Hall brought to the Pinter plays produced at the RSC's Aldwych theatre a cool correctness, a deliberation of style which made each dimming of the lights, each slight gesture, each intonation, part of an overall pattern. The Pinter-Hall evenings at the Aldwych provided the high style of the 1960s, a sharp contrast to the energetic, imaginative but often somewhat rough theatre which abounded elsewhere. Their later triumphs included *Landscape* and *Silence, Old Times* and, at the National Theatre, *No Man's Land*; but the production which indicated what was to come, was that of *The Homecoming*.

By almost any standards, *The Homecoming* is a disturbing play, in that the central character, Ruth, deliberately chooses not to be a respectable wife and mother on a university campus in the States, but to be a high-class whore established in a Soho flat by a family of male chauvinist pigs. The title is capable of several interpretations. It can mean, simply, the return of Ruth's husband, Ted, from the States to his home in North London, where his father, a widower, lives with his uncle and brothers. Or it can mean that the arrival of a woman provides the equivalent to home life for the male family: there is one splendid scene where the family puts on its best behaviour for after-dinner coffee. Or again the title could be explained as a return from the intellect to the emotions, from a cold, ordered life to a passionate

PINTER

disordered one. *The Homecoming* was a perplexing and challenging play, asking questions, upsetting moral premises, daring its opponents to tag it with labels of obscenity. It out-stared the 'dirty plays' controversy; and perhaps the secret to its success lay in the non-emotional, very deliberate style of its presentation.

In later years, Hall's directing of Pinter's plays came under some attack for being over-stylised. A very fine production of *The Homecoming* by Kevin Billington in the late 1970s treated the play on an almost completely naturalistic level. The pauses, the ambiguities which seemed so tellingly mannered in the mid-1960s, were made to feel simple and forthright in Billington's hands. But by then, the war had been won, or rather it had changed battle-grounds; and the victory, such as it was, was attributable to the original RSC production.

The story of Harold Pinter's new play is stark and horrible. Teddy, the successful son of a singularly beastly family, comes home from America to pay them a short visit, bringing with him the wife whom none of them have met. Four of the family live in the decaying old North London house – Teddy's father, an aged bully given to sudden spurts of violence; his brother Sam, a taxi-driver of a tidier and more pacific way of life; and Teddy's two younger brothers, Lenny, a successful ponce with girls working the Greek Street area and Joey, a boxer haunting the gym in the vain pursuit of recognition.

Teddy has somehow become a Doctor of Philosophy in a mid-Western American university, and his wife, Ruth, as we first see her, is the ideal consort for an American professor, cool, attractive, well-dressed, well-poised, the mother of three children. At first, their impact on the family is what you would expect from the contact of quiet, civilised people with the rough relations they have grown away from. The general level of reserve is dented here and there by bouts of exaggerated affection or familiarity pressed too far, but it maintains an orthodox course on the whole.

And then, in a brilliant Pinterian stroke, an extraordinary change takes place. Ruth gets up to dance with Lenny, and at once they go into an amorous clinch. Teddy watches impassively. Lenny is followed by Joey, whose success with Ruth is so immediate that he finally takes her up to his room. The last scene is devoted to a family conference at which they discuss a plan to install her in one of Lenny's Greek Street flats and share her favours when she is off-duty. When it is settled, Teddy leaves for America as unperturbed as if his wife were going to her mother's for the weekend.

I've recounted the plot in such detail because Mr. Pinter keeps insisting that there's no more in his plays than what you see. It would be easy to read into this story something about original sin, perhaps, or the dangers of rising above one's station. But if I understand Mr. Pinter's principles rightly, it's simply the story of a woman who found life in an American university intolerable ('it was all sand and rocks, and there were lots of insects') and the prospects of life on the game more attractive.

However you care to take it, it's monstrously effective theatre. Perhaps Mr. Pinter keeps us waiting a little too long before he springs the trap, dickering with half-suggested family scandals; but once he does, he raises all the expected *frissons*. Mr. Pinter isn't to my way of thinking an *important* playwright, in the sense that he has any message to offer us or any trail-blazing innovations in technique. But he has this enormous capacity for generating tension among his characters in which the audience becomes irresistibly involved; and to do this is surely the playwright's first responsibility. I defy anyone not to feel concerned with the events presented to them in *The Homecoming*.

B. A. Young: *Financial Times*
4 June 1965

Mr. Harold Pinter's first full-length play for five years gives us an opportunity to see where this master of intangible menace has now got to: it is a homecoming in more senses than one ...

Now: to what home has Mr. Pinter come? Not, I think, a very happy one. The first act of the two displays all his dazzling dramatic legerdemain, his ability to transmute the smallest of small-talk into dialogue quivering with sinister, half-caught meanings, his skill at establishing a relationship between two characters and then violently wrenching it out of shape, his very considerable stagecraft.

But, in the interval, his invention seems to flag. Long stretches of the second act seem to be no more than the actions of a tired man keeping the ball in the air; the positive motivelessness becomes negatively aimless and shallow; he seems to be imitating his own style, asking himself what Pinter would do now, and then doing it.

Bernard Levin: *Daily Mail*
4 June 1965

Boredom can set in fairly early with the rationalist. I enjoy myself the outrageousness and am quite happy with the baffling message of motiveless evil lurking in wait. But to me (and to me only it may be) Mr. Pinter reverses the chief pleasure in the theatre: which is to sit with fellow-humans (the audience) either fully in-the-know or in keen curiosity as to the general state of affairs and then to see the players, probably not in full knowledge or in misguided expectations make a mess of or redeem events through their 'own' devices and character. In Pinter, the thing is the other way up. It is *we* who are in total ignorance: the actors who are exchanging wreathed smiles and knowing nods of complicity.

Why, for instance, does the chauffeur uncle have a heart attack? He was such a nice fellow and his boring anecdotes and self-regarding patter are beautifully managed by John Normington. Was it because he didn't have the courage to stand out against the arrangement whereby his niece-in-law was to be set up in prostitution? Arguably Paul Rogers the hectoring old widower also has a heart attack but doesn't die. His whine 'I'm not an old man' addressed to the enigmatic and only too willing daughter-in-law (Vivien Merchant, all poise and polish) finally brings down the curtain.

Most enigmatic of all is Michael Bryant's Teddy (the homecomer) who remains a complete blank and makes off to America again without protest or visible sign of relief at being rid of a tiresome wife. Ian Holm, with enormous gusto and volume, bounces us into feelings of interest for Lenny, the cock sparrow brother with most enterprise. Peter Hall produces with a splendid sense of what can be got out of the veiled innuendo and non sequitur. The result is often very comic in a wry way. The grey and black horror of a living room designed by John Bury is not the least of the ingredients. But it leaves us feeling cheated.

Philip Hope-Wallace: *Guardian*
4 June 1965

Mr. Pinter guides us into his strange wasteland of 20th-century loneliness and then deserts us. We are soon lost in his labyrinth of dead ends, unmade roads and confusing signposts.

He is more cruel, gruesome and deliberately offensive in this two-act horror than in his previous plays. On its face value, it is callous and empty enough: what lies in its Freudian depths one dreads to think.

Anthony Seymour: *Yorkshire Post*
4 June 1965

This intensely unattractive play is the first full-length drama Mr. Pinter has written since *The Caretaker* in 1960. In the intervening five years, he has devoted himself to one-actors like *The Birthday Party* and *The Collection* in which he developed more and more his special tricks of atmosphere and menace.

We have all come to recognise these Pintermimes a mile off – with those long, unblinking pauses, the aura of something horrific behind the humdrum action, the sense of suppressed violence beneath the banal utterance.

Herbert Kretzmer: *Daily Express*
4 June 1965

Hamlet

Royal Shakespeare Company, Stratford Memorial Theatre:
19 August 1965

·

'*Hamlet*,' said Peter Hall in an interview with the *Daily Mail* (11 August 1965), 'must be re-thought every decade or so.' His *Hamlet* with David Warner was a particularly careful and radical new interpretation; and the changing images of Hamlet himself over the years suggest much about the social climates of the times as well as of altering theatrical fashions. At the risk of oversimplifying, one could suggest that prior to the 1960s, Hamlet was always played in Britain as a hero with heroic qualities – courage, intelligence, elegance – defeated by events; whereas during the 1960s, he was presented as an incomplete person, Bryden's 'unfinished hero', whose inadequacies made matters worse. John Gielgud's Hamlet, for example, in 1929/30 epitomised a scrupulous sensitivity which was too delicate to cope with the crudities of plain revenge; Olivier's and Burton's during the 1940s and early 1950s were honest, straightforward, athletic princes, not over-subtle and perplexed by the deviousness and 'rottenness' of political Denmark. In the 1960s, however, Hamlet's failures as a person, his bunglings and hesitancies, seized the imagination of directors, of which the most extreme example was Charles Marowitz's twenty-minute *Hamlet* (performed as part of the Theatre of Cruelty season at LAMDA) where the prince was shown to be simply rather callow and immature, unable to break from the domination of his parents. Other countries too had their changing Hamlet archetypes: 'Hamlet', we were told, 'is Germany', and Hamlet's inability to dispose of Claudius was linked to the failure in the 1930s to get rid of Hitler. The RSC's studio *Hamlet* with Ben Kingsley in 1975 expressed a similar view, with Denmark presented as a sinister prison state in which Hamlet was trapped, like a Franz Kafka, whose only doubtful hope of escape lay in a desperate assassination.

David Warner's Hamlet was not an anti-hero. He was certainly gauche and immature, but not stupidly so. He was regarded as a representative of an idealistic student generation, whose presence was making itself felt in British theatre, through the growing fringe movement, and elsewhere in society, culminating perhaps in the *événements de mai* in 1968 in Paris, in the protest movements against the war in Vietnam and in the flower-power movement. This Hamlet was highly topical; but this is not to suggest that it was also superficial, for a feature of the production was the way in which the familiar words had been reconsidered and invested with fresh interpretations. The verse-speaking was criticised partly because the lines sounded unfamiliar, with unexpected stresses, consistent with the interpretation but not with tradition. It was almost like listening to a new play.

In offering us a Hamlet of our times, Peter Hall presents David Warner as an immature young undergraduate, powerless at what his elders are doing with his world, pipe-dreaming and crossly complaining with his red Wittenburg Varsity scarf wound tightly around his neck.

We are offered Hamlet as a coward, a boy who doesn't know what has hit him, who is prodded into action only when he cannot escape it (to save his own skin).

He is a Hamlet who knows he will never have the courage to kill Claudius as he knows he should. He is a Hamlet with a 'Ban the Bomb' button.

It is a consistent portrait that Peter Hall offers us through the lank body and contemporary voice of David Warner, but, of course, it robs us of the real Hamlet.

There is no intellect in this man, nothing princely. We see nothing of the great Elizabethan dilemma: the Hamlet 'adrift from old faiths and not yet anchored in new'.

David Warner is at his best with sex (as one would expect in a teenage portrait of Hamlet). There is the young man's deep revulsion from sex in his rejection of Ophelia after he sees what his mother could do in his dead father's bed.

He has another fine moment when, having accidentally killed Polonius, he brags to his mother what he is going to do to Rosencrantz and Guildenstern. He has had the taste of blood, the taste of action, but it soon passes.

But whatever its other merits, one must turn one's back on a performance in which the verse is spoken so execrably.

I would as lief the town-crier spoke Shakespeare's lines as hear David Warner. He delivers the soliloquies as though he were dictating to the literary pirates jotting down the first-quarto version of the play.

He butchers the rhythms, stresses unimportant words, affects new and strange ways of speaking the English language. On his delivery of the part alone, he must stand condemned.

As one would expect, Peter Hall has staged the play with great care, skill and deliberation. He has mounted it in huge spaces, great panelled rooms, vast bare sets relieved with solitary but solid objects – a cannon, a heavy table.

Julian Holland: *Daily Mail*
20 August 1965

The world it inhabits is that of confident public life. This Elsinore is not a dream castle honeycombed with Gothic corridors, but a busy centre of government and social glitter opulently reflected in the tapestries and marble floors of John Bury's set. The cold war with Norway gets full emphasis – the first thing that strikes the eye being a massive cannon trained on the stalls: and when Fortinbras appears – a blond demigod in a silver breastplate – it is like the sun coming out. Hamlet himself, trapped in this hive of bustling militarism and courtly display, is from the start in a condition of existential panic. He has no clear identity: all he knows is that the solid appearance of the court is a façade for shifting values and lies. No one can be trusted; and the Ghost's call for vengeance is an invitation to involve himself in the life of action from which lies originate. 'They fool me to the top of my bent' is his key line.

It makes sense, and it connects with a widespread current attitude towards public life. And yet how much the play has had to be tailored to fit the interpretation! Horatio, for instance, almost vanishes so as to preserve Hamlet's isolation. Brewster Mason's Claudius is an unshakably bland politician, and Tony Church's Polonius a smooth adviser with a clubland drawl — both Establishment figures. As such they are well played, but large areas of the parts have simply been left out. Polonius *is* a silly old man, Osric *is* a fop. Claudius *does* suffer from remorse and can be publicly unnerved. But not in this production: even at the climax of the play scene Claudius registers no more than offended dignity. When he calls for lights, he is rebuking Hamlet for a social gaffe.

Such distortions are not made crudely; there is no facile attempt to draw a parallel with modern political disaffection. All the same, David Warner's Hamlet would make better sense if he had no cue to passion and were simply wrestling with the Danish equivalent of the Tory magic circle. He does not seem to have fallen into melancholy as a result of his mother's re-marriage: rather he is temperamentally a neurotic intellectual — patrolling the corridors prematurely haggard like Chekhov's eternal student wearing a shabby old gown and steel-rimmed glasses; back from the sea voyage, his costume suggests a turn-of-the-century motoring outfit. His soliloquies (well motivated) come across as an almost pedantically articulate attempt to impose a meaning on his inner chaos; but they hardly advance his development as a character.

Essentially what Mr. Warner presents is yet another variant on his Henry VI — a sweet-natured child entrusted with a task beyond his powers. ...

The Times
20 August 1965

Mr. Warner's Hamlet ignores convention, which is sufficiently an aristocratic thing to do, since it is only the established, the bohemian and the poor who can afford to do so without social and financial loss. Those who go to this *Hamlet* expecting to be gratified with the smooth formalities of Saville Row will be sadly let down, but if they accept the proposition that Hamlet could conceivably have been dressed, would in fact today be dressed, by Cardin, they will like me be excited, satisfied, beautifully astonished and profoundly moved.

What matters, of course, is not the sober cut of the gentlemanly suiting, but the inner authority. Mr. Warner has that all right, and when the occasion demands he can interpret it in glittering physical terms. He may stoop from his outrageous height, wave his arms like a scythe, howl to the moon, and go after the king at a most unrefined gallop, but, if the immediate situation dictates it, he is spare, controlled, deadly, and most royally confident.

For a long time in the duelling scene he stands perfectly still, hardly troubling to move his sword, smiling unforgivably, while the active, sweating Laertes tries in vain to get at him from all angles. If, as people seem to believe, one of the functions of Hamlet is to make the commonalty feel their commonness, I have never seen the thing better done. It is an assertion of distinction based not on artificial considerations, but on an obvious superiority of nerve and skill.

Mr. Hall has imagined the ghost as a vast, insubstantial wraith that moves in and out of the shadows with supernatural regularity and ease; it glides silently as if independent of human means of locomotion; and is quite terrifying even before Patrick Magee begins to speak with his graveyard voice. It is so huge that it can fold Mr. Warner (the tallest actor on our stage) in its arms as if he were a child, and an undersized one at that. This is important, for it is overwhelming grief for his father's murder that inspires Mr. Warner's Hamlet.

When Mr. Warner speaks the great soliloquies he comes to the front of the stage and rakes the first few rows of the stalls with ravaged eyes, searching distractedly for a comfort that is not there or anywhere. Besides the enormity of his private sorrow, affairs of state are a secondary consideration. So much so that in a sensational treatment of his last speech, Mr. Warner makes Hamlet's dying vote for Fortinbras a joke.

Harold Hobson: Sunday Times
22 August 1965

Mr. Warner's voice can match his aspect. It can be brusque, nasal, grating or linger monotonously on the note. It is the voice of a baffled youth at war with himself, caught in the busy 'prison' that is Denmark, unable to urge himself to action, finding that he has a way of expressing himself poetically, and shying from the idea in embarrassment. He will argue closely and very, very slowly, with himself and with the members of the audience he is anxious to draw into his soliloquies ('Am I a coward?'). The sound of the thing does not matter, though now and then he starts, like 'a guilty thing upon a fearful summons', when a speech insists upon making its own music.

It is, on its deliberately small scale, a very intelligent lost-soul Hamlet. He thinks his way into every line, and we are obliged to go with him, though at the première I kept on wondering whether it could be a translation into prose, an answer to an examiner's demand for a paraphrase.

J. C. Trewin: *Illustrated London News*
28 August 1965

...the revenge he really wishes, and achieves, is on himself for not being the great Hamlet his father was. The key to every *Hamlet* is its ghost. A solid ghost demands an active, believing hero, thwarted by events; an insubstantial one, all light-effects and echoes, a brainsick prince, nerveless and Oedipal. The apparition which swims above the walls of John Bury's Elsinore (a superb inferno of bitumen ramparts and lakes of black marble, whose throne-room swarms with faded frescoes of sad grey Rubens flesh like a wax museum of elderly lasciviousness) is something new: a giant helmeted shadow ten feet tall which dwarfs his shuddering child in a dark, commanding embrace. 'This was a man', Hamlet tells Horatio enviously: for once we are shown the other side of the Oedipus complex. This Hamlet is less jealous of his mother's bedfellow than of his father's stature. As the hollow voice beneath the stage cries 'Swear!', his son lovingly measures his length on the ground, as if on a grave; but the voice moves, he cannot cover it. Clutching violently at his mother on her bed, he looks up to find the huge presence of his father towering between them. Every recollection of his mission is a reminder of his sonship, his immaturity.

His pretence of madness is half an admission of this. He shelters in childishness, seeking to appear not merely insane to be responsible for his actions, but too young, His disguise is not just dishevelment but the wilful untidiness of an undergraduate, the half-baked impertinence of the adolescent who would test his parents' love to the limits of tolerance. He slops ostentatiously through the castle in a greenish, moth-eaten student's gown, peering owlishly over his spectacles to cheek his elders. He knows his position as heir to the throne protects him, and abuses it as far as he can. The easiest disguise for an adolescent with a problem too big for him is that of a problem adolescent.

Hamlet (RSC, Stratford)

It's a conception which requires a special kind of actor, young enough to play both buffoon and tragedian. The image may have been Hall's, but clearly it shaped itself around the peculiar talents of David Warner. His Hamlet grows out of his Henry VI and Valentine Brose in *Eh?*: an angelically gawky Danish stork, recognizable compatriot to Kierkegaard and Hans Anderson, who tries on ideas and emotions for size as he tries on the Player King's crown – it slips down over his nose. As he denounces the firmament to Rosencrantz and Guildenstern for a foul and pestilent congregation of vapours, he watches to see if they find his pessimism as impressive as it sounds. Do they believe it? Does he? Or are his emotions as false as theirs? They laugh, swinging teasingly on his long student's scarf, and he turns chastened to the arriving players, to test his rage and grief against those of Pyrrhus and Hecuba.

Warner is the first Hamlet, surely, young enough to play the prince as a real student, learning as he goes along. It's this that gives the production its marvellous new life: he feels each line back to freshness, lives each scene for the first time. He simply does not know what to do about Ophelia when he meets her. In his trouble, he has forgotten that she is a separate person, with her own emotions. He falls back shocked and fumbling at her reproaches – this, and her mad scene, are the points at which Glenda Jackson's sharp, self-possessed personality are put to good account.

It's hard to convey the excitement of seeing him make each discovery, seeing the play's machinery dismantled and fitted together before your eyes ... This is a Hamlet desperately in need of counsel, help, experience, and he actually seeks it from the audience in his soliloquies. That is probably the greatest triumph of the production: using the Elizabethan convention with total literalness, Hamlet communes not with himself but with you. For the first time in my experience, the rhetoric, spoken as it was intended to be, comes brilliantly to life.

Ronald Bryden: *New Statesman*
27 August 1965

Armstrong's Last Goodnight

National Theatre at Chichester and the Old Vic:
6 July and 12 October 1965

British theatre during the early 1960s could justifiably boast about its
remarkable group of young dramatists. If some of them promised
more than they actually delivered, this was in a way to be expected,
for they promised so much, and with such variety of styles and ideas.
In the two years spanning the first performance of *Armstrong's Last
Goodnight* (at the Glasgow Citizens in 1964) to its last with the
National Theatre at the Old Vic in 1966, we were able to see (to take
two extremes) the first plays of Joe Orton and Edward Bond, Pinter's
The Homecoming, Osborne's *Inadmissible Evidence* and *A Patriot
For Me*, Marcus's *The Killing of Sister George*, and many other
intelligent, original works.

I have chosen *Armstrong's Last Goodnight* from this number, not
because it is necessarily the best of them, but because it illustrates so
exactly the buoyant ambitiousness of the period. The original
inspiration came to Arden after reading Conor Cruise O'Brien's
book, *To Katanga and Back*, concerning his experiences as a United
Nations representative in the Congo, during the post-independence
civil war. The play's relationship, however, to the events in the
Congo is far from direct. Arden associated the civil war – and
Lumumba's attempt to bring Tshombe into line – with the treatment
of border barons in sixteenth-century Scotland. In both cases, a
central, national government was trying to impose its authority on a
sturdily independent outlying region; and the civilised Sir David
Lindsay, the herald of King James V, who negotiates with and then
betrays the border baron, Armstrong of Gilnockie, resembled
(though not closely) the pacifying role of O'Brien.

If Arden's concern for the new nations of Africa represented one
side of his world view, his determination to relate it to Scottish
history was another; for he did not want British audiences
complacently to assume that the troubles in Zaire and elsewhere in
Africa could not happen, and had never happened, here. He wanted
to show them as part of an overall pattern. *Armstrong's Last
Goodnight* anticipated both the crusade for devolution in Scotland

167

JOHN

and Arden's subsequent passionate denunciations of the British presence in Ireland.

To achieve his aims, it was essential for Arden to convey a sense of regional differences. He did so by a very bold method indeed. He constructed a heavy Scottish dialect, almost a new language, based upon the medieval Scots of Dunbar, Henrysson and Lindsay himself (who wrote *The Three Estates*). He ran the risk that this language would be barely comprehensible even to audiences above the border, for in addition to including obsolete words, Arden invented some of his own. But one Scottish language was not good enough, for Arden's play was about regional difference; and so the border baron, Armstrong, had to speak this new language with a thick local accent and local words. Arden's remarkable achievement, helped by precise directing (from John Dexter and William Gaskill in the National Theatre's production) and vigorous acting, was that this language succeeded in all its aims – by being understandable, dramatically and linguistically, and by conveying a sense of foreignness. The National Theatre's production also illustrated a new sophistication in handling stage areas – for one side represented the king's court and the other the border castle of Gilnockie, with the intervening area suggesting a journey of more than a hundred miles.

John Arden's play, first produced at the Glasgow Citizens Theatre, seems to have lost something essential on the long journey South to Chichester. John Dexter and William Gaskill's production has more polish, more attention to detail, but less sheer emotional impact. The Armstrong clan, in particular, is curiously lack-lustre and muffled beside the bluff Davy Crocketts we saw in Glasgow. I must also admit to preferring Iain Cuthbertson as John Armstrong to Albert Finney. Mr. Finney emphasises the sullen, brutish side of the character; he appears to take one line of the play, that he is 'violent, proud and abominably selfish', entirely literally. He misses the warmth and generosity of heart. At the end, when poor Finney dangles dead from a tree, it is hard to feel particularly concerned.

Armstrong, I should explain, is a sixteenth-century laird who by constant raids on towns over the border, nearly lands Scotland in war with England. Essentially, the play is a conflict between him and the king's herald, Lindsay, played by Robert Stephens. It is in effect a conflict between anarchy and order; between emotional and cerebral attitudes to life; between base crude humanity and the politicians. John Arden's achievement is that he suggests these and other ideas through live robust characters whom he never tries to simplify. He has an obvious (and intense) moral concern for his problems, but he never uses his people for moralising. It is quite impossible to endorse either of the protagonists. If Armstrong has a marvellous sense of freedom about him, he is also egomaniac and dangerous. Lindsay has all the right humanistic ideas; but in the end, he too turns to deceit and betrayal for a solution. ...

Stephens and Finney are the prominent trees in a veritable forest of Arden. This is, indeed, a complex, ambitious play. It grows outward, layer by layer, from its solid kernel of personal conflict. Everything is related to everything else; nothing is black, nothing is white; it is impossible to make any absolute standards on people, on problems. But, after all, there is no reason why a play should reveal all its secrets at one session, any more than a complex personality should reveal his psyche to a stranger. Those who think that a play is a message, tantalisingly put into code by its author, may well be disappointed. John Arden has more respect for his audience's intelligence than to manipulate them like decodification machines.

Benedict Nightingale: *Guardian*
7 July 1965

One thing can be said straight away about John Arden's new play, *Armstrong's Last Goodnight*. No composition that I have seen done in Chichester has been so well suited to the open stage here.

Mr. Arden has used the medieval method of having 'mansions' permanently set on the acting floor.

One of these is a palace representing the court of the Scottish King James V. The other is a castle representing one of the impregnable fortresses from which the marauding Border chiefs conducted their raids – into England if possible but into the southern Scottish counties when occasion served.

At the back of the stage is a third set-piece, the Forest which stands for the wild Border country. All this is ideally suited to the Chichester lay-out. ...

If your idea of a well-spent evening is to listen to slugs of talks in an ersatz dialect of medieval Scots for more than three hours here is your play. You get some decorations thrown in – a bit of murder, some elementary pageantry and a realistic hanging.

But speaking quite personally, I don't know why anybody wanted to write it or anybody wanted to put it on.

W. A. Darlington: *Daily Telegraph*
7 July 1965

Last night at the Old Vic I had one of the greatest surprises of my playgoing life. I paid a second visit to John Arden's *Armstrong's Last Goodnight* – and enjoyed it. ...

The whole atmosphere of the piece is subtly changed. The action seems closer knit, the dialogue less uncouth and more easily followed, the characters more human and individual.

How much of this startling change is due to the more intimate kind of staging I cannot guess.

It is pretty clear, though, that great credit must go to Albert Finney, who restaged the original Dexter-Gaskill production for the warmth and humanity the piece now has.

W. A. Darlington: *Daily Telegraph*
13 October 1965

... There was no arguing with my feelings: I had had an almost complete change of heart. A play which had seemed distant and dead, now seemed close and warmly alive.

My job as a critic lay plain before me. First I had to describe the phenomenon and then try to explain it.

The first task was simple and easy. The second was neither, and within the limits of time and space that are the morning critic's conditions of work, I could only arrive at a conjectural explanation.

Albert Finney, the leading actor in the play, had re-staged it for the proscenium-stage at the Old Vic, and my guess was that his experience during the Chichester run had enabled him to spot weaknesses in the original production by John Dexter and William Gaskill, and to put in something stronger of his own.

It was a plausible theory enough, but it didn't altogether satisfy me, and next day I began to wonder whether my change of opinion might not perhaps be purely subjective, in which case it must be I, and not the production, that was different.

Had I, for example, been in a jaundiced mood at Chichester, and had I now regained my serenity? I gave the idea an honest looking-over and dismissed it. I am not moody by temperament.

Had I then allowed myself to be prejudiced in some way by the barbarous nature of the play's action, the remoteness of its historical background, the roughness of the dialect which the author had invented for the occasion?

No, it couldn't be that. The play was already in print when the Chichester performance took place, and as I had taken care to read it, I had known exactly what the play was like before it began. What was more, I had formed the entirely favourable opinion that the play was specially well suited to the open-stage conditions of the Chichester Theatre.

So far as I could tell, then, the change did not lie in me, but in something – presumably something rather subtle, since it was so difficult to spot – that Mr. Finney had done to it. And I dare say I might still be wondering if the post hadn't brought in a letter from Mr. Finney himself.

It was a very delightful letter, reflecting an attractive modesty in the writer. I am not going to quote from it, because it was written with no thought of publicity; but I must give you the gist of it, because it solved the problem on which my mind had been at work.

He waved aside my suggestion that it was cleverness on his part in re-staging the play that had altered its impact. He had, he said, kept close to the original Dexter-Gaskill production, and added a word of admiration for the quality of his predecessors' work.

It was the Old Vic itself, he went on, that had caused the improvement to which my reaction had been so immediate and so powerful. He did not enlarge on this theme, but it was quite clear what he meant. Once again, and this time in a play which I had thought ideally fitted for the open stage, the greater intimacy, the closer concentration of a proscenium theatre had brought an increase in vitality.

W. A. Darlington: *Daily Telegraph*
25 October 1965

The new season of the National Theatre opened last night with a play which should ensure for Mr. John Arden his long deserved status as a contemporary classic.

Violent, argumentative and disillusioned, his plays are essential expressions of our age. *Armstrong's Last Goodnight* is a direct descendant of *Sergeant Musgrave's Dance*. Like the earlier play, it is a moral-political parable, set in a small community of many conflicting interests, and using the facts of our own contemporary history to teach a timeless lesson in public and private morality. Both Armstrong, the self-appointed ruler, and Lindsay, the political idealist, are descendants of Musgrave: both pay the price, Armstrong with his life and Lindsay with his integrity, for ignoring the bitter realities of political necessity. 'Ane trustless tale grew out of this conclusion', Lindsay meditates under the gallows of Armstrong; and the ending is a bleak reflection on inevitable and wasteful sacrifice.

The Times
13 October 1965

Arden's recurring theme is the denial of function. We are not the uniforms we wear, he reiterates, but the naked, complex, contradictory animals inside them. Musgrave, in *Sergeant Musgrave's Dance*, exposes the reality of soldiering by hoisting a skeleton in uniform before the townspeople. The incorruptible police chief in *The Workhouse Donkey* is defeated by the human deviousness of the town he tries to clean up. At the beginning of *Armstrong's Last Goodnight*, the King of Scotland's civilized herald removes his surcoat before embarking on his mission to pacify the marauder. 'Do you remember the story of the Gordian knot?' he says, 'There was ane emperor, and he went with ane sword and cut it. He thocht he was ane god, walken. Why in God's name could he no be a human man instead and sit down and unravel it?'

Naked into the conference chamber, in fact. Arden says his inspiration for this comedy of personal diplomacy came from Conor Cruise O'Brien's account of his mission to Katanga. It's a pity he couldn't use that gorgeous tale as it stood, but libel apart, his sixteenth-century Border setting gives him the Northern imagery he loves, and takes him to the heart of the ballad tradition which is really the centre of his talent. The North, the ballad, are his symbols for pre-social reality: the fury and the mire of human veins which defeated Musgrave's pacifism, Chief Constable Feng's law.

To bring out the resonances of his history, Arden has imagined that James might have chosen as envoy the brightest jewel of his court, his tutor Sir David Lindsay, and has steeped himself in the marvellous language of Dunbar and Lindsay himself, lovingly recreating it into a theatrical speech thorny with images, knotted with strength, rough and springy as an uncombed fleece. Dramatically, it works superbly. The author of *The Thrie Estaits*, the

173

poet who with Dunbar brought Scots dialect to such urbanity, is just
the man to recognise Armstrong's value, to try to bring him within
the king's peace by humane reason, man to naked man. Equally, he
is just the man to see the humour and irony of his abortive attempts
to snare this sly white savage of the moss, and the tragedy of his
inevitable failure – that all civilization can do with white whales is to
kill them. Armstrong, is simply too much for reason to cope with.
Having forsworn the sword, Lindsay is eventually driven to untie his
Gordian knot with a royal noose.

Ronald Bryden: *New Statesman*
16 July 1965

Saved

Royal Court Theatre: 3 November 1965

Saved was Edward Bond's second play to be shown at the Royal
Court, the first being *The Pope's Wedding* in a production without
decor in 1962. It provoked the most violent reactions, for and
against, but mainly against, of any play in the post-war period.
Simply on the grounds of its language, it would have been banned by
the censor; and so William Gaskill, who had taken over from George
Devine as director of the Royal Court, decided to turn the Royal
Court temporarily into a club theatre so that it could be staged,
beyond the reach of the Lord Chamberlain's Examiner of Plays.

But it was not the language which outraged audiences and many
critics, but one particularly horrific scene in which a baby was
stoned to death in a pram. The realism of Bond's writing, his superb
evocation of a flat, arid, hopeless and deprived social life in South
London, compelled everybody who saw the play to recognise that
atrocities were not confined to fascist camps or to the more lurid
reaches of melodrama, but took place in supposedly civilized
countries as well. Since seeing *Saved* on its second night, I have
never been able to read a newspaper account of child- (or
wife-) battering without remembering that one scene, and for that
reason alone (although there are others), I have always ranked *Saved*

among my most powerful and haunting theatre experiences.

I was then working in the script department of a film company and also wrote an occasional column for *London Magazine*; and I was so alarmed by what seemed to me the disgraceful reception of *Saved* that I almost physically dragged along my friends to see the play, canvassing support for it in any way I could. Such unprofessional partisanship was shared by many other admirers of the play, and seemed particularly necessary when the Royal Court, after a minor alleged breach of the club licensing laws, was hauled into court. Olivier was among the many notable witnesses who spoke in the play's favour; and, in retrospect, I am inclined to think that the battle over *Saved* won the war against stage censorship, abolished in 1968.

The partisans of the time, however, were inclined to underrate or deliberately overlook the very rapid changes in outlook and taste which had occurred over the preceding five or six years. Although Hall had won his battle with Littler over *The Marat/Sade*, the 'dirty plays' controversies raged on, and every month, it seemed, added another *succès de scandale* to the list – Rudkin's *Afore Night Come*, Orton's *Entertaining Mr. Sloane* and *Loot*, Fred Watson's *Infanticide in the House of Fred Ginger* and Giles Cooper's *Everything In The Garden* with its implication that all families caught up into living beyond their incomes in a consumer society offered potential recruits to prostitution. If *Saved* had been an isolated example, perhaps its opponents might not have been prepared to drag out their dislike of it to such lengths; but, as it came within such a powerful trend, they felt determined to take a stand. The seriousness of Bond's vision – though bleak and often humourless – defeated them in the end; for Bond was quickly recognised, even by those who disliked his work, to be a major new British dramatist.

The scene is a South London park, though the stage is totally bare, sloping down to the audience, where a burly young man stands fishing in confident tranquillity. Beside him a sturdy but more sensitive companion squats on the grass. They talk in a desultory way, sensitive Len, irritatingly confident Fred, by nagging on about Pam, the slut Fred has stolen from Len, and about Fred's sexual prowess in general. They break off for a detailed description, graphically mimed, of how to tear a worm in pieces and squeeze the bits on to a hook.

Presently, enter Pam, pushing a smart pram containing Fred's baby, which has previously been heard crying, and ignored, for twenty minutes at a stretch as a background to domestic bickering. Taking it for a walk is now being used as a pretext by Pam searching out Fred, who is fed up with her. More bickering is brought to a close by Pam flouncing off, leaving the baby behind. Poor Len is much distressed, Fred indifferent.

Next enter four louts, led by a pinched psychopath, last seen hurling filth jokes at an unknown elderly woman. A to and fro of sneers and jeers is followed by prolonged phallic obscenity with a long blue balloon. Tiring of this, the louts gather round the pram. For a moment, flickers of humanity seem to spark and gutter in their stunted souls. But then the psychopath says you can put a baby to sleep by pulling its hair – and pulls it, quite gently at first. The others join in; one of them punches it, also quite gently at first. But soon they are pummelling it, fists and faces working. They tear off its drawers and nappies – are disgusted to see that it is dirty. They roll it over and rub its face in its own excrement, dancing madly round the pram. They pick up handfuls of sharp stones and bombard the tiny, filthy, bleeding body. Len has been standing by, horrified, but too frightened to intervene; now he is terrorised into stoning the baby. But they realise that the baby is dead, and scatter. In wanders its mother and hazily pushes the pram off.

This scene is the *pièce de résistance* of Edward Bond's *Saved*, the third offering of the Royal Court's new management, produced and presumably chosen, by the English Stage Company's director, William Gaskill. I have described it at length, and as impassively as possible, because it, and the play which frames it, represent something of a crux in modern drama: a clear demonstration of what is permissible, what is not, and why. ...

... even amidst its horrors further doubts arise. Why does the baby, which has previously howled for quarter of an hour at a stretch, utter no sounds? For practical reasons, obviously – and a perfunctory reference to its having been dosed with aspirin only underlines the contrivance. And after the killing, when the reluctant mother Pam returns, how are we to believe in her sudden concern for the child? How even more are we to accept that she never so much as glances into the pram to notice the mangled little corpse? Again the perfunctory statement that 'I can't bear to look at you' only underlines the contrivance. It begins to be impossible not to think that the whole scene of the killing is contrived. Cruelty and viciousness, on stage, are no strangers to the theatre. But was there ever a psychopathic exercise so lovingly dwelt on as this, spun out with such apparent relish and refinement of detail?

Here is the crux for modern drama. It is becoming more sharply and urgently associated with contemporary life than it has been for centuries, if ever. Things as horrible as this baby-killing, and worse, happen every day; but it is not enough merely to enact them. Without the shaping hand of art, the result is only reporting. And when to reporting is added the intensification of stagecraft and powerful acting, and the prolongation of sadistic antics far beyond the time needed to make a valid point, in circumstances carelessly rigged, the conclusion is inescapable, that we are being offered not a keenly understanding, and therefore implicitly compassionate, study of deprived and unfortunate people, but a concocted opportunity for vicarious beastliness – still, I naively suppose, a minority taste.

J. W. Lambert: Sunday Times
11 November 1965

I spent a lot of the first act shaking with claustrophobia and thinking I was going to be sick. The scene where a baby in a pram is pelted to death by a gang is nauseating. The swagger of the sex jokes is almost worse.

But it has to be said that this isn't a brutish play. It is a play about brutishness, which is something quite different. The swagger belongs to the characters, not the author. Edward Bond has planted a foul piece of social evidence in our files. If we prefer to turf it out, I shan't be the least surprised, but it is a sizable testimony. *Saved* is a study of reduction of personality that makes no excuses and offers no kicks, executed with hard-headed humanity and a brazen technique. The play is about English thuggishness: it is our Fascist document, the one we don't want to know about. 'Gangs all over the place', says the murderer in the play when he is about to go to jug; 'police don't do their job'. It wasn't my fault about Belsen, I only worked there.

Saved is about people who are at the very bottom end of human possibility. The well that most human beings drop down only through temper or drink or madness is the place where the characters spend their lives. They are thick, vengeful, incoherent and terrified. They are frightened of one another, but even more of themselves, because they have no insight and no sense of cause and effect ...

Two distinctions. If the events in the play provoke incredulousness, this doesn't mean that they are incredible; not when newspapers regularly have stories about old ladies in tobacconists' shops who have been coshed over the head for less gain than a quarter of toffees, not when divorce judges so often mercifully prise apart couples who haven't spoken to each other for thirty years.

And though the vernacular language may make the play look like a 'slice of life', a phrase that is used to mean a very inferior slab of theatrical fruit cake, the truth is that the prose is skilfully stylized. It uses a hard, curt unit of dialogue, a statement of panic masquerading as an attack, hardly ever more than five or six syllables to a line. People don't elaborate; they stab in the dark, the dagger turns into rubber or a wisp of fog, and the bad dream has already left them behind.

Again and again in *Saved* a violent act or expression is cut off from the feeling that gives it meaning. The destruction has no rage in it, the desires are empty boats and the obscenities aren't erotic. 'No one tells you anything real.' Personality can only be asserted by walking out, and a row is not a sequence that can be remembered but a seething knot of which no one can find the end. The girl's father, ironing his shirts as he has done for years because his wife won't, says proudly to his daughter's boy friend that he came back after a row just to show her; 'Why should I soil me 'ands washin' and cookin'? Let her do it. She'll find out.' 'Yer do your own washin' ' objects the boy. 'Eh?' the old man says, encountering the truth for a second and losing it again. 'An' cookin' ', the boy insists, but this is too much reality to cope with. ' 'sfree country', the characters in *Saved* will often say; no, it isn't, not if you live in this cage.

What happens when people have no curiosity, and when they feel that education is a boat that left them behind? What happens when they find relationships so impossible that they treat people as disposable? The thing that makes *Saved* most painful to watch is the fact that the characters who won't listen to other people's desperate voices are in despair for lack of a listener themselves. In the first half of the play, it is a baby that is crying its heart out while its mother and grandmother sit by the telly vying with each other in not bothering about it. In the second act, the same sound comes from the mother, weeping in bed while her dad and her boy friends leave well alone.

When people in this play try to make anyone understand their feelings, they can describe nothing, and they know it. They are like men in exile carrying around a brick in the hope of showing what their country is like. In the last scene, the egocentricity of the characters has made communication finally impossible. The boy friend is mending a chair, the mother wins an inch from her daughter by pinching the *Radio Times*, the daughter takes it back again, and the father is doing his pools. The mime is life-in-death, the most horrific thing in the play.

Penelope Gilliatt: *Observer*
11 November 1965

I now know that there is at least one kind of play that I cannot take, whether it is good or not.

That is the 'slice of life', when the slice comes from life at one of its more bestial levels.

Such plays, in fact, as *Entertaining Mr. Sloane*, or last night's new offering at the Royal Court, *Saved* by Edward Bond.

The key scene in this piece is one in which a gang of young South London roughs work themselves up into a savage frenzy in which they stone a baby to death, as delinquent children might stone a puppy or kitten.

The effect of this scene on me is precisely the opposite of what the author intended me to feel. I had no sense of horror, no dramatic illusion.

I knew there was no baby in the pram, just as I could see there were no stones in the actors' hands. My only emotion was cold disgust at being asked to sit through such a scene.

W. A. Darlington: *Daily Telegraph*
4 November 1965

The last scene of the play consists of four minutes of complete silence.

There they sit, the father planning to leave his wife as soon as she is old enough for it really to inconvenience her; the vengeful mother; the girl who lost a baby she didn't want anyway; the boy who wanted to help but found no one to help.

All that is said is 'Fetch us a hammer'. No one does. One feels that this was the scene that started the author writing.

There must be many such rooms and many such silences – of total, personal indifference. How did they get that way?

It is a muddled and muddling play. But it is certainly a moral one. It is impossible to be indifferent to the characters' indifference.

Peter Lewis: *Daily Mail*
4 November 1965

The infanticide is entirely unmotivated and unexplained and is preceded by a series of obscene actions performed on the body of the baby that cannot be touched on in print. From first to last, Edward Bond's play is concerned with sexual and physical violence.

It is peopled by characters who, almost without exception, are foul-mouthed and dirty minded and barely to be judged on any recognizable human level at all. Nobody in his senses will deny that life in South London or anywhere else for that matter, can be sordid, sleazy and sinister. Nobody, furthermore, will deny that it is one of the functions of the theatre to reflect the horrific undercurrents of contemporary life. But it can not be allowed, even in the name of freedom of speech, to do so without aim, purpose or meaning.

Herbert Kretzmer: *Daily Express*
4 November 1965

The production is painstaking, the writing often powerful, the acting meticulously naturalistic. Barbara Ferris gave a frighteningly exact performance as the girl and I don't want to see the play again.

Jeremy Kingston: *Punch*
10 November 1965

Suite in 3 Keys

Queen's Theatre: 25 April 1966

It seemed odd at the time, and still stranger now, that the last plays of Noël Coward should have received their premières in London after such plays as *Saved*. The gap between Coward and Bond seems much longer than a generation; and the presence of both illustrates the diversity of the theatre of the 1960s. Coward, who also acted in the three plays, had not appeared in the West End since 1953; and his previous play, *Waiting In The Wings*, had not been a great success in 1960.

During the mid-1960s, however, there was a marked revival of interest in Coward's plays. In 1963, Hampstead Theatre Club had staged *Private Lives*; while in 1964, the National Theatre invited Coward to direct *Hay Fever*, which was a great success. Coward's personal appearance in a new play in the West End seemed to be the final phase in a long return to fashion. But it felt very much like a farewell occasion, not just to Coward himself but to the era which he in particular represented. The main play of the three, *A Song at Twilight*, was a protracted swansong, and its story about a famous writer blackmailed in his old age by the threatened release of some homosexual love letters evoked memories of how some other authors of Coward's generation had been treated by their biographers and friends – Maugham and T. E. Lawrence among them. The short season at the Queen's was respectfully received; and one critic of Coward's generation, Lionel Hale, went so far as to say during a BBC critics' discussion that no contemporary dramatist could match Coward's skill as a writer; but, for me, it was very much a generation occasion, highlighting the differences in ideas, skills and beliefs between pre- and post-war theatres. The pure, unselfconscious enjoyment of Coward's art came later, with an anthology evening of his songs, *Cowardy Custard*, at the Mermaid Theatre in 1972, which Coward attended in one of his last London visits before his death in 1973.

Three minutes before the first act curtain of *A Song At Twilight*, Noël Coward comes to a halt in his fretful pacing, shocked and slightly sickened, like an ill, old man who has walked into a wall in the dark. That leathery, lizard profile of an elegant amateur boxer has been made up now to look smudged and flabby.

The hair is just a few chalky streaks, the lean rangy body bulges into a pot-bellied bulb like a thermometer, and the tendons of the neck stand out in ropes as the blunt chin yearns upwards like a straining snail. It is an extraordinary apparition, as if Lord Butler were imitating Somerset Maugham, and somehow the monochrome face floats about the stage with the peculiar black-and-grey ghostliness of a television image in a coloured room.

Mr. Coward's latest impersonation, Hugo Latymer, is Garry Essendine 30 soul-sapping years on, a famous satirical writer run to seed after a lifetime of self-indulgence and self-advertisement. The news which knocks the wind out of him is the threat by a former mistress to release to the world his homosexual love letters. The elaborate camouflage of normality is about to be stripped from him when his physical and mental energies are at their lowest ebb. ...

... courageous and uncompromising as *A Song At Twilight* is, so far as it goes, it is a gesture which stops short in mid-flourish. The first act is nearly all padding during which it is difficult to make out whether Hugo's second-rate Cowardisms are meant to be deliberate or accidental. Certainly, the pseudo-highbrow vocabulary, full of difficult, dead words like 'prescience', 'obloquy', 'egregious', 'vitiating' and 'gratuitous', sounds strained and hollow. The jokes are served out in quotes as with tongs and have to be immediately apologised for. The insults are repetitive and depend upon a few over-worked, italicised adverbs, such as '*interminably* witless' and '*inexpressibly* tedious'.

It may be that Mr. Coward is intentionally satirising the conversational style of his earlier heroes. But if so, the method is too tentative and uncertain to achieve its aim.

And the second act tells us nothing about what it is like to be a homosexual in an unsympathetic society. We learn that Hugo's wife has known all along and that his mistress was never deceived. But what about the rest of his friends, his associates in show business and literature? Did he have only one male lover? Most of us can think of quite a few celebrities who flaunt their normality to millions of admirers, yet whose real sexual habits remain an open secret among thousands in the know. If *A Song At Twilight* was not written to demonstrate the strains, the misunderstandings, the comedy and the tragedy of the double life, then what was its purpose?

Alan Brien: *Sunday Telegraph*
17 April 1966

He has had the inspiration of casting himself as far older than he really is – as a celebrated author living out a cheerless decrepitude among his laurels in an expensive Swiss hotel suite, with a German wife-guardian (Irene Worth) and an unexpected caller in the shape of Lilli Palmer, as the actress who was his first affair.

For a long first act, it is the old tennis match of barbed courtesies between old, embittered lovers. The desolation of wealthy old age is beautifully conveyed.

He, with his regime, a doubtful eye on the gastric tract which makes every delicacy joyless, his ration of cigarettes and liquor, accepts it.

She, with her face-lifts, her glandular injections, her auburn rinse, frankly defies it. Both courses seem equally unattractive.

Then, with an old-fashioned but still effective manoeuvre, drops the bombshell that she has letters proving him to have been a homosexual all his life.

Here the parallel with Somerset Maugham becomes extremely pointed ... though you can take it or leave it. There are many possible interpretations.

But the end of it, as Coward with tremendous understatement sits reading the letters, leaves us with the bleak husk of a man which is, in its quiet way, terrible. No compassion is asked for.

Peter Lewis: *Daily Mail*
15 April 1966

... Mr. Coward seems to have drawn upon some hitherto untapped source of creative energy to make *A Song At Twilight* his most interesting play since the war. He appears in it himself – for the first time in a play of his own since 1947 – and plays an elderly, frail and cantankerous novelist whose bitter satires have brought him a knighthood, but whose life and works are less than great because too much of his energy has gone on concealing the fact that he is a queer.

Jeremy Kingston: *Punch*
27 April 1966

In *Shadows of the Evening*, the first of his two new plays at the Queen's, Noël Coward pursues the serious purpose that motivated his examination of a homosexual author in *A Song At Twilight*.

This time Coward is fascinated by death. What are the reactions that intelligent, articulate, sophisticated people will adopt when confronted by its immediate inevitability?

When George Hilgay, a rich publisher living in Switzerland, is stricken by a disease that will kill him in three months, his mistress calls for help to the wife he has deserted. Should they tell George about his fate?

Their mutual animosity dwindles in the face of their common problem, but their dilemma is resolved when George announces that he knows exactly how long he has to live.

Trying to be gay and normal about it, they plan a night out in a casino, but George rebels against the façade and the pretence.

Superficially the publisher skirts the issues many of us would feel in a similar situation. Being an agnostic, he can take no refuge in religion, he cannot stand the prospect of dying in an atmosphere of tight-lipped heroics and what he wants of those who love him is their help in overcoming fear.

It is not a particularly profound play, but in the hands of Lilli Palmer as the semi-hysterical mistress, Irene Worth as the strong but rejected wife and Noël Coward, looking pathetically fragile as the dying publisher, it works on the level of a moving, well-told short story.

Milton Shulman: *Evening Standard*
26 April 1966

Of the two short plays, one is solemn and one is gay, but both amount to vigorous restatements of Mr. Coward's values – loyalty, emotional honesty and stoicism in the face of the inevitable. All admirable qualities which nevertheless stick in the craw when fired off at point blank range as they are in the first play – a triangular reunion for a dying publisher, his mistress and long-estranged wife.

The two women attempt a façade of friendship to gladden his last months, but he insists on the truth and rejects their deception – 'The silences between us will lengthen', he says: it is one of a number of strongly felt lines, but these are outweighed by the see-saw passages in which he delivers homilies and then apologises for preaching. Nor, in spite of Mr. Coward's strenuously preserved nervous tension, is the piece particularly well-played.

Less ambitious, *Come Into the Garden, Maud* is a good deal more stage-worthy. It presents a blue-rinsed battle-axe (a gorgeously vulgar performance by Irene Worth) dragging her docile millionaire spouse round the cathedrals and impoverished nobility of Europe. Finally the worm turns and he makes off with a glamorous Italian grandmother who is still young at heart. Situation and characters alike are good solid stereotypes, but they still have plenty of life in them. Mr. Coward himself sheds 10 years and plays a spry, grinning butter and egg king, which is an agreeable change after his previous dilapidated roles.

The Times
26 April 1966

... [George Hilgay] is civilised, intelligent, witty and suave, and he wishes to die well.

Mr. Coward makes this exceedingly moving. In many respects, his play penetrates as deeply into personal problems and emotions as anything now to be seen in London, or that we may expect to see for a considerable time. It is written with authority and power; some moments in it are heart-breaking in their pathos.

Harold Hobson: *Sunday Times*
1 May 1966

Noël Coward's *Suite in Three Keys* was brought triumphantly to completion at the Queen's last night with two one-act plays – *Shadows of the Evening* and *Come Into the Garden, Maud*.

And the nature of the triumph proves one thing all over again – that what the public hopes for from Coward is gaiety, wit and laughter.

He may prefer himself in his more serious mood – two out of the three plays in this series are sombre in theme, with an accent on age.

Shadows of the Evening indeed has no gaiety in its theme, since it deals with a man who learns that he must die within a matter of months and shows him making up his mind to do it bravely.

The applause when the curtain fell on this play was respectful but nothing much more. After the second one, *Come Into the Garden, Maud*, it was ecstatic, noisy and prolonged.

We were suddenly back again in the old days when a Coward first night was a guarantee of wild excitement. It was delightful to see how pleased people were that he had been able, once again, to arouse that excitement.

W. A. Darlington: *Daily Telegraph*
26 April 1966

Rosencrantz and Guildenstern are Dead

National Theatre at the Old Vic: 11 April 1967

Noël Coward's style provided many links with British theatrical traditions. His acting developed that cool nonchalance associated with Sir Gerald du Maurier in the 1920s, which was itself a continuation of a manner for which Sir George Alexander and his productions at St James's Theatre during the 1900s were especially noted. His literary style too retained the slightly dashing poise of the dandies of the 1900s, with its use of irony, sometimes delicate, sometimes heavy-handed, its delight in snubs, a dash of cynicism and more than a dash of sentimentality. Coward provided the 1930s equivalent to Edwardian society drama.

Left-wing writers of the 1960s (such as David Mercer) would skilfully imitate this style, to ridicule it, as part of upper-class affectation. Its mannerisms suggested a social corruption, which was not a hard polemical point to make, for corruption was always part of the charm. Other dramatists, however, delighted in the style for its own sake; and developed it for their own purposes. Simon Gray and Christopher Hampton were two young writers who emerged during the 1960s, whose plays were distinguished by their commands of witty dialogue – ironic, cool, sophisticated, and very much in the Coward tradition.

Tom Stoppard shared this elegance of language; and his first play to attract widespread attention started its life as a fringe play at the Edinburgh Festival in 1966, and was taken up by the National Theatre. *Rosencrantz and Guildenstern are Dead* was an ambitious play. If the poise and precision of its dialogue evoked comparisons with the society comedies and dramas of the past, its themes were very much of the 1960s. If the Hall-Warner *Hamlet* showed the prince as someone at loss amidst the corruption of the Danish court, Rosencrantz and Guildenstern in Stoppard's play were even more perplexed; they could not even begin to know why the prince was upset or what was upsetting him. Their deaths were as arbitrary as their lives; and the comedy of the play partly comes from the fact that the audience knows so much more about their dilemmas than they do. They could also have been compared with Vladimir and Estragon in *Waiting for Godot*, whiling away their times waiting for something to happen. In this play, Stoppard managed to change the tone of this debate, from deep and sometimes gloomy seriousness, to light-hearted good humour, flippant but charming. He provided the National Theatre with a notable success at a time when the company particularly needed it, after various rows which caused John Dexter to leave the artistic management and Kenneth Tynan to abandon his scheme to produce Hochhuth's *Soldiers*.

As a first stage play, it is an amazing piece of work.

I know of no theatrical precedent for it, but among other things it might be called a piece of literary detection. From the labyrinthine picture of Elsinore, Mr. Stoppard has blown up a single detail and wrenched enough material from it to create a drama.

The shadowy history of Rosencrantz and Guildenstern always sticks in the mind as a classic instance of the fate that befalls little men who are swept into great events. Much is said against them in the course of *Hamlet*, but they hardly deserve it: they are too insignificant to escape anonymous servitude.

For most of Mr. Stoppard's play they are shown in private – abandoned in an ante-chamber of the palace waiting for the next call, spinning coins and playing word games, desperately latching on to the First Player as the only character who will speak to them.

From time to time, the court sweeps on to conduct its incomprehensible business and sweeps out again, leaving the interchangeable nonentities stranded like driftwood on the beach.

What emerges is a compound of Shakespearian criticism, Beckett-like cross-talk, and the mathematical nonsense comedy involving two cyphers. The couple have no memory of the past, no understanding of the present, and no idea where they are going.

All they have is words, and the endless word games they play represent both a way of passing the time and an indefatigable attempt to make sense of their predicament.

Mr. Stoppard manages to relate the material to the Shakespearian action – as where a quick fire question game (as exciting as a tennis match) is used as a preparation for an interview with the prince, who promptly wins the game and set (' "We were sent for", you said, I didn't know where to put myself').

But the real triumph is in relating the partners' preoccupation with free will to the players, whose profession insists on fixed destiny and who stage a rehearsal of the *Gonzago* prologue forecasting the fatal voyage to England. On the voyage, Mr. Stoppard secures an existential conclusion in which the partners discover their death warrant and choose to deliver it so as to emerge, if only for a second, into lives of their own.

There are times when the author, like his characters, seems to be casting about for what to say next. But for most of the time he walks his chosen tight-rope with absolute security.

In its origins this is a highly literary play with frank debts to Pirandello and Beckett; but in Derek Goldby's production, these sources prove a route towards technical brilliance and powerful feeling.

Irving Wardle: *The Times*
12 April 1967

If the history of drama is chiefly the history of dramatists – and it is – then the National Theatre's production of *Rosencrantz and Guildenstern are Dead* ... is the most important event in the British professional theatre of the last nine years.

Rosencrantz and Guildenstern are Dead is the best first London-produced play written by a British author since Harold Pinter's *The Birthday Party* in 1958. It has been well – even enthusiastically – received. This is fortunate for the reputation of the British public, for not to appreciate it is to merit a gamma in the College of Theatrical Enjoyment, and a gamma minus in the University of Life.

Its ingenuity is stupendous; and the delicacy and complexity of its plot are handled with a theatrical mastery astonishing in a writer as young as Mr. Stoppard, who, whilst demonstrating a spirit deep, foreboding, and compassionate like Beckett, shows a sleight of hand as cunning as Feydeau's. Tragedy is made, not by situations, but by men. Macbeth would not have been troubled by Hamlet's problem: with a little help from his wife he would have polished Claudius off before breakfast. Nor would Antonioni's hero in *Blow-Up* have been perplexed by the circumstances of Rosencrantz and Guildenstern. He would have plunged with eagerness into the relationships between Hamlet and Ophelia, and no doubt he would have contrived some revealing photographs.

But it would never have occurred to him to worry over why he had been sent for. Like them on the periphery of violence, he would have been content with cheerful and self-regarding agnosticism. But Rosencrantz and Guildenstern are without this precious gift of indifference, and there are millions of people in the world who resemble them: people, from Oedipus downwards, who cannot bear not to know the answer to questions they would be happier if they never asked.

Tossing coins in a romantically decaying Elsinore, engaging in philosophic speculation, indulging in word games that are sometimes dazzling in speed, timing and judging of climax, they are all the time uneasy because no explanation has been given them why they have been summoned to the palace. The court rushes in, speaks some words from Shakespeare that are incomprehensible to these young men who do not know the plot, and rushes out again. The court, the king, the queen, Hamlet himself come and go like a whirlwind, blowing to all quarters of the globe what shreds of self-possession Rosencrantz and Guildenstern have hitherto been able to preserve.

Their uneasiness rises to panic. They ponder, examine, weigh and argue about every word Hamlet says to them, and in their mounting distress can make nothing of them. Yet they are not unintelligent, and in a particularly shining passage, they make a brilliant summary of possible reasons for Hamlet's distress; but it helps them not at all in their own. Rosencrantz is frank, simple and impetuous, Guildenstern dark, intellectual and Italianate. Both are equally baffled and helpless before the blank, terrifying and unanswering wall of life. It is a situation many people know well.

Harold Hobson: *Sunday Times*
16 April 1967

Well, it is all very clever, I dare say, but it happens to be the kind of play that I don't enjoy and would in fact much rather read than see on the stage. It is the kind of play too, that one might enjoy more at a second hearing, if only the first time through hadn't left such a strong feeling that once is enough.

W. A. Darlington: *Daily Telegraph*
12 April 1967

Easy as it is to find echoes of Sartre, Beckett and Kafka in the introspective exchanges of R. and G., it is as an exceedingly funny play, underlining some of the more idiotic plot devices in

Shakespeare, that this piece will best be cherished. Derek Goldby's production, crammed with wit, irony and stunning balletic and comic effects, catches every nuance of the play's many-layered statements.

Milton Shulman: *Evening Standard*
12 April 1967

In outline, the idea is extremely ingenious; in execution, it is derivative and familiar, even prosaic. As an artist, Stoppard does not fight hard enough for his insights — they all seem to come to him, prefabricated, from other plays — with the result that his air of pessimism seems affected, and his philosophical meditations, while witty and urbane, never obtain the thickness of *felt* knowledge. Whenever the play turns metaphysical, which is frequently, it turns spurious, particularly in the author's recurrent discourses upon death: 'Death is not romantic ... and death is not a game which will soon be over ... death is not anything ... death is not. It's an absence of presence, nothing more ... the endless time of never coming back'. This sort of thing is squeezed out like toothpaste throughout the play, the gravity of the subject never quite overcoming the banality of its expression: 'The only beginning is birth, and the only end is death — if you can't count on that, what can you count on?' Compare this with Pozzo's lines in *Godot*: 'One day we were born, one day we shall die, the same day, the same second, is that not enough for you? They give birth astride a grave, the light gleams an instant, then it's night once more' — and you will see how much Stoppard's language lacks economy, compression, and ambiguity, how far it falls short of poetry.

There is, in short, something disturbingly voguish and available about this play, as well as a prevailing strain of cuteness which shakes one's faith in the author's serious intentions: 'Eternity's a terrible thought', reflects one character, 'I mean where's it going to end?' Hamlet spits in the wind, and receives his spittle back in his eye. There is a good deal of innuendo about the ambiguous sexual nature of the boy playing the Player Queen. And the two central figures are whimsical to the point of nausea.

It is, in fact, the characters of Rosencrantz and Guildenstern that account for a good deal of my queasiness about the play. In Shakespeare, these characters are time servers — cold, calculating opportunists who betray a friendship for the sake of a preferment —

whose deaths, therefore, leave Hamlet without a pang of remorse. In Stoppard, they are garrulous, child-like, ingratiating simpletons, bewildered by the parts they must play – indeed, by the very notion of an evil action. It is for this reason, I think, that Stoppard omits their most crucial scene – the famous recorder scene where they are exposed as spies for Claudius – for it is here that their characterological inconsistency would be most quickly revealed. Since the author is presumably anxious to demonstrate the awful inevitability of a literary destiny ('We follow directions – there is no *choice* involved. The bad end unhappily, the good unluckily. That is what tragedy means.'), it hardly serves his purpose to violate the integrity of Shakespeare's original conception. But I suspect the author has another purpose here – that of amusing the audience with winning heroes – and the necessity to be charming is not always easily reconciled with the demands of art.

Robert Brustein: *The Third Theatre*
(Jonathan Cape, 1970)

Oh! Calcutta!

Round House: 27 July 1970

Theatre censorship was abolished in Britain in 1968; and there were those who thought that its abolition would open the flood-gates to a high tide of pornography, 'permissiveness' and 'dirty plays'. Others felt that the very absence of an establishment target, like the Lord Chamberlain, would take away some incentive from the rebels who had previously wanted to defy the social codes; and perhaps lead to a decline in 'dirty plays', or at least a discovery of a civilised equilibrium in which sex would take its place among many other emotions as a proper subject for the theatre.

There did seem to be fewer scandalous successes after abolition, nothing to compare with *Entertaining Mr. Sloane*, *The Marat/Sade* and *Saved*. Nor did a sea of sex shows sweep over the West End. One or two productions of this character, such as *Council of Love* and *Pyjama Tops*, had runs which in the former example was short and in

the latter rather long. The test case for the new permissiveness was *Oh! Calcutta!*, which was indeed still running in 1979. This was Kenneth Tynan's attempt to bring together a show to fill a vacant place where, in his words, 'a civilized man (could) take a civilized woman to spend an evening of civilized erotic stimulation'. He had assembled a remarkable group of writers and artists to provide such an evening, including Joe Orton, Sam Shepard, the composer Johnny Dankworth and the designer Allen Jones. It was first produced in the States, where it was received with a mixture of curiosity, enthusiasm and impatience. Clive Barnes suggested that it was the sort of stuff 'which gives pornography a bad name'.

My impression is that London received *Oh! Calcutta!* with considerable calm. Various attempts to rouse public indignation against it petered away into nothing; and although it was certainly a commercial success, it never looked like taking the town by storm.

Oh! Calcutta!

Irving Wardle's review for *The Times* which starts so
enthusiastically and ends so damningly expressed the thoughts of
many people who would have preferred *Oh! Calcutta!* to have been
more successful than it was. Its sequel, *Carte Blanche*, was an
outright disaster. It was perhaps too much to expect that sexual
freedom, if such a thing exists, could have been achieved overnight;
but it was surprising that, after so long a campaign and so much
heraldry, that the event itself should, as it were, go off half-cock.

POLITICS OF MORALS (Headline in *The Times*)
The opening in London of Mr. Kenneth Tynan's 'entertainment',
Oh! Calcutta! should bring home to people what is happening. Its
game is basically the sort of exhibition of sexual voyeurism that used
to be available to the frustrated and the mentally warped in the side-
turnings of a certain kind of sea-port. If Mr. Tynan and his friends
wished to satisfy themselves by this sort of thing in strict private, I
suppose the rest of us would have no cause for any reaction, except
pity. But, in fact, they seek to thrust it down the heaving throats of
the majority ...

Ronald Butt: *The Times*
23 July 1970

So much dirt and so many lofty sneers have been heaped on this
show that one's first impulse on emerging uncorrupted, undepraved
and quite well entertained is to declare the whole thing to be
marvellous. I have seen better revues than *Oh! Calcutta!* but none
based on ideas that strike me as more sympathetic. Namely, that the
ordinary body is an object well worth attention; and that there is no
reason why the public treatment of sex should not be extended to
take in not only lyricism and personal emotions, but also the rich
harvest of bawdy jokes. ...
... In many ways, it is a ghastly show: ill-written, juvenile and
attention-seeking. But it is not a menace.

Irving Wardle: *The Times*
28 July 1970

What is new about *Oh! Calcutta!* ... is its cool insolence. This is an
elaborately got-up musical revue that peddles publicly to middle-

class audiences the sort of material previously confined to the saloon bar or the sleazier strip club. ...

... it presents sex as an endearingly improper, absurd and eminently kiddable human activity. ...

... the shock effect is at the opening when the 10 men and girls of the company come on stage and undress. They don white robes while the slotted panorama behind them glitters with projected slides. Eventually, movie film is played on their bodies as they parade, proud as peacocks, totally nude. Given their figures, the effect is quite stunning ...

... There is poetry in its celebration of the human body, and much to laugh at in its mockery of sex. So far as I can judge, I was neither depraved nor corrupted by its impudent humanity ...

John Barber: *Daily Telegraph*
28 July 1970

... *Oh! Calcutta!* is five years too late to be the great liberating sensation it was obviously intended to be....

...What we are left with is a so-called erotic revue which is anti-erotic and in which nearly every sketch is embarrassing – not because it is rude, but because it isn't funny with it.

Peter Lewis: *Daily Mail*
28 July 1970

But though I, in my depraved way, felt a bit let down after all the fuss, I certainly would not think *Calcutta* corrupting or even depraving. We have it on the highest authority that to the pure all things are pure. Children would be the last to take offence. One black nude looks good as she sings (unintelligibly into a yowling mike). Generally, the ladies come out lolloping or lissom. The men seem to shrink from such total exposure. Generally, there were stretches which seemed more like a long, dirty schoolboy joke than 'elegant eroticism'. But *chacun à son goût* ...

Philip Hope-Wallace: *Guardian*
28 July 1970

The Philanthropist

Royal Court: 3 August 1970

Christopher Hampton's first play, *When Did You Last See My Mother?*, about two ex-public schoolboys sharing a London bedsitter and discovering how to cope with their adolescent lonelinesses, was written when he was only eighteen, and produced in 1966. It was a remarkable play from so young a dramatist; and although it was never a popular success, it was regarded by many critics as the most promising first play of any written since the war. But often brilliant talents fail to develop after such an early success particularly if the original inspiration has come, in part, from intense personal experience.

Hampton, however, even in his first play, obviously liked the craftsmanship of playwriting. The dialogue and structure were precisely, carefully worked, even, in places, formal. It seemed likely that he could apply this skill to subjects at a greater distance from his own life. His second play, *Total Eclipse*, was a study of the relationship between Verlaine and Rimbaud; and retained the care with language, although the biographical play structure was, of necessity, somewhat less tightly-knit. The play, however, which was palpably successful on all levels, with critics and public alike, for it received a long run at the May Fair Theatre after its première at the Royal Court, was his third, *The Philanthropist*, written when Hampton was still only twenty-four.

The Philanthropist was sub-titled 'A Bourgeois Comedy'; and in a sense it was odd to see an apparently conventional comedy – set in a drawing room, among a young, middle-class and slightly trendy group – at the Royal Court, so long a home for anti-bourgeois plays. But *The Philanthropist* was a cleverly double-edged work, being both an excellent bourgeois comedy at its face value, and a criticism of the genre. The hero is a philologist, Philip, fascinated by the games language plays; and in one scene, he becomes innocently absorbed in the 'wit' of a successful writer, Braham Head, once left-wing, now right-wing, rich and outrageous. 'Your use of paradox', Philip says, 'You've got it down to a fine art, it's a reflex action. You've digested that it's an extremely simple and extremely effective technique.' Braham is offended: 'I think there's nothing cruder than an excess of subtlety', he retorts, thus precisely illustrating Philip's point. But paradox and irony, parallelism and eccentric words in conventional contexts, have for a long time been the gloss on English comedy. Hampton, in writing his bourgeois comedy, described the tricks of the trade and pointed out how easy they were.

But *The Philanthropist* was not simply a literary criticism play, inbred and over-technical; in that Hampton was tackling the wider theme of how politeness takes over from friendship, how the style swamps the man and how drawing room manners protect people from becoming too involved even in those circumstances which threaten their lives. It is a comedy in which the evasions of social conventions are innocently undermined by a quiet, well-intentioned don whose job is to observe them. Hampton's open-mindedness, his unwillingness to indulge in polemic and his reluctance to rely on easy quasi-political analyses strengthened this quiet, deliberately low-keyed play. The background events, however, are not low-keyed, for this bourgeois comedy takes place in a world of student and political revolt, with the events of 1968 close to the minds of audiences and actors alike.

Holding his two companions at gunpoint, a desperate young man berates them for having ruined his life and then pulls the trigger against his own head. There follows a small click, and the trio launch into an embarrassed discussion of his play and its rather obvious debts to Pirandello. The aggrieved hero concedes that perhaps his hero might have staged a more effective suicide; to illustrate which he puts the barrel into his mouth and blows his brains out.

My difficulty in discussing Christopher Hampton's new play is to relate this marvellous first scene to the rest of the piece. We next see the two bereaved friends preparing for a dinner party. Apparently they had an awful job cleaning up. From every point of view, they agree, the evening was disastrous; and, anyway, his play was no good, far too cerebral. Nervous giggles. They are university teachers, meeting in the room of a bachelor don. Shortly afterwards one of them languidly drops the news that the entire Cabinet has been mown down by a mad lieutenant-colonel posing as a woman in the Visitors' Gallery. (The play is set in the future, but, after the CS gas incident, perhaps the near future). How will the country carry on? Not that it will 'make much difference; not to us anyway.'

It is tempting to take this as a key line, and to view the play as an indictment of academic society: a rock pool where selfish bachelors laze the time away and allow their feelings to atrophy in over-protected seclusion from the world outside. Inset within a framework of bloody external events, and with rebellion simmering in the student population, Mr. Hampton's characters devote their time exclusively to casual bedhopping: and they are not particularly strenuous even in pursuit of that.

However, this view disregards the fact that we are offered imagined acts of farcical violence, not the real thing: and also that much of the sex is handled in a far from farcical spirit. As in his previous plays, Mr. Hampton has far too much respect for individuals to cut them into schematic units. And what he has produced here, in spite of its harsh implications, is a gently mocking comedy of academic manners.

Its hero is an amiably dispirited philologist who has spent his life in giving way to stronger personalities. ... Alec McCowen plays him beautifully; casting involuntary backward glances for support whenever anyone asks him for a decision, and adopting primly attentive postures towards the people who pour through his room, telegraphing inner panic from behind a rabbity smile. It is the best part to accommodate McCowen's nervy talent since *The Small Back Room*.

The rest of the comedy serves as an obstacle course for Philip: bullied by the ghastly right-wing novelist he asked to dinner, hauled reluctantly into bed by one of the girls, and grievously mauled by the fiancée who discovers this lapse. In every case, you see Philip smashed by yet another more powerful antagonist; and resorting to a style of literal-minded candour that only heightens their wrath.

He ought to cut an irritatingly pathetic figure: but thanks to the balance of Robert Kidd's production and to the writing, he remains (to a male observer, at least) much the most sympathetic. For where he has insight, the others only have appetites: the bitch fiancée (Jane Asher), the colleague who has reduced apathy to a fine art, the ghastly novelist (played by Charles Gray with superb predatory relish) are all decisive figures and their lines crackle with aggressive wit. But, theatrically, they are no match for Philip's stumbling gaucheries and sudden flashes of bleakly pedantic truth.

Irving Wardle: *The Times*
4 August 1970

A philanthropist is literally someone who likes people. But the philanthropist on view in this play is a man who doesn't want to hurt people's feelings – which is rather different.

As a result, he is a man whom almost nobody likes. From his quiet corner as a university lecturer, he sows disaster all round him.

His polite interest or praise is taken for cunningly veiled insult. He ruins his relations with every woman he meets. He sleeps unwillingly with one because he does not like to refuse – but afterwards he explains to her that he does not find her attractive.

This combination of good intentions and the crassest tactlessness is possible in green youth, but this is a man of middle-age who has never grown up.

In fact only the deftness of Alec McCowen makes the character briefly credible. His agonies of innocent embarrassment are well done.

But not even he can make such a humourless, not to say, boring character, worth an evening's attention.

Peter Lewis: *Daily Mail*
4 August 1970

I do not understand why Christopher Hampton should subtitle his new play, *The Philanthropist*, as a bourgeois comedy.

It is rather a caricature of university existence and those who inhabit it: the caricature is the medium for the message taken from his earlier play, *Total Eclipse*; that the only unbearable thing is that everything is bearable. For here he creates (or distorts) a society which has regressed into patterns of enormous self-absorption. Nothing outside the perimeter of personal relationship touches: alliances based on friendship and sexual interest are the last bastions.

To unravel this theme, he depends too much on a wilful exaggeration, the fatal glow of blandness. His central character and concern is a philology don whose obsession is words, their sounds and shapes, not their effects. He abstracts, and his failure depends on an inability to be or find himself. But to reinforce this impression of an over-closed community and to parallel the progress of the man's unhappiness, Hampton introduces two external shocks.

An undergraduate playwright shoots himself dead, nine cabinet ministers, we hear, have been gunned down in the House of Commons. Both events are briefly used to illustrate the characters' indifference to outside phenomena, to the happening outside the closed circle, the tight community. Both are caricature, unnecessary interjections.

But when the play reaches its hard taut centre Hampton lifts it into a different plane of conviction. The don may be a man whose mild indecisive life-style is close to preposterousness, but his relationship with his girl is not. A fatal time of one-night sexual stands and permutations is used to establish both the nature of his apartness and the girl's realisation that she has committed herself to someone she can like and not want. Inevitable that the don's reaction should be a first awareness of his wretchedness and a kind of stoicism which enables him to suffer himself without cracking.

Hampton now writes with a cool, slightly sour, witfulness, though his female characters tend to be walking attitudes. His gift for satire rather than caricature is shown gloriously, if extraneously, in the introduction of a John Braine character spewing out disgust and taking offence from anything in sight. If the play marks a regression from the fabulous *Total Eclipse*, it nonetheless emphasises that Hampton is now writing better than Wesker, Osborne or Mercer.

Nicholas de Jongh: *Guardian*
4 August 1970

With *The Philanthropist*, Christopher Hampton becomes the best dramatist the Royal Court has turned up since Edward Bond. He is, of course, a very different kettle of fish, and it is a kettle of fish which is easier to comprehend at first go.

It is the story of an extremely diffident don who loses all his girl friends by being too sincere.

His honesty upsets them, though he means well. And he ends up inevitably alone.

Mr. Hampton took the idea from Molière's *Le Misanthrope* and acknowledges the debt with *les trois coups* to raise the curtain and with chunks of Palestrina between scenes.

But if a debt is owed to anyone apart from the young author and the players who serve him so well, it is surely the Royal Court's policy of harbouring promising playwrights. ...

... the new piece is at once clever, effective and serious. It shows an easy theatrical assurance and recognises that there are other things as well. Out of its blandly intelligent and witty cynicism comes a genuine and moving desperation, especially in Alec McCowen's blind sincerity as the hero with such an awkward instinct for truth.

As a philologist, he suspects that he is a bore, he worries about meanings and his feelings. He is a bachelor, alone and academically loitering, and on the verge of marrying a student. But he keeps putting his foot emotionally in it. He is no good at campus promiscuity.

The thing that marks out Mr. Hampton's talent is not just his ability to make his people real and to give them likely things to say. It is his knack for changing mood. He can be flip and feeling by turn. And the turns are generally skilled.

What starts out as a smart conversation piece, rivalling early Coward in its self-conscious sophistication, becomes a scathing comment on intellectual high society without at any point straining for a moral.

It strains for an acceptable final curtain and also for cynicism in the dialogue. This cleverness is apt ultimately to shrink the hero into a merely sexual impotence. Never mind, it makes a brilliant third play.

Eric Shorter: *Daily Telegraph*
4 August 1970

A Midsummer Night's Dream

Royal Shakespeare Company at Stratford: 27 August 1970

Throughout Peter Brook's career, which shows such command and originality with so many different styles, there has been a constant thread – his love of the spontaneous and the immediate, his search for the living, as opposed to what he called the 'deadly' theatre. He recognised, of course, the limitations of the merely improvised production, for if actors do not know what they are going to do next or what effects they are trying to achieve, they can become inhibited or (which is as bad) self-indulgently narcissistic. He was also too good a technician to admire the sloppy or uncontrolled production. He therefore sought to provide a context in which it was possible for actors to feel free without being at a loss, where audiences could react with surprise and sometimes shock, and where the art of the theatre would never fall into the mechanical repetition of a set production.

A Midsummer Night's Dream was the last production of his years at Stratford, although he did return for occasional productions later. After his *Dream*, he went to Paris to form the International Centre of Theatre Research, in which he tried to break away from the conventional restrictions of the theatre – such as first nights, set rehearsal schedules and bureaucracy. He took his troupe to the Sahara, made them improvise plays without scripts and indeed without having a common language with their audiences. These ideas became crystallised in his mind during a short pre-Stratford run of *The Dream* at the small Midlands Arts Centre in Birmingham.

In an interview with Judith Cook, published in *Directors' Theatre* (1974), he said: 'I wanted everybody to understand that it was the actors always playing and improvising, it was never a production fixed by a director in a certain way for the actors to obey. I wanted a context in which the actor could continually come back remaking the play, and to make this live is a very difficult idea of improvisation – it isn't total freedom, nor is it total restriction with discipline, it is something mysteriously blending the two ... although we'd been working for ten weeks with juggling, swings, sticks and plates, and had been working in a very precise place with a very definite relationship to an audience at the Stratford Theatre, we went out to Birmingham taking no props, no accessories of any kind, with the actors working from what was at that moment their living knowledge of the play after that much rehearsal. The improvisation was an improvisation to find, on the spur of the moment, the outside forms that made this shared sense come to life for the people who were there. It was a tremendous occasion for everyone, because it was the first time we had seen the *Dream* alive in the way we'd been working on it.'

This anecdote is particularly interesting because it illustrates that one real strength of Brook's *Dream* was the actors' knowledge of the text. The most eye-catching feature of the production, however, was Brook's use of acrobatics and juggling, his refusal even to attempt a woodland *Dream* and his realisation of 'magic' in terms of humming tubes and one spectacular red feather suspended in the air which Sara Kestelman's Titania used as a couch. Nobody in Britain had ever seen a production of *A Midsummer Night's Dream* like that before; and nobody but Brook would have attempted it.

After a good, if not vintage season, Stratford rounds off its year with a masterpiece. By which I mean that Peter Brook's version of *A Midsummer Night's Dream* marks the apex towards which the RSC has been moving for the past two years, and that it brings Brook himself to a new point of rest. You could not have predicted what he would do with the play : but after seeing the production you feel that you ought to have known, as it is a simple and inevitable crystallization of what has gone before.

Like the RSC's previous shows, it is set in a bare lofty room. The difference is that Brook's designer (Sally Jacobs) has converted it into a gymnasium with ropes and trapezes suspended from the flies and a railed gallery running round the top. This serves several purposes.

It provides an environment for the *Dream* which removes the sense of being earthbound : it is natural here for characters to fly. Also it offers a range of entirely man-made images (even the trees are coils of wire let down on fishing rods) that set off the natural images of the text. Again it provides the greatest extension so far of the company's efforts to develop bodies as well as voices.

In this sense, the production relates back to Meyerhold and his mechanics : the ideal of a troupe of crack gymnasts skilled in clowning and all the tricks of the circus. In this way, Brook's company give the play a continuously animated physical line, occupying the whole cubic space of the stage as they shin up and down vertical ladders and stamp about on enormous stilts. Some of the effects are breath-taking : like the nuptials for Titania and Bottom (David Waller) where the stage is deluged in confetti and a purple-gowned Oberon swings across on a trapeze to the roar of Mendelssohn's Wedding March.

A smaller example is Puck's magic flower, here shown as a spinning juggler's plate which he and Oberon nonchalantly toss from wand to wand.

However, Brook is at least as much concerned with the voice as he is with the body. And what he offers is another answer to the question of false stage rhetoric. It consists of a running musical accompaniment (by Richard Peaslee) mainly scored exotically for percussion, autoharps, tubular bells, bongos. These punctuate the action to provide atmosphere and a sense of occasion. He also uses the guitar. The effect these have on the text is to make it natural for characters, at moments of high emotion, to pass over into song : sometimes lyrical, like the lovers, sometimes barbaric, like John

PETER BROOK'S
A MIDSUMMER NIGHTS DREAM RSC

Kane's war dance 'Up and Down' as Puck.

The interpretation to which these styles give substance is one of social harmony expressed by means of emphasizing the parallels between the three groups of characters. We are accustomed to seeing them as inhabitants of different worlds. Brook shows them as members of the same world. Aegus's loss of his daughter is matched by Oberon's loss of his Indian boy. 'This same progeny of evils comes from our debate', says Titania; and as Sara Kestelman delivers it, reclining on the huge scarlet ostrich feather that serves as her bower, the line is meant to embrace the whole action.

Thus Theseus is doubled with Oberon, both played with sovereign magnanimity by Alan Howard, Hippolyta doubles with Titania and Philostrate with Puck.

Brook has done two things here. He has made some reversals simply to produce a thrill of the unexpected, as in the beefy male fairies and a Snug (Barry Stanton) whose lion really does alarm the ladies. And he has altered other traditional emphases to express the main theme. You see this first in the Bottom-Titania wedding, an occasion for real sexual revels and not a joke against an outclassed clodpole.

But the point comes out most strongly in the mechanicals' play. The joke this time is not against them. The audience are not invited to join with the nobility in sneering at these crude performers. The play is a meeting between friends. At Pyramus's line 'I come without delay' all the lovers join in the song. And the event closes on a note of calm social harmony. 'Meet *we all* by break of day', Oberon says to the assembled stage. And the cast leave by way of the aisles shaking hands with the house. A marvellous evening.

Irving Wardle: *The Times*
28 August 1970

In a production of *A Midsummer Night's Dream* that will surely make theatre history, Peter Brook last night at Stratford-on-Avon tore through all conventional ideas about how the play should be staged.

He found new ways of giving form to its latent poetry and power.

For setting, he offers a dazzling white box. The actors too wear white — or else plain colours as vivid as conjuror's silks. The only furniture is four cushions, also white.

Several trapezes hang from the flies. Iron ladders at each side of the stage extend to the railed platform where musicians, zither, guitar or bongo-drums, are stationed.

The naked harshness of this environment is used by Mr. Brook as a means of exposing the actors' words and emotions. Its coldness suits the palace scenes admirably, and we are at once seized by the pathetic vehemence of the lovers' protests.

And when the rude mechanicals come on, the white courtyard is exactly right for a gang – it might be their lunch-hour – in flat caps, string vests and braces. Here suddenly Bottom, refused the role of the Lion, downs tools and sulkily walks off the stage and up the theatre aisle.

It is one of many stunning effects. The midnight wood is created with a galaxy of tricks. The trees are steel spirals held on fishing rods from above, and in the helical coils the lovers will be enmeshed.

Above, the fairies scrape washerboards and shake thundersheets to give the wood its awesome sounds. Oberon's enchanted herb is represented by a silver dish spinning on a wand, and passed from Oberon's wand to Puck's when both are on moving trapezes.

And when Titania sees Bottom translated, suddenly Mendelssohn's Wedding March blares forth and the stage fills with confetti the size of plates.

In any description, such devices must sound mere gimmickry. I can only report that they held me enthralled as the mood of the play leapt – one never knew what would happen next – from horseplay to startling bawdry, from poetic dignity to seething eroticism and to alarming chases up and down the ladders.

Old lines whose familiarity had bored one for years came up fresh and comic or distressingly apt.

For it was Mr. Brook's triumph to generate an atmosphere in which only the poetry mattered ...

John Barber: *Daily Telegraph*
28 August 1970

How can you perform the *Dream* in a white walled circus ring in blinding light with trapezes flying overhead?

Why, the fairies, swinging over the heads of the mortals, are the trapeze artists.

The mixed-up lovers, clawing each other up and down ladders in white bell bottoms and tie-and-dye dresses, are the tumblers.

And the rude mechanicals, bursting into the ring with their saws, planks, string vests and the roaring of Pyramus and Thisbe's lion, are the slapstick clowns.

Once you get used to it, it seems natural.

Peter Lewis: *Daily Mail*
28 August 1970

My own last contact with [Peter Brook] was through the medium of a television set, an odd, uncanny vision, which bothers me still. There he sat, hunched, furrowed, brooding, and, with every appearance of terrible intellectual struggle, enunciated more convoluted platitudes than one would have believed possible in so short a time. Was it really the Big British Peter? If so, what would his next production be like? As humourless and pretentious as this? Well, the answer is at Stratford, a *Midsummer Night's Dream* to strain the faith of admirers. The mountain has laboured and brought forth, among other things, Mickey Mouse.

This, presumably, is what his Bottom is meant to evoke. Why else should he have a tiny black bulb for a nose, small black ears instead of the conventional ass-head, and huge black clogs for feet? The actual purpose of the innovation isn't so clear; but then nor is much else in the production. It takes place in a slightly smaller version of the plain white box we've seen so often at Stratford: ladders lead up the sides to a gallery at the top. Those players who aren't onstage stand up there, gazing down on those who are, and intermittently grate, scrape and bang at the rails, making rough music. Music of a slightly smoother kind is provided by two small percussion sections, also aloft. The trees of the forest are represented by enormous springs dangling down from what look like aluminium fishing rods, Puck's magic flower by a steel plate twirling on a steel wand; players noisily wave big blunt saws and hurl shrieking silver and blue torpedoes at each other. It is a bizarre, metallic business: Shakespeare as he might have been conceived by a science fiction addict, or, indeed, performed by enthusiastic Vegans; the *Dream* 2001.

Perhaps this is the point. The romantic imagination nowadays isn't so exclusively filled with visions of spotted snakes, musk-roses, luscious woodbine and the other exotica invoked by the spirits in the play. We have seen Oldenburg as well as Rousseau, read Ballard as well as Keats. There's no reason why the nightmares of a technological age should not include processed minerals as well as animals and vegetables. But this little perception cannot justify the production as a whole, and there are other oddities still to be explained. Why Mickey Mouse? Why should the young bloods be dressed in what look like Marks and Spencer blouses and the fairies in baggy silver pyjamas, like Japanese wrestlers? What are we to make of a Puck in billowing yellow silks and a blue skullcap, who swings on a trapeze above the bickering lovers at a time he's supposed to be off-stage and still manages to mistake their identity afterwards? 'I'll put a girdle about the earth/In forty minutes', cries this fantastical Chinese rabbi from his perch, grinning foolishly; and we do not believe him for a moment. Only a humourless man could have staged this. There are also times when one feels that only a cynical one could be in control. The archetypal Hollywood mogul, thinking a scene dull, will call for gratuitous tit; and some of Brook's innovations seem analogous. Does the verse limp, the acting labour? Very well, put the speaker on a swing or stilts, make him scramble up ladders or wrestle with his betrothed on the ground, let him deliver his lines as if they are a pop-song, or, if they're meant to be sung already, sob them like a raga. All this happens in Brook's perverse dream, and more.

... The oddity of it is that Brook's controversial friend and influence, Professor Kott, is never more persuasive than when he condemns the sentimentality with which the *Dream* has been swaddled since Mendelssohn and before: in no other Shakespeare play (he suggests) is 'eroticism expressed so brutally'. The effect of Brook's interpretation is to sentimentalise it once again, and in a new, more insidious way. His manic decoration has deprived it of suffering, fear, horror, and, apart from one moment, when Bottom's phallus is crudely mimed by the fairies, even of lust.

Benedict Nightingale: *New Statesman*
4 September 1970

Long Day's Journey Into Night

National Theatre at the Old Vic: 21 December 1971

Olivier's last major part for the National Theatre, James Tyrone in O'Neill's *Long Day's Journey Into Night*, came at a particularly crucial time for the company. After several comparatively weak seasons by their standards, when the old management team of Dexter, Gaskill, Olivier and Tynan had broken up and the new associate directors had not settled down, the National Theatre had taken a great gamble. They knew that the new theatre which was being built for them would contain three auditoriums, which would require a larger company and a greater output of productions. Accordingly, they had decided to take over the New Theatre (now the Albery) in the West End. Their financial resources were low, and they had hoped to catch the summer tourist trade. Unfortunately, this season too was a comparative failure; and left them still deeper in debt.

Olivier had been struggling with ill-health for years; and, unknown to him, the National Theatre Board under its new chairman, Lord Rayne, had been discussing the problem of his successor, but very quietly and discreetly. In the summer of 1971, Peter Hall was approached to sound out his reactions to the thought of taking over Olivier's job as the National Theatre's director; but Olivier did not hear about this offer until the following March.

In the meantime, however, Olivier had taken command of his company again in a very characteristic fashion. His performance of the ageing actor, Tyrone, ranked with his finest at the National Theatre; while the production, though disliked by the American critic Robert Brustein (then writing for the *Observer*), led the way for a remarkable revival of the company's fortunes. The next two years were distinguished by several outstanding productions, such as *Jumpers*, *The Front Page*, *The Misanthrope* and *Equus*; but the standard overall was high, with, for example, Jonathan Miller's austere 1920s *Measure for Measure* touring the regions in a mobile production, unable to find a place in the crowded schedules at the Old Vic. *Long Day's Journey Into Night* was also one of the few National Theatre productions to reach a national audience successfully through television; and the impact of Olivier's performance could be felt over the following years, in productions which had little to do with O'Neill or even American drama. As with his Richard III and Othello, Olivier had provided an unforgettable impression of a character who represented a certain recognisable strand in human nature, an ageing, battling, cantankerous old warrior whose past wars were no less real to him because they were fought on the stage rather than the battlefield.

Although Olivier's Tyrone is scaled down to the surrounding company, it is a performance of intense technical and personal fascination. Personal in the sense that James Tyrone was an actor with the kind of career which Olivier spent his life avoiding: a strong talent destroyed by years of imprisonment in profitable type casting. We see Tyrone at a stage where he is all too well aware of this; and the dejection that settles on Olivier's frame from the start – his body hunched and his mouth cracked into a small crooked line – expresses a sense of defeat that encompasses the whole of his life and not merely his family. There are touches of the old ham: as when he smugly intones a few of Prospero's lines and turns to his son in naked appeal for applause; and where Olivier pulls out a pair of his own incomparable physical tricks in staging two contrasted descents from a table. But what marks out his performance most from the others is its breadth; all the components of the man are there simultaneously – the tight-wad, the old pro, the distracted husband, the ragged Irish boy – and there is the sense not only that O'Neill is showing off the different sides of the character, but that Olivier is consciously manipulating them for his advantage.

Irving Wardle: *The Times*
22 December 1971

On a second viewing the National Theatre's production of Eugene O'Neill's *Long Day's Journey Into Night* looks as commanding as ever. It has, if anything, deepened and strengthened with time, since the cast now look even more like members of a real family chained together by guilt, recrimination, jealousy and a strange, self-torturing love.

Indeed it is this emotional ambivalence that makes the play so moving. Not simply the fact that O'Neill compresses his whole traumatic family history into a single New England day thus giving the play an Aristotelian unity; nor merely that we know the play to be written 'in tears and blood'. But the fact that, however appalling the accusations one character may fling at another, the love that binds them together can never be entirely killed. The dreadful James Tyrone (miserly as Balzac's Grandet) may consign his tubercular son to a cheap sanitorium; the sottish Jamie may warn brother Edmund that the dead part of him rejoices in his sickness; the mother may degrade and humiliate them all with her morphine injections. But, paradoxically, the deeper they sink their teeth into each other's necks, the greater their love seems to grow.

Love and waste: these are the play's two enduring themes. Olivier's James Tyrone is still a massive performance, moving from an initial nervy jocularity to a throttled, brick-red despair at his wife's relapse to a thrilling, soul-baring intensity in his cups. But the lynchpin of the interpretation is Tyrone's inescapable feeling that he is a great actor manqué and when Olivier sweetly croons 'We are such stuff as dreams are made on' he magnificently evokes a vanished acting style and makes you believe this old matinée idol had the makings of an American Kean. For a genuinely great actor to play a nearly great actor is the hardest technical feat of all: Olivier does it to perfection.

Constance Cummings's wife, bent white arms clinging tenaciously to her sides, gives one a similar feeling of wasted life and also plots more carefully than before the woman's collapse into fogbound reverie. Ronald Pickup's Edmund, uncorking his bottled intensity with terrifying power during his colloquy with his father, and Denis Quilley's Jamie, full of fake Fifth Avenue charm, compound the feeling of energy fatally misdirected. Michael Blakemore's production also does O'Neill the great service of disregarding many of his stage directions and only allowing the cracks and fissures under the surface to emerge as the day grinds on. Such, in fact, is the quality of acting and direction we seem to be not merely watching great drama but to be eavesdropping on life itself.

Michael Billington: *Guardian*
11 September 1972

... we should gratefully seize any opportunity we still have for seeing Laurence Olivier – who remains in total control of that powerful stage presence and extraordinarily detailed and bold stage technique. I don't say that his James Tyrone has quite the bravura of his Othello, or even of his Shylock – that dignified but slightly gooey Rothschild with teeth like reversed orange peel, in a production that sometimes resembled a sneak preview of the Dreyfus Case. But from a mellow, vocally fruity start, the performance builds up to a fine old frenzy. Who can quickly forget the moment when this boozy, irresponsible, affectionate, pinch-pursing poseur, realising that his wife has hit the morphine again, buries a suddenly scarlet, puffy face in her bosom with a great cry of 'For the love of God!' It is one of those times, rare in the theatre, when you feel you have intruded deeply into somebody's privacy; and the sight is so painful and your own presumption so great that you just have to look away.

Also the play is a marvel of sustained emotion. By comparison, most of our contemporary dramatists seem starved and parched, scrawling their petty anxieties on tiny, disposable canvases. ... Possibly Michael Blakemore's production damps down the flames a little for inhibited British audiences, on the grounds that they might find its Irish-American intensity a trifle melodramatic; but, if so, the crises and climaxes have a greater impact when they do come. Thanks to him and Olivier, to Constance Cummings's touchy, glazed wife, and to Denis Quilley and Ronald Pickup as the tormented Tyrone boys, it will all be remembered for a long time to come.

Benedict Nightingale: *Harper's Bazaar and Queen*
September 1972

If the National's version of *The Front Page* lacks the requisite energy, its rendering of *A Long Day's Journey* lacks the necessary pain and passion. One can understand how English actors might confuse an Irish-American family with a family in Ireland, and introduce a hint of brogue in place of a New England accent. But while the unconvincing dialects are annoying, what is most disappointing is the inability of the cast to penetrate the suffering of these benighted characters. The relationships of the four Tyrones should be as nagging as a toothache; but what we get instead of painful accusations and apologies is a beautifully spoken, rather polite series of conversations among reserved and well-mannered householders.

Playing Jamie and Edmund, Denis Quilley and Ronald Pickup, though excellent actors, failed to investigate the confessional poetry of their parts or their symbiotic interaction on each other; and while Constance Cummings, as Mary Tyrone, seemed to be moving towards something extraordinary in the terrain of her particular hell, she hit a detour somewhere in the third act, and couldn't recover direction in time for her final speech. As for Sir Laurence Olivier – one of the finest actors in the world playing one of the world's greatest parts – he attacked the elder Tyrone like a character in classical comedy, speaking his lines as if they were verse, and displaying ease only with the miserly side of the character. One had to remember back to the great performance of Fredric March in the original production – self-justifying, raging, mixing reproaches with conciliation and compassion with despair – to recall the torment out of which this part, indeed this whole play, was initially conceived.

What one missed most from the English production, finally, were the pity and the terror of the work – the sense of journey into an awful, almost unacknowledgeable past where hope is blighted by memory. The generic word for this is tragedy. And I am beginning to conclude, on the basis of more evidence than the inadequacies of this production, that tragedy is not a very natural expression of the English theatre at the present time, even at the highest level of performance. Perhaps there is a price to be paid for the extraordinary civic organisation of contemporary England in that the security provided by public order is dulling the nation to the resources of the inner life. To be sure, there is a tragic skeleton in the British closet called Ireland – and the younger dramatists are now trying to rouse some shame and indignation over England's part in the past and present difficulties of Ulster. But perhaps because Ireland is separated from England by a sea's breadth, nobody here seems sufficiently upset by these accusations to enter into guilty explorations of the self.

America, on the other hand, is not in agony as a result of her past, and the afflictions of our nation are directly traceable to the errors and crimes of our history. As a result, I believe, we are becoming, perhaps without quite knowing it yet, a truly tragic nation. Our tragedy is a compound of Vietnam, of deteriorating cities, of poverty and suffering and racial strife, of drug abuse and violence, of political assassination – and further back, a heritage of the original sin of our country, the institution of slavery. A people who till recently smiled at itself daily in the mirror, and demanded happy endings to its plays and movies, is now being forced against its will, to examine its soul and live with the knowledge that past sins are not easily redeemable, even with the best intentions.

This is the knowledge that forms the basis for the tragic arts. It is small comfort, to be sure, to say that our present agonies are giving us a tragic dimension, for tragedy, being purgative rather than remedial, has never been known to solve a social problem or answer a political question. Still, if we can develop the courage to create and absorb tragedy in art, we may yet achieve the toughmindedness we need to grapple effectively with the more insoluble difficulties of our society. And anyway great art has always been a spiritual satisfaction rather than a utilitarian instrument – one of the few consolations left us in a bad, yes, a disastrous time.

Robert Brustein: *Observer*
10 December 1972

ATV filled an entire evening with the National Theatre's Michael Blakemore production of *Long Day's Journey Into Night*, thereby laying up a goodly store of professional credit. Olivier, the finest actor alive by a nautical mile, is the supreme modern master of words.

David O. Selznick used to send memos saying that he could understand Olivier's whiplash delivery, but that nobody else could. Decades later, every mesmerised listener is still convinced that he can understand Olivier, but that nobody else can.

Olivier runs at the far limit of what we can apprehend and we are persuaded that it is only our attention which slows him into audibility: if we relaxed, he would accelerate into a scream. And yet in this play, whose every phrase seems to be chosen for its dead weight, and whose poetry resides in nothing that can be said, he undoes all expectation and finds the deep inner silence in which O'Neill's father remained unreachable, even by memory. I didn't see the performance on stage, but can't imagine that his projection in the theatre could throw it closer to me than Peter Wood's cameras brought it with an easy glance. A career-clinching interpretation. Magnificent.

Constance Cummings I thought very fine: she achieved, by taking flesh-transforming thought, the parody of transparent saintliness that this junkie mother must present – for here too, and pre-eminently, O'Neill's gaze is clouded and perfumed by romance. No problem about where she gets the dynamite. She practically secretes the stuff. In O'Neillian physiology, morphine floods the bloodstream as a matter of course: synthetic and gorgeous, an artificial paradise updated to the age of hypodermics, it's a symbolic blast.

Gaping first and coasting later, Miss Cummings hour by hour thinned the marble veneer of her cinquecento skin and pumped the pulp behind it full of poisoned bliss. The men looked on, waiting for the crash. Ronald Pickup and Denis Quilley both realised, and both demonstrated, that the play's fateful youths are not the last of the ancient Greeks but the first of the twentieth-century walking wounded. They looked implicated, as they should: O'Neill forecast uncannily that drug addiction would be the aestheticism of modernity – art for the artless.

Long Day's Journey Into Night was the play in which booze went out of date as a brain sweetener, upstaged by the clinically refined destruction of pure powders. Another nostalgia, a further romance. O'Neill was the only decadent to be transitional.

Clive James: *Observer*
29 April 1973

The Misanthrope

National Theatre at the Old Vic: 22 February 1973

Perhaps the most surprising production from this Indian summer of Olivier's regime was *The Misanthrope*. Molière is notoriously difficult to translate into English. A previous National Theatre production of *Tartuffe* had been most disappointing. It is hard to capture Molière's wit; and rhymed couplets in English have a tendency to sound like pantomime doggerel, each thought clipped off in its prime by a too obtrusive rhyming word. It is equally hard to match the British equivalent of Louis XIV's court; and the whole high style, within which Molière's comedies took their place, partly ridiculing the manners, partly applauding them.

Tony Harrison, the translator/adaptor, took the exceptionally daring step of updating *The Misanthrope* to the reign of de Gaulle, the contemporary example perhaps of a sun king. This gave him the opportunity to match some of Molière's topical allusions. His verse had a remarkable freshness and sparkle; and although his *The Misanthrope* may have missed the darker side of Molière's play, the sadness of an honest man who lacks, and scorns, social, polite trainings, and suffers for it, it was at least very funny. Few Molière productions in English raise more than occasional smiles.

John Dexter's production was stylish and visually spectacular; and what most remains in my mind are the performances of Diana Rigg and Alec McCowen, an unlikely but beautifully balanced partnership, who relished Harrison's lines. There were delights as

well in the surrounding cast, particularly Gawn Grainger's Oronte;
and one indication of *The Misanthrope*'s success is that attempts
were quickly made to match it. Harrison was commissioned to adapt
a play by Racine, *Phaedre*, for the National; while the Rigg/
McCowen team was brought into a new West End production of
Shaw's *Pygmalion*. But the unexpected delight of Harrison's updated
Molière could not be repeated.

John Dexter's production of Molière's *The Misanthrope* opens with
an irresistable *coup de théâtre*. The curtain rises upon a faintly lit
stage; stiffly voluminous silvery drapes hang above an unlit
chandelier, suggestive of the baroque swathes that frame portraits of
Louis XIV's proud left leg. A figure sits with his back to a classical
façade listening to some twiddly string music. One prepares oneself
for an evening of 17th-century brocade. Enter the first character who
switches on the chandelier, switches off the record player and we are
in a smartly furnished *beau monde* interior of 1966.

It is a revelation that elegantly prepares us for Tony Harrison's
remarkable achievement as a translator. He has turned Molière into
English couplets that dance with colloquial vigour. With seeming
effortlessness they convey Alceste's bitter outbursts and his
cackhanded attempt at politeness; they adapt for the spacious
declarations of what a man might be and what he is; brilliantly suit
the twittering of a pair of marquises, the irony and the courteously
worded insults. For the pompous Oronte (Gawn Grainger) Mr.
Harrison provides an entrance speech of gruff, clipped
monosyllables, and throughout the play he makes great use of jokey
slang for the rhyming word.

In Molière the references are to the King; here they are to Charles
de Gaulle and the Elysée: we are in the world of political hostesses
and Gaullist chicanery and it is against this contemporary dishonesty
that Alceste rails. It is a funny, civilized, witty play but Molière
steers the comedy again and again to the very edge of the tragic.
Alceste will not be comforted, won't appeal against an unjust
judgement; he would cut off his nose and offer it as proof that other
men are spiteful. His love for Célimène is self-love and it is
interesting that at the end of the play he rushes off the stage, still
raging, somewhat like Malvolio. For such a character no happy

ending could be contrived because it would threaten the preconceptions that sustain his being.

Jeremy Kingston: Punch
7 March 1973

Mr. Harrison has composed a version in rhyming couplets which is
wholly free from echoes of the Christmas pantomime: and I can
think of no other writer who has managed to bring this off. What
strike you on a single hearing is the freedom with which Mr.
Harrison preserves normal speech rhythms and conversational
syntax within a rigid metrical scheme. All the rhymes are good.

Stylistically he scores both classically and idiomatically.
'Moderation', says his Philinte, 'is where wisdom lies. What we
should be is reasonably wise.' The pun on 'reasonably' would not be
disdained by Pope. At the far end of the scale, here is Célimène
turning down Alceste's proposal for a retreat to the wilderness: 'I'd
be terrified! Just you and me and all that countryside.' Isolated
quotations on paper cannot convey the flow and vitality of the work;
but in performance it leaves everyone from Miles Malleson to
Richard Wilbur standing.

... *The Misanthrope*, an inexhaustibly great comedy, invariably gets
people arguing; and arguing at its expense. The only objection that I
rashly offer (and which the production does something to answer) is
that, like Eliot's Hamlet, Alceste has no 'objective correlative' for his
misanthropy. There is a vast disproportion between the evidence of
human corruption put on stage, and the violence of his denunciation.
Hence, you may say, the source of all comedy. But Alceste is a bigger
man than that: he is ridiculous, and he is an honest intelligent man:
and the comic force of his tirades would be all the greater if they
were directed against something more than artificial manners and a
trivial court-case.

One possible assumption is that Molière was unable to name
Alceste's real complaints without insulting the palace. That
constraint no longer applies, and in this production, everything is
done to build up the power of the Elysée. Célimène is subtly altered
from a mere pleasure seeker to a quasi-political hostess; dropping
her frivolous charm when that subject comes up. Left alone at the
end (a marvellous moment, prolonging the character's life beyond
the span of the play) she walks upstage and looks out towards the

Elysée as the lights fade. Oronte (Gawn Grainger) becomes a highly sinister personage, his sickly smile reversing into tight-lipped official threats. Even the off-stage debate over his poem becomes a sinister midnight summons from the Académie terminating with a walkout by Malraux.

All this adds to the substance of the given action, and endorses Alec McCowen's terrier-like reading of Alceste. It is possible for Alceste to be played sympathetically; an almost passive figure who tears people apart with reluctance. What McCowen does is to show him as a maniacally frothing figure who nevertheless has right on his side. You get the full force of this during the poem scene with Oronte. McCowen cracks his knuckles with embarrassment and attempts a diplomatic appraisal. Then, when this fails, he goes off like a volcano, 'Jesus wept, it's bloody rubbish'. He is right (the poem has become a lovely little-mag parody), but the reaction is wildly disproportionate.

Irving Wardle: *The Times*
23 February 1973

John Dexter's modern-dress production of *The Misanthrope* at the Old Vic will obviously be an enormous popular success. It is stunningly elegant to look at in Tanya Moiseiwitsch's chic, glossy, Lelouch-like setting; it is throughout extremely funny, and Tony Harrison's acute, dexterous translation is full of modern allusions (to de Gaulle and Malraux, for instance) that enable audiences to chuckle at their own sophistication. Yet under all this gloss and shine and expertise, I feel the pain and agony at the heart of this great play gets lost ...

Dexter's production ... weakens Alceste's case by making the surrounding society look anything but vicious or corrupt: only if one believes that there is something inherently evil about Veuve Clicquot, pot, fancy clothes or mohair rugs can one believe that Alceste has an iron-clad case. He should be raging against degradation; here he seems to be attacking merely frivolous hedonism.

Moreover, technically brilliant though Alec McCowen's performance is, it suggests that Alceste is a nervy, suppressed hysteric rather than a fatally disappointed idealist. It is marvellous to see and hear Mr. McCowen sliding into falsetto in moments of anger, delicately flexing his fingers when trying to get out of an awkward situation, narrowing his eyes to venomous slits in preparation for another tirade. But the laughter seemed to me constantly directed against the over-reacting hero rather than against the world around him. Even his final self-imposed exit, which should have the weight of Malvolio's 'I'll have revenge on the whole pack of you', produced a ripple of amusement.

I blame the amiability of Dexter's production rather than the actor; and indeed I have no fault to find with Diana Rigg's skittish, alluring, narcissistically frivolous Célimène or Gawn Grainger's balding, pot-bellied, marvellously seedy Oronte. But this production seemed to me flawed by the National's tendency to treat each play as a separate, one-off affair rather than as the product of any sustained social vision. In short, I think this is basically an uncompromising, disturbing left-wing play here given a pleasing, decorative bourgeois production.

Michael Billington: *Guardian*
23 February 1973

What is unusual in the production, apart from its sheer brilliance, and capacity to dazzle, is that it is heavily biased on the side of the Establishment. Célimène and the two marquis may not be models of rectitude but they are at least people with whom one could pass an evening without becoming involved in a violent quarrel, whilst the mere presence of Alceste is a constant and noisy accusation of villainy against everyone but himself. Alceste may verbally subscribe to the highest ideals, but Alec McCowen makes it perfectly clear that he is a man with whom no one could possibly live. This, in case anyone misses it during the opening scenes, is made unmistakably clear in the fourth act, when Alceste, thinking himself betrayed by Célimène, shows no grief of heart, no disappointment of love, but only the screaming excesses of a vile ill-temper. The point is emphasized by immediate contrast with a brief scene of affection, which is played by Jeanne Watts and Alan MacNaughton with infinite delicacy, and it is put beyond all possibility of doubt by the last scene of the play. Molière ended *The Misanthrope* with the complete discomfiture of Célimène, and her dismissal from the stage. At the Old Vic, everyone else departs, and Diana Rigg's superb and deserted heroine is left sadly contemplating the desolation of her empty house, alone but with all our sympathies. The contemporary theatre is thick with left-wing triumphs and even with self-inflicted left-wing defeats, of which we have had three in three successive nights. But the National Theatre's *The Misanthrope* is that rare phenomenon, an unchallengeable right-wing victory.

Harold Hobson: *Sunday Times*
25 February 1973

Equus

National Theatre at the Old Vic: 26 July 1973

The success of Peter Shaffer's *Equus* matched that of his *Royal Hunt of the Sun*: but I was one of a minority of critics who disliked and distrusted the play's premise. There seemed to be a too-easy acceptance of the Romantic conflict between reason and passion, cold scientism which murders to dissect and religious inspiration which is life-giving even in its moments of destruction. I also felt that these themes had been tackled with greater force during the mid-1960s, in *The Marat/Sade*, in Mercer's early plays and in various fringe productions, emanating from the Theatre of Cruelty season.

There could, however, be no complaint with John Dexter's production, with the actors miming the horses, with Alec McCowen's Dysart and Peter Firth's Alan Strang. *Equus* quickly became a popular play with rep directors, who told me that it was an excellent introduction for regional audiences to metropolitan sophistication. It had the firm structure of a well-made play; but it also allowed actors to mime. It could be played on any kind of stage – it was very effective 'in-the-round' – and the scene where the boy and girl were naked gave no offence. The nudity was obviously necessary to the play. In places like Belfast – or in the mid-west of Canada – or in Windsor, *Equus* was a useful play in order to test public reactions to such matters as nakedness on stage: and for that reason, among others, it was scheduled for productions all over the world, internationally and nationally popular as few contemporary British plays have been.

Peter Shaffer's *Equus* is sensationally good. Like *The Royal Hunt of the Sun* and *The Battle of Shrivings*, it is based on a direct confrontation between reason and instinct. Like them also, it suggests that, though organised faith is usually based on neurosis, a life without some form of worship or belief is ultimately barren. But it's a far better play than either, if only because the intellectual argument and the poetic imagery are virtually indivisible.

It deals with the psychiatric exploration of a hideous crime. A 17-year-old boy has blinded six horses with a metal spike; and we watch as the doctor patiently pieces together the evidence that will explain this act of cruelty. Gradually we learn that the boy's mother, a religious fanatic, has filled his mind with images of Biblical cruelty; that his father, a taciturn printer, cannot communicate with him about anything; that his sexual instincts have been aroused by horseflesh and that he has come to love one particular animal as a god; that, impotent when seduced by a girl in the stables, he has wreaked a terrible revenge on the all-seeing horses around him.

A classic case-book drama then? Not at all. For, though Shaffer pieces the evidence together with an accelerating detective story tension, his real concern is with the relationship between the psychiatrist and the boy. Humane, clinical and efficient, the doctor realises that by restoring the boy to 'normality', he is in fact killing the motivating force of his life. 'Passion', he explains, 'can be destroyed by a doctor, it cannot be created'. And the question the play asks is whether by rooting out the brainsickness and abnormality of individuals, we don't ultimately deny their humanity. ...

Intellectually, the one gap in the play is that Shaffer advocates 'worship' and passion (in a very Forsterian way) without suggesting what we do if that passion is socially destructive. To 'cure' murderers and return them to our society may be a denial of their instincts, but isn't it socially necessary? ...

Michael Billington: *Guardian*
27 July 1973

Peter Shaffer is a writer of formidable intelligence and traditional stage technique whose consistent purpose has been to invoke the primal dramatic forces which would blow his own equipment sky-high. In style, one can never predict what kind of piece he will write next; but his theme remains constant. Whether he is opposing

Christian and Aztec culture in *The Royal Hunt of the Sun*, or a philosopher and an anarchist poet in *The Battle of Shrivings*, Shaffer is repeatedly mounting a tournament between Apollo and Dionysus under various coats of arms.

The argument of these plays is lacking in sinew; but the really sad thing about them is that while they are intended to celebrate the Dark Gods, it is always Apollo who wins. Mr. Shaffer, a Western intellectual, was born into his service; and when he tries to conjure up Dionysus all he can offer is a projection governed by the Apollonian rules of reason and control.

Equus, although a far better work than *Shrivings*, repeats the same inescapable pattern. It is based on the case of a stable boy, aged 17, who unaccountably puts out the eyes of six horses with an iron spike. Why? Mr. Shaffer attempts an answer through the authoritarian medium of the institutional psychiatric interview.

Characteristically, the interviewer is the modern equivalent of a spoiled priest, much afflicted by Laingian doubts; but however equal the terms on which they agree to meet (playing a game of mutual interrogation in the early scenes), the fact remains that Dr. Dysart is in charge and can at any minute terminate the session and dispatch Alan back to his solitary nightmares.

Within this framework, taking in discussions with the parents and flashback re-enactments with the boy, the play starts unravelling the enigmatic atrocity. Son of a pious mother and an agnostic father, Alan developed an early obsession with Christian sado-masochism; while a wild ride on the sea coast gave him a parallel fixation on horses. The two obsessions merge in his private cult of 'Equus' and on taking a weekend stable job, he consummates his worship in orgiastic night-riding. ...

Clearly the play's main concern is neither with the doctor nor the patient, but with the god-like image of Equus. One senses Mr. Shaffer straining to the limit to summon this awful presence. But, not for the first time, he owes whatever numinous results he does achieve to his director, John Dexter.

As with the unearthly masks in *The Royal Hunt*, so with the horses in this play. They are played by standing actors wearing hoof-lifts and wired silver heads through which performers' own faces remain visible. The effect is totally stylized (while also fitting the centaur imagery), but it secures in full the magical transformation which is the special province of the mask. In the night ride, on a manhandled revolve, and in the climactic blinding, with silvery muzzles converging questioningly from the shadows of the stable, the play instantly fills the theatre with the sense of a potent and ancient force returning to life.

The text, however, does no such thing. The image of the horse is poetically inexhaustible, and Mr. Shaffer draws on its ambiguity (dominion and servitude) to link his pagan and Christian material. But here, as in the surrounding detail, what comes through is not a fiery symbol, but the sense of a painstaking and profoundly dissatisfied intelligence carefully slotting things together. ...

Irving Wardle: *The Times*
27 July 1973

There are horses, as the erudite will guess, in Peter Shaffer's *Equus*. I hope that Mr. Shaffer will forgive me if I say with apparent, but not real, flippancy, about a play which is far from flippant, that in *Equus*, Mr. Shaffer, like the splendid animal which at Kempton Park last Wednesday utterly outran Lester Piggott, proves himself a very Daring Boy. For what he says in *Equus* is so non-conformist that a large proportion of his audiences, though they will be stunned and blasted by the power of the play, will go away pretending either that Mr. Shaffer does not believe what he says, or says something quite different from his plain and (to the present age) unacceptable meaning.

... What becomes clear in the course of the play is not whether the boy can be cured, but whether he ought ever to have become ill. On these points, Mr. Shaffer is categorical. Any psychiatric cure, he says, is a dangerous sham. In a shattering speech at the end of the play, the psychiatrist, in intense distress, admits – no, proclaims in the voice of a prophet – that the boy's cure has been effected only by a complete disembowelling of all that in him is potentially finest: that, in fact, though in appearance at peace he leaves – and necessarily leaves – the hospital a human being crippled and ruined.

What has been taken from him is the capacity for worship, the realisation of the supernatural, the transcendence of material things, without which, in Mr. Shaffer's Dionysiac, religious, ecstatic view, life is empty and hollow ...

Harold Hobson: *Sunday Times*
29 July 1973

... Taken realistically the play is a dud; Alan seems to have grown up in a social vacuum and Dysart's problems are manufactured. Theatrically, it is a triumph, and though one's first impulse, as with *The Royal Hunt* is to give credit to the director, John Dexter, and his choreographer, Claude Chagrin, this is probably unfair. The images they so stunningly fleshed out were the author's first of all. Mr. Shaffer writes fair to indifferent prose, but he imagines magnificent scenes. Here he has actors pawing the ground in silver masks, horse and rider combined, to tell us all we need to know about the boy's obsession. One understands how Gulliver must have felt among the Houyhnhnms.

There is more than spectacle to Mr. Dexter's production; for it is a precise instrument for the generation of tension, and it nourishes a memorable acting duet. The doctor has to be partly an audience surrogate; we take our bearings on Alan from him. For this task, Alec McCowen's dapper irony is ideal and expected: what one forgets is his capacity for rhetoric. He can engrave words elegantly on the air but he can also – as he does at the close of this play – erect huge fortresses of passion ...

Robert Cushman: *Observer*
29 July 1973

The play pullulates with dishonesty. Dishonesty towards its avowed purpose, the explication of 'a dreadful event' by making that dreadfulness seem fascinating and even admirable. Dishonesty to the audiences, by trying to smuggle subliminal but virulent homosexual propaganda into them. Dishonesty towards the present state of the theatre, in which homosexuality can and has been discussed openly and maturely. Dishonesty to psychiatry, which is depicted as a castrator of bodies and souls. Dishonesty towards normality (whatever that is), by making its representatives and defenders, for the most part, pathetic or unappetising. Dishonesty to art, which does not abide such facile equivocations as 'You will be cured', 'You won't be cured', 'You will be cured and less healthy for it', to say nothing of the fudging over of that horse-blinding by doing it as a nude scene, and to horses that are mere metallic masks. Greek tragedy showed no acts of violence either, but found a poetry that could richly convey them. It would not have settled for a Dysart (the psychiatrist) who says feebly – as he assumes, for no good reason given, the boy's sick identity – 'I stand in the dark with a pick in my hand, striking at heads', followed by the no less feeble lines about *his* now having a permanent, painful chain in his mouth. Has Dysart become both Alan Strang and Equus?

In any case, the final dishonesty here is toward the very thing meant to be championed: homosexuality. Not only is it obliged to masquerade as zooerastia (also known as bestiality), it is accorded a false and misleading image. What is the equivalent in basic homophile terms for the key incident of *Equus*, the blinding of the horses? I can find no valid analogies, yet the fundamental obligation of a metaphor or a symbol is to create a thorough, functioning correspondence. *Equus* fails all the causes it seems to espouse, except for the dubious cause of spectacular theatricality.

> John Simon: 'Hippodrama at the Psychodrome'
> *The Hudson Review*: Spring, 1975 (Volume XXVIII, No. 1)

Flowers

Regent Theatre: 27 March 1974

Lindsay Kemp is not an acquired taste. Most critics seem to know instantly whether they like or dislike his work; and refuse to be budged. His position in contemporary British theatre is, in some respects, similar to Kantor's in Polish – both rebels, with very powerful private visions, who manage to attract devoted followers, amateur and professional, from whose loyalties their companies are formed. Such mixtures do not encourage subsidies; particularly not if, as in Kemp's case, there is an aura of decadence. The open sexuality (mainly homo-, but also on occasions hetero-), the gawdiness of the images, the wilful tawdriness and the refusal to give moral self-justifications encouraged those who were unresponsive to Kemp's work to label it self-indulgent. Self-indulgence is indeed one of its characteristics; but there is also self-discipline, imagination, buoyancy and a cheerful irreverence for propriety. The images of *Flowers*, like that of Kemp's *Salome*, are haunting.

Flowers was first seen in London at the Bush Theatre; and I must 'declare an interest', in that I have been connected with this fringe theatre since it began. Kemp and his company rehearsed in my flat; and so naturally I felt a concern for the success of a production which I had seen evolving. These reasons, however, would have inclined me to omit this production from my selection, were it not for the number of directors, actors and dancers who have told me how much their work has been influenced by Kemp. Apart from his impact on punk rock – and on the style of such singers as David Bowie and Kate Bush, Kemp's productions were surprisingly popular in Yugoslavia and Canada, as well as surviving disastrous reviews in Australia to become scandalous successes.

There is another reason, however, for the inclusion of *Flowers*, apart from its genuine originality and merit. It represents a kind of theatre – glamorous, sensational, sleazy and notorious – which both the West End and the subsidised theatres after the war ignored. It was almost a throw-back to turn-of-the-century show-biz, the seedy music-halls which Shaw deplored and the decadent glories of the Alhambra and the Hippodrome. When Kemp states that he has always wanted to be a great star, there is something more exact than naive in his remark; for stardom – including the ballyhoo of long entrances down winding staircases which he both evokes and satirises in *Flowers* – is essential to his kind of theatre. *Flowers* was, I thought, especially startling in the confined circumstances of the Bush Theatre, with its open stage; rather than in the long, skinny auditorium of the Regent with its proscenium arch stage – but there again, of course, I must declare an interest.

'The beauty of a moral act depends on the beauty of its expression', is a typically perverse statement made by Jean Genet. The most that can be said for Lindsay Kemp's *Flowers*, described as 'a pantomime for Jean Genet' is that it occasionally achieves a visual beauty of expression. Undulating bodies, luridly spotlit, augmented by smoke and wet umbrellas, make an arresting image. Here and elsewhere, Mr. Kemp does create acceptable theatrical equivalents of the febrile, rancid prose of the dedicatee.

But at its worst, *Flowers* descends to 'high Kemp'. Transvestite drag acts, replete with glitter, do not suggest *Notre Dame des Fleurs*. Judged as mimes, the company are mediocre. To a purist, the ear-splitting organ and sound-effects, are unacceptable; so is the selective

LINDSAY
KEMP's FLOWERS
Felix Topolski

use of props (if the wine glasses and battle are real, why should the wine be invisible?).

The ballet dance to the music of *Giselle* is sacrilege: according to Marceau, mime must be earthbound, whereas the element of ballet is the air. The only legitimate ingredients of mime are movement and silence: its function is to make the invisible visible, and this demands efforts of imagination from the audience, as well as from the performer. I shudder to think what Etienne Decroux would say of these queer capers.

Obviously, Mr. Kemp's intentions are not very serious. He wants to provide a spot of decadence as entertainment.

Frank Marcus: *Sunday Telegraph*
31 March 1974

I may be unjust, but I cannot help feeling that the guarded reception of Lindsay Kemp's *Flowers* ... has something to do with lack of courage. To review favourably an entertainment which is passionately steeped in the conviction that homosexual love, preferably homosexual love amongst criminals and outcasts, is the only kind of love that deserves the name: that what we have known as love from the days of *Romeo and Juliet* to those of Terence Rattigan's *In Praise of Love* is only a game: favourably to review such a work lays the reviewer open to all kinds of social and personal suspicions.

But no critic should be intimidated by the fear of misrepresentation or slander. *Flowers* is a quite extraordinary creation, extraordinary as *Notre-Dame des Fleurs*, whose lyrical verbal ecstasy it translates into mime, is extraordinary. It creates with a terrifying and revolting beauty the awful world of the Place Blanche and Pigalle and the *milieu* that dangerously fascinates Genet; the perverse cafés; the horrible public lavatories (when he was poor Genet knew every public lavatory in Paris that had a seat instead of a hole); the readiness to spill blood and the worship of the naked male body; and invests these things with that blasphemous reverence for the Mass, and that haunted confusion between the criminal and the saint that makes him unique amongst the great masters of French prose.

Through this obscene and evil world, so glorious to Genet, moves Mr. Kemp's timid and infinitely sad Divine, tottering like a more than consumptive lady of the camellias, doomed to an exhausted passion and a bloody end. No man can hate more than I do the things that Genet admires; but I can at least tell whether the man who presents what I hate is an artist or a fraud. Neither Genet nor Mr. Kemp is a fraud; they both believe what they claim to believe. I wish that they believed something different. But that is a vain desire. We have had many productions of Genet in this country, all of which, I think, I have condemned as false to their author.

I do not intend to speak with an unfelt modesty. It might have happened to any drama critic to have read Genet in Paris whilst his work was condemned by the French censorship, and was yet unknown in England: or to have become on terms of friendship with him; but in fact, it was only to me, sundered from him in sexual tastes and in religion, that it actually happened. It is with confidence that I say that this mime, in which the exceeding slowness of Mr. Kemp's performance is a mark that, in Genet's world of transcendental viciousness, he has passed from time into eternity, is a true rendering of Genet's shocking, unmatchable prose; the work of Lucifer rejoicing in being hurled from Paradise, but remembering his former, purified splendour; a masterpiece of the irreclaimably damned.

Harold Hobson: *Sunday Times*
31 March 1974

Incense and organ music greet you as you enter; and that neatly captures the whole atmosphere of scented rhetorical camp. We start with writhing prison-cell masturbation done with more balletic style than physical accuracy; move on to a Montmartre funeral full of black umbrellas, turquoise smoke and hefty, spotlit buttocks; edge our way into a gay bar where that talented mime, Lindsay Kemp, does a very funny slow entry in fox fur, lilac dress and pearl-encrusted skull-cap like a shortened version of Bea Lillie; and proceed, via rape on a hurtling express, a good deal of wide-mouthed agony and send-ups of the sleazy drag underworld, into the violent climax where Genet's angelic-looking lover dies, as he wrote 'in a pool of her vomited blood'.

I don't doubt the genuine agony on which the work is based: what I distrust is the masochistic delight in suffering for its own sake and the rhetorical inflation of human feeling. Scene after scene ends with a spotlit agonised face trying desperately hard to look like a screaming Bacon cardinal; and there's one fearfully precious moment when hero and boy-friend heart-rendingly pluck at a flower which brought to mind a marvellous Polish clown I once saw who gazed wistfully and longingly at a rose and then proceeded to eat it. Moreover, the delight in shock-tactics, such as copulating with a boy with a crucifix, is the product of profound naïveté rather than worldly sophistication.

A pity because at the best Mr. Kemp, who devised and directed, has a self-mocking humour that lightens the agony and the ecstasy; and his bald, plump, pouter-pigeon tragedy queen is a genuinely funny creation ...

Michael Billington: *Guardian*
28 March 1974

I usually grind to a halt half-way through the novels of Jean Genet because there are so many words I do not know, but I get the message clearly enough to recognise that Lindsay Kemp's *Flowers*, which I went belatedly to see last week – and went two nights running, actually paying the second time – mirrors truthfully Genet's individual fusion of sex, masochism, religion, blasphemy, beauty and squalor.

Kemp devised this dragodrama ... and he performs in it with a talented company. The devising is brilliant, the direction is masterly, the performance is overpowering. Productionwise, it is the most stunning show in London.

I kick myself for having been kept away from *Flowers* for so long by a summer surfeit of ballet and a distaste for the pallid pathos of mimes like Marceau, whom I presumed Kemp would resemble. Well, they have something in common, and Kemp's silent slow-motion arias are so long-drawn-out that they could be thought embarrassing. Yet I find them as necessary to the whole as, say, the appearance of Martha Graham with her company when she was over seventy.

Andrew Wilson's electronic score, with a collage of popular and classical music, sacred and profane, contributes enormously to the savage spectacle. The set, with its upper gallery, is mysterious. The ragged costumes could not be bettered. The make-ups are the most original and poetic since Kathakali.

Unforgettable scenes are the frigid reception of Kemp on his first slow entry into the dive, dressed as a raddled old bride, then the arrival of the Byronic groom, Neil Caplan, and the waltz that converts the pimps and whores into romantic dreamers; the mocking of the Crucified, which shocked me till I realised it was the modern equivalent of Breughel and Bosch designed to arouse pity and terror; the Cavafy-like falling in love of the two angel boys, Caplan and Tony Maples, staring into each other's eyes at the cafe table, impervious to the strip-teasing whores (from Tudor's *Judgement of Paris*); the final unmasking in a welter of blood.

I have never seen strobe lights used to greater effect than in the last scene. It really was as if the Veil of the Temple were rent in twain. We could use a producer of Lindsay Kemp's genius at Covent Garden, at the Coliseum and at the National.

Richard Buckle: *Sunday Times*
14 July 1974

The Norman Conquests

Greenwich Theatre: 9 and 21 May, 6 June 1974

Alan Ayckbourn was already well-established as a writer of (to use Michael Billington's words) 'extremely ingenious farces based on a dazzling theatrical legerdemain', before *The Norman Conquests* were written. These three plays represent, however, the height of his ingenuity, for he took an apparently conventional situation – three related couples changing partners over a country-house weekend – and extracted three different angles from it, by simply setting the plays in three different places – the garden (in *Round and Round the Garden*), the sitting room (in *Living Together*) and the dining room (in *Table Manners*). The three plays occupy the same time span, and so what happens in one play is taking place off-stage in the other two.

The formal mechanics of Ayckbourn's writing, however, provides only one delight; and if *The Norman Conquests* were only clever and nothing more, we would probably forget about them. But Ayckbourn is also an acute observer of how people behave and his characters, in this play struggling and middle-class, carry with them an unforced credibility. The tentative vet, the lecherous librarian, the domineering sister and her trapped small-business-man husband are recognisable but original characters: we never doubt that they could exist. The quality of observation lends substance to the wit; and it also allows Ayckbourn considerable freedom within his formal structure. The writing in *The Norman Conquests* shows Ayckbourn's variety, his capacity to show the sad, as well as lighthearted, aspects: and there are traces in these plays which foreshadow the rather bitter comedies which he was later to write, such as *Just Between Ourselves* and *Joking Apart*.

Although the plays can be taken in any order, I have kept to the pattern in which they were first seen by London audiences at Greenwich. The productions afterwards transferred to the Globe Theatre, with the same cast.

Alan Ayckbourn, a mathematical genius of a manipulator when it comes to writing comedies of manners, has set himself a stupendous task: a trilogy, no less, in which the events of the same turbulent weekend are covered in, respectively, the dining room, the sitting room, and the garden. The setting is a small country house; mother (unseen) lies bedridden upstairs; a resident daughter with a steady boy friend looks after her; the remaining characters are a son and daughter, with their married partners. They are the house guests. The catalyst is the son-in-law, Norman (Tom Courtenay) a manic assistant librarian whose pursuit of women is not entirely selfish.

As if this almost Cubist scheme were not complicated enough, the author asks us to judge each play independently and only after having seen them all to pass a retrospective judgement on the trilogy, named collectively *The Norman Conquests*.

Very well, so be it. *Table Manners* may not be as rich in texture and as wild in invention as other Ayckbourn plays, but it is still ten times better than similar types of plays currently on view ...

Already one speculates on how Mr. Ayckbourn will manage to avoid repetition in the two plays to come, and whether the sparse plot will sustain them. Personally, I have complete confidence in this master-magician and his adroit director, Eric Thompson.

Frank Marcus: *Sunday Telegraph*
12 May 1974

In his use of obsession, Ayckbourn is like Feydeau: the characters' most earnest obsessions generate our loudest laughter. But as in

Ayckbourn's other plays, they also generate sadness in the audience.

Each of the three couples is unsatisfactorily matched, and no one's situation is improved by the end of the weekend; unless you regard the harbouring of illusion concerning oneself and whomever one desires or thinks one desires, as unsatisfactory. His plays are, technically, light comedies; but however delightfully, they convey despair, although Mr. Ayckbourn's acerbic view of the characters never quite permits us to be moved by them as individuals.

Charles Lewsen: *The Times*
11 May 1974

... I'm not sure that even this weekend, whose dining-room (*Table Manners*) I saw, witness some fine old ding-dongs, lovingly detailed infighting, boisterous emotional square-dancing and even a spot of fisticuffs, can really stand up to that sort of attention. Some of the interest of a new comic play does, after all, come from wanting to see what happens; after seeing only one of these three, you know that nothing ever really does, from that Saturday to Monday.

Nevertheless, it's a taut, polished, jolly evening, verging at times on the farcical. The device of having one character sitting on a dwarfishly low chair at a dinner table provokes a paralytic hilarity, as does the deftly choreographed breakdown of a careful seating plan with each new arrival at the table. Lines can be corny – 'Ever been to Bournemouth? Oh ho. Great place. Laugh a minute'. – but spoken by Tom Courtenay, still stir great gusts of laughter.

Alan Ayckbourn in a programme note expatiates affectionately on his dynamic hero, Norman the Assistant Librarian, his ambitions of conquest on all his female relations and his attempts to bring happiness to all. But Norman's interest seemed strongest to the people on the stage: Michael Gambon's Tom, the shambling and melancholy vet, is subtler and more original; and Felicity Kendal's Annie treads a delicate tightrope of jaunty pathos. And Penelope Keith's Sarah, a rigid yet palpitating bundle of powder blue-dressed or pink-floral-housecoated nerves, face a mask of blank desperation, hands automatically remaking the shattered napkins as fast as the rest of the family wreck both them and her attempts to impose formality on the chaos of the table, is the best thing in a strong cast, well directed by Eric Thompson.

Janet Watts: *Guardian*
10 May 1974

235

Mr. Ayckbourn makes life even more complicated for himself. Not for him the megalomaniac demands on his audiences of a Shaw, an O'Neill or a Wesker: he wishes each play to be judged independently. Here I must admit a difficulty. I found it impossible to expunge from memory the knowledge of the three couples and their predicaments, as shown in the dining room in the first play, *Table Manners*.

In *Living Together*, set in the sitting room, I recognised instantly the notorious beige fur rug, on which Norman had dallied briefly with his sister-in-law the previous Christmas: the repercussions of which incident set the plot in motion. Wisely the author rations the appearances of the funniest character, the bossy neurotic Sarah, but does this diminish the enjoyment of audiences unfamiliar with the first play?

On the other hand, the dull eternal fiancé (Michael Gambon) is given greater chances; his agonisingly long pause before deciding whether to have black or white coffee is sublimely funny. Only a brilliant playwright can make dullness amusing. Similarly Reg (Mark Kingston), the hearty inveterate inventor of impossibly complicated games reaches a peak when trying to prove the absurdity of chess by demonstrating physically the movements of a knight and a bishop.

Leaving aside the precise dramatic function of the invalid mother upstairs, which has yet to be justified, the serious centre of the play is the marriage of Norman and Ruth. Tom Courtenay is not funny in himself: he *acts* funny. The contrast between his wild behaviour ('I can't help being magnetic') and his sad, soft voice suggests a Jacques trying to play Touchstone. His angry wife (Penelope Wilton) is made comic by myopia: to be taken seriously, you must be able to focus on the object of your derision. Felicity Kendal, pushing the pockets of her grey cardigan almost to her knees, remains delectable but unaltered.

This is perhaps the one area where Alan Ayckbourn has yet to convince me that he can write comedies. In farce, the plot is predominant; the characters are two-dimensional. In comedy, the characters must change in the course of the play. By adopting a three-tier structure, he has made things very difficult for himself. If the characters change in the same way in all three plays – which they must do to some extent – the result could be repetitious for those who come to see the entire trilogy ...

The essence of Ayckbourn lies in behavioural comedy. His eye is needle-sharp; his knowledge of the minutiae of domestic life unerringly precise. Social criticism is implicit – and all the more effective for being so. If he chose to be more pretentious, and bored or accused us with half-digested Marxist didacticism, he would no doubt be the darling of our major subsidised theatres and have theses and assessments written about him.

Frank Marcus: Sunday Telegraph
26 May 1974

His special gift is for combing the mechanical dexterity of farce with the attention to character of comedy; and you see this here to perfection. *Living Together* charts the same disastrous suburban family weekend as its predecessor, *Table Manners*: the difference is that the off-stage events in one play are now brought on-stage. Thus, the mysterious mushroom-cloud that hung over Sunday breakfast in the first play is explained once you've .see Tom Courtenay's uncontrollably randy Assistant Librarian getting plastered the night before on dandelion wine, having a blazing row down the phone in the midst of a hideous family game, and rushing to assault his bed-ridden mother-in-law with that special murderousness the British reserve for their relations.

But although the plays interlock like bits of Meccano, they are independently funny because the jokes are always tethered to character. My favourite figure in the two plays is Tom, an incredibly dumb vet, so dense he can't even play the straight man in a Knock-Knock joke; yet his habits of answering a question ten seconds after the conversation has moved on or always ending up on a chair that mysteriously brushes the ground would not be at all hilarious if transferred to any other person. Moreover, Ayckbourn has the true comic writer's unerring gift for rows: he knows exactly how civil war can break out over the right to pour coffee and understands perfectly the fury of a myopic spouse unable to insult a husband she can't see.

Michael Billington: Guardian
22 May 1974

Thought for the week: superficial differences, not basic similarities, make people, and life, interesting. Stripped down, any individual is a bunch of identical physical mechanisms, and psychological impulses towards self-preservation, self-defence and self-perpetuation.

But out of these blind and repetitive processes have mysteriously

237

flowered the interplay of character, circumstances and perception which fills human lives with beauty and terror, pain and passion. What these processes seldom offer is any lasting sense of fulfiment. That is the business of art.

Music works with the pattern and timbre of sound. The visual arts deploy colour, line and mass to the same end, until very recently relying upon the representation of people and places, real or idealised, to augment its magic. The verbal arts work mainly through stories: unfolding variations on a handful of infinitely ancient myths, anecdotes embodying aspects of human and superhuman nature.

A straight re-telling of an ancient myth has its own charm; but almost all stories are in fact new versions of some tale first grunted out by a beatle-browed cave-dweller. And now that we are becoming so timidly self-aware about these distant signals, it is increasingly clear that the less an artist has them consciously in mind, the better his art is likely to be.

The very title of *Mourning Becomes Electra* throws a false shadow over O'Neill's tragedy. Eliot much marred several of his plays and our reception of them, by his nudging hints about their derivation, not to mention the tiresome intrusion of the Eumenides into *The Family Reunion*.

Like, shall we say *The Cocktail Party*, Alan Ayckbourn's superb comic trilogy, *The Norman Conquests*, is another variation of the age-old story of a group thrown into confusion by an outsider. But, like, shall we say, Pirandello in what I incline to think his finest play, *Lioïa* – he has not felt obliged to solicit the votes of fretful culture-snobs with any of the many relevant mythical parallels. Yet now that the last of the trio, *Round and Round The Garden*, has triumphantly joined *Table Manners* and *Living Together* at Greenwich, we can easily feel, in this brilliantly composed comic achievement, an elemental pain shivering darkly through the uproarious comedy of manners.

... each play miraculously makes perfectly good sense if one has not seen the others; but each naturally gains in comic density through cross-references, and with each play, knowledge of the characters grows, affection for them deepens.

Norman, the outsider, setting about seducing his own wife and his two sisters-in-law is no exurbanite Don Juan; part-Pan, part-Puck, he is also a bearded assistant librarian whose buffooneries inextricably mingle malice and a wish to liberate, whose mischief is laced with desperation. It is a measure of Tom Courtenay's skill as an actor that we never tire of him, of his stature as an artist that he is also ready to act almost as straight man to the others – to Felicity Kendal's fetching, inhibited little spinster, Penelope Keith's tense epitome of good bourgeois values gone wrong, Penelope Wilton's brusque and myopic businesswoman, Mark Kingston's bouncy but defeated extrovert, and Michael Gambon's wonderful study of vampire diffidence.

Absurd to smudge the quality of their performances, in Eric Thompson's direction, by quotation or description. Mr. Courtenay is not painfully funny merely because he cleverly mimes Norman's efforts to get his hand on a woman's breast, or Miss Keith because she amusingly keeps shoving that hand away. The seductive rhythms of a game with a tennis ball have a tense rhetoric not to be conveyed in words. Shall I persuade you of Mr. Ayckbourn's wit by quoting a line like 'I believe you would too'? Or of his merciless ear, merely by reporting that dreadful motoring talk ('You ought to have taken the A247 ...') which vies with gastronomic prattle as the most dispiriting by-product of the affluent society?

In short, these plays, and their current performance, have an organic inner power, a truly classical grip. Structure and invention serve observation and understanding. What has long seemed likely is now clear: Mr. Ayckbourn, the Kingsley Amis of the stage, is the most remarkable British dramatist to have emerged since Harold Pinter – with whom he has more in common than may seem instantly probable.

J. W. Lambert: *Sunday Times*
9 June 1974

The flaw that defeated *The Norman Conquests* was the author's determination to make each of the three plays stand on its own feet. That design made it impossible for the characters to develop. We accept with delighted surprise that the events of the weekend are illuminated from the dining room, the living room and the garden. To the best of my knowledge, no critic has remarked on the absence of the crucial bedroom – preferably that in which the invalid mother holds court. Was it artistic constraint or lack of nerve which prevented Mr. Ayckbourn from taking us there?

Frank Marcus: *Sunday Telegraph*
23 June 1974

Mr. Ayckbourn ... deals in conceits (for how else would you describe the three-fold reiteration of the events of a single weekend). Norman is a man – or at any rate an assistant librarian – and his conquests sexual. His attempted conquests, I should say, though he lays siege during the trilogy to all three of the women in the cast, only one of them actually capitulates and that his own wife. His avowed intention is to seduce his sister-in-law. He is, however, thwarted by his other sister-in-law, a monstress. It was always a question whether Mr. Ayckbourn could convincingly complete his scheme by contriving a plausible encounter between Norman and this last lady. He begged it, until the final play, *Round and Round the Garden*, and then he blew it.

Although it has always been difficult to fault Tom Courtenay's performance of Norman, it has never been possible quite to believe in it. In the earlier plays, he was a manic presence who promised to improve, and even to become comprehensible, on closer acquaintance.

This last and most schematic of the three drags him firmly but disappointingly into the centre. He propositions the ladies, and is rejected by them, more for the sake of his author's pattern than from internal logic.

Robert Cushman: *Observer*
23 June 1974

Hamlet

The Other Place, Stratford-on-Avon: 24 April 1975

I have not chosen this last *Hamlet* production for this book merely because of the tragic circumstance which overshadowed it, the suicide of its young director, Buzz Goodbody. She was certainly a great loss to the theatre, and of her several fine productions for the RSC, *Hamlet* remains most vividly in my mind. But she would have disliked a merely pious tribute; and the inclusion of this *Hamlet* is on merit alone. I have seen no other *Hamlet* which has moved me so much, which gave me a greater sense of a claustrophobicly evil society – all outward smiles and inner malice – and which expressed Hamlet's dilemma more vividly. Every age (as we have partly seen) has its own interpretation of this dilemma – as the hero who fails, as the 'unfinished man' screwing up his courage to become a hero, as the tortured adolescent haunted by Oedipal longing and passions. Buzz Goodbody's production gave another perspective: her Hamlet, brilliantly played by Ben Kingsley, could not take any action because he had lost faith in any possible good which could come from his deeds, whatever they might be. The state, and indeed the world, was so rotten that no kind of swift social surgery, in the shape of an assassination, would help it to recover. This Hamlet could not believe in a benevolent god, only in avenging demons; and his will was weak because he had no latent optimism on which it could grip.

The RSC's Stratford studio theatre – a mere shed with banks of seats – provided the most casual of sets, with almost no scenery at all; but by lighting through the roof girders, and by casting moving shadows across the wall, we were made to feel inside an army barracks or some makeshift prison camp. *Hamlet* was one of several fine studio productions – another being Trevor Nunn's *Macbeth* with Ian McKellen and Judi Dench – which became a feature of the RSC's repertoire in the 1970s. The Other Place was more than an experimental small theatre: it became an alternative to the main theatres, where the emphasis was upon informality and close actor-audience contact. Not all the RSC directors used the casual surroundings with Buzz Goodbody's skill, but all of them became aware of the potentiality of The Other Place.

... this production opened to the public last month several days before Buzz Goodbody's death. It is therefore a completed work and not a patchwork job by her RSC colleagues. 'Speak what we feel, not what we ought to say' is Shakespeare's advice for such occasions; and I am obeying it when I say that the production redoubles belief that the theatre has lost a superb talent at the very moment that it was moving from promise to fulfilment. It is a long time since I have been so gripped by this play.

Like her *King Lear* of last autumn, it is a studio production played in modern dress on a stage equipped with little apart from grooved white panels and a Kabuki bridge leading to the rear exit of the auditorium. The result is certainly a piece of directors' theatre, but – again like *Lear* – also an occasion for delicate and truthful acting. You can sense the company's relief in, for once, not having to hit the back wall of the circle. There are many startling changes of emphasis. Bob Peck, as the First Player, sits beside Hamlet quietly delivering the Hecuba tirade into his ear. Nor have I previously seen Polonius upstaged by an obsequiously contemptuous Reynaldo: Charles Dance, who doubles this tiny role with a commandingly sardonic Fortinbras, is a young actor of whom we can expect to hear more.

However delicate the personal nuances, the overall view of the play is the bleakest I can recall; not only is society poisoned, but neither Hamlet nor anyone else has any chance of setting it right. This society is established by the first entrance of George Baker's Claudius, a genial figure in a business suit, who addresses the house, like a company director at a shareholders' meeting. As the poison starts rising to the surface, you can chart its progress from Mr. Baker's smile; a sickly leer in the play scene, where he staggers involuntarily to his feet as if about to vomit, and a crooked grin at the end where he faces Hamlet with mute defiance: it is like the death of Iago. And from Fortinbras's smile as he picks up the weapons, it appears that he will be continuing from where Claudius left off.

In the production's deathly perspective, human affection appears a short-term affair. The Polonius family are presented as exceptionally loving: even Andre van Gyseghem as the old man softens his garrulous admonitions with tender physical contact. But, under pressure, all the humanity gives way to murder and maddened sexuality. Likewise Mikel Lambert's Gertrude, immediately after the promises of the closet scene, throws herself into Claudius's arms.

Ben Kingsley's Hamlet, above all, embodies the sense of reductive biology. He is set apart from the others not by nobility of bearing but by intelligence. Where the others are blinkered, he can see it all coming, and the variety of his performance amounts to an effort to escape from this knowledge, either in brief spurts of gaiety or in scurrying away from opportunities of vengeance; but always returning to a trance-like obsession in which the remaining characters already appear as so many standing corpses.

Irving Wardle: *The Times*
17 May 1975

White screens all around, Claudius and his court in pinstriped suits, an uneasy conspiratorial co-operation between the bureaucrats and the great-coated military, the inspirational inter-scene use of snatches from Brahms's A-flat piano waltz; there is a Strindbergian intensity about the production that pays particular dividends in the domestic scenes. For once, you can actually believe that Hamlet's 'neglected love' is as contributory a factor to his madness as is the shaking, shattering revelation of his father's murder. And Ben Kingsley, so intelligent and explicit at every turn, builds his fury and resolve as powerfully as he describes the growth by leaps and bounds of his own existential imaginings. His thoughts fly not up, but out and beyond each physical situation he himself manufactures. 'Now might I do it, pat' – and he is immediately scurrying away to the corner of the acting area; the tears for Hecuba, Yorick's skull, the little plot of land – in contemplating them fiercely, his own terrible circumstances crowd around for him to beat against.

The closeness of the actors results in genuine physical involvement as well as the chance to enjoy special details. The Ghost, beautifully spoken by Griffith Jones, walks among us with a natural imperiousness; when the doors are locked on the final bloodbath, the little theatre is slammed shut before the chilling silence is interrupted by the crashing arrival of Fortinbras (presented by Charles Dance as more of a determined, ugly professional than is usual). And, close.to, we can *feel*, as well as see, how this Hamlet enwraps his friends: Mr. Kingsley is superb at signalling both the generosity and sensitivity of the character towards those he holds in affection.

This performance is surrounded by others of equal distinction. George Baker as Claudius is ruthless but never supercilious. With Gertrude (Mikel Lambert) at Ophelia's funeral, he carries a small posy similar to that distributed by the girl in an earlier scene. Ophelia's decline – Yvonne Nicholson, pert and sexy, all but disfiguring her face with lipstick – is a matter of much horror for Mr. Baker, and his performance demonstrates yet again what a great part this is (his chief soliloquy is suddenly a re-focused view of the whole Elsinore mess that, in these circumstances, leaps memorably from the tyrannous claustrophobia for which he is responsible), Stuart Wilson is a frenetic and greatly affecting Laertes: his attachment to Ophelia is clearly more than sisterly and his 'show' of grief nothing of the sort; emotions are running as deeply here as anywhere in the play and his participation in the rigged duel is reluctantly, even suicidally, undertaken. Mr. Wilson is the best Laertes I have seen. The pleasures and subtleties are innumerable. ...

Michael Coveney: *Financial Times*
19 May 1975

... Mr. Kingsley is far away from the cliché expectations of Hamlet – he has none of the fair-haired youthful suffering attractiveness which a generation of preconceived ideas had led us to expect. This is a mature, grim, semitic Hamlet who uses his years to strange advantage.

Unable to suggest the disgusted and tormented vulnerability of the still young, this is a Prince of absurdity. That is to say, 'Oh, what a rogue and peasant slave am I' becomes the play's key speech. A dejected, slightly quizzical acceptance of the world's vileness and complexity, of its clashes between seeming and being, whose passions are brief and sudden, as if he had almost accepted that he could never kill a king. Resignation is all. Only when he wrenches out the words 'it hath made me mad' in a slow, agonised burst of vehemence do we sense that kind of desperate grandeur of which the great Hamlets are made, of the tension between feigned and real madness. But within its own terms, this modern dress man fulfils a mood of contemporary resignation which is most suitable, even if the histrionic demands are not altogether fulfilled.

Nicholas de Jongh: *Guardian*
17 May 1975

Three Sisters

Cambridge Theatre: 23 June 1976

Although Jonathan Miller's production of *Three Sisters* was not a studio production – it opened at the Yvonne Arnaud Theatre at Guildford and transferred to the Cambridge – it had many of the attributes associated with the small theatres. It was very much an actors' production, rather than a designer's or a director's: it was staged with the minimum of cost and its transfer to the West End represented a triumph of artistic integrity over poverty of means. Miller once said that the best work within rehearsals was done during the coffee breaks. He believed that acting was ultimately a matter – not of correct moves, gestures or intonations, not of military drill – but of putting the mind in the right place, of thinking appropriately. Casual discussions, with insights about the play flashing from actor to actor with some prompting and contribution from the director, was the best means towards a collective understanding.

Three Sisters demonstrated Miller's particular approach at its best. Its great merit lay not with the individual performances, fine though they were, but with the confident interplay among the actors, listening, responding and reacting, as if each performance were a fresh experience. Its immediacy was striking; and Miller's skill at conjuring up this group response was illustrated in comparatively small, as well as large, ways. Although the set was rudimentary, Miller's visual sense was shown in his exact placement of props, in his careful groupings which emerged from the acting and did not seem to be superimposed on the cast, as well as in the overall style. Miller, who had had experience before with small-scale mobile productions at the National Theatre, was able to adapt this felt knowledge to the demands of the West End, a rare achievement indeed.

Two months after its first showing in Guildford, Jonathan Miller's production arrives in London transformed from a fine production into a great one; and the first in my experience that fully acknowledges the objective nature of the piece.

To varying degrees, every other performance I have seen falls into the trap of presenting the action from the sisters' own viewpoint: three Grade A girls, well equipped for life in Moscow but pathetically defeated by the mediocrity of provincial life and too high-minded to protect themselves against a wastrel brother and his ruthlessly acquisitive wife.

Miller questions all this. The sisters are always sneering about the town, but what do they know about it as they entertain no society outside the officers' mess? They gush idealistically about work, but once they get a job they do nothing but complain of boredom and headaches, Masha has married a local schoolmaster, but does all she can to ignore him. As for the usually villainous intruder, Natasha, the worst one can say about her is that she knows exactly what she wants. It is not her fault that she cannot speak five languages: in fact, as the sisters' cultural horizon contracts, so Natasha's expands, and by the end of the play, she is speaking passable domestic French and making headway with 'The Maiden's Prayer' and what is wrong with her affair with Protopopov if Masha is permitted to entertain Vershinin?

What makes this reading worth discussion is that Miller has succeeded in justifying it in performance with no textual distortions and no crude reversals of sympathy. On the whole, one still prefers the sisters to Natasha. The Chekhovian balance still operates, prohibiting final judgement on any of the characters. Likewise, nobody has Chekhov in his pocket, least of all the members of the Prozorov family.

What is true of all these General's children is that none of them possesses any courage. John Shrapnel's Andrey takes it out viciously on class inferiors, but succumbs to apathetic guilt among his equals. Susan Engel's Olga puts a protective arm around the old servant, but withdraws it and stands mutely abashed when Natasha orders her out of the room. Angela Down's Irena, the most selfless performance, renounces all the accustomed lyricism and presents from the start a character incapable of love; a dogmatic adolescent, charming only when she reverts to childhood, and greeting the news of the Baron's death with a rasped 'I knew it', as though a picnic had been rained off. That this is deliberate appears from her passionate breakdown on the night of the fire, which is the single, most moving passage in the show.

Nowhere does the sense of paralysis appear more openly than in the Masha/Vershinin relationship. Nigel Davenport and Janet Suzman project the full intensity of the attraction, but it is clear that neither of them intends to do anything about it. Vershinin's philosophizing on the future comes over as a deliberate strategy for letting the present take its course: while Miss Suzman, a hunched figure, hands usually buried deep in her skirt pocket, appears armour-plated in self-sufficiency. After Vershinin's parting embrace, her arms immediately snap back round her own body, as the only physical contact she can rely on.

There follows a marvellous moment when she goes up to the

complaisant Koolygin, gently removes his false beard and attempts to caress his face. As always, she fails. And as always, Anthony Brown greets the attempt with a hopeful smile. It is details of this kind, pervading the show, that compel one's assent. Sebastian Shaw, as the drunken doctor, making his desperate confession while vainly looking for somewhere to pour away the water in which he has just tried to drown himself; Peter Bayliss's Soliony saying Yes to another brandy and secretly adding it to the one he has got already; Peter Eyre delivering the Baron's final request for coffee as a firm order to keep Irena away from the duel.

Mostly these are instantaneous flashes within a rapidly changing stage picture. Since its opening, the choreography has developed amazingly: witness the speed and complexity of the interrupted party, with Masha executing a wild scarf dance and June Ritchie's Natasha covering every corner of the room with her officious clockwork strut, tapping on shoulders until she has brought the fun to a stop. Or, for sequence of mimes, consider her wordless 'Lady Macbeth' entrance in the fire scene. Here, it is more ridiculous than ominous; so ridiculous, in fact, that the sisters imitate her and dissolve into helpless laughter, at which point Masha announces her love affair which instantly drives them all back to their separate corners. Patrick Robertson's platform set is used in depth and is better viewed from the circle than the stalls. But neither sightlines nor the vile Cambridge echo can do much to blur this glorious evening.

Irving Wardle: *The Times*
24 June 1976

... other directors swathe Chekhov in atmosphere – Jonathan Miller allows the atmosphere to arise from the interaction of characters and ideas. As a result his *Three Sisters* ... is much less about a romantic yearning for Moscow and much more a ceaseless Darwinian debate about the idea of a perfectible future. Anguish is there all right; but it's intensified by the characters' awareness of their own expendibility.

Miller also has the first rate Chekhovian director's ability to illuminate character through tiny behaviourist detail. Janet Suzman's marvellously witty, aggressive, tough-minded Masha, like a Mensa veteran hungering for a challenge, positively luxuriates in Vershinin's cigarette smoke while a moment later testily scything her way through Soliony's unbearable cigar fumes. ...

But the real eye-opener is Angela Down's Irena, which is not the usual besotted ingenue, but a girl who passes in the course of the play from hopeful youth to soured middle age; you can almost see the light in her eyes go out when, after the Baron's death, she realises she's doomed to become another spinsterish Olga.

My only quibble is that, though the production looks splendid from above, the placing of the downstage furniture sometimes impedes the front-stalls sightlines. But I don't want to quarrel with a production that makes you hear the text as if for the first time, that achieves a rich balance between ideas and emotions, and that invests every role with importance. ...

Michael Billington: *Guardian*
24 June 1976

Dr. Miller ... treats Dr. Chekhov with the deference due to a senior consultant. He ignores the historical and geographical factors, and subjects the characters to psychological investigation in depth.

His diagnosis is surprising. In spite of their constant protestations of anguish, he finds his three heroines suffering from lack of feeling and inability to act. Thus, their longing for Moscow is a pipe dream worthy of the inmates of Harry Hope's saloon.* He strips them ruthlessly of glamour. Masha (Janet Suzman) is an impetuous, tight-lipped neurotic; Irina (Angela Down) is pale and frigid: it is her admirers who endow her with the bloom of youth.

This method has the result of making the nasty characters less unpleasant. Natasha (June Ritchie) may be shrewish, but she knows what she wants and is practical, and Soliony (Peter Bayliss), forever rejected, is pathetic rather than villainous. Koolygin (Antony Brown) is the most kindly, albeit absurd, person on the stage.

There are many felicitous touches. The play survives the clinical examination with flying colours.

Frank Marcus: *Sunday Telegraph*
27 June 1976

There is a Slavic fatalism veering tempestuously between resignation and hope that Anglo-Saxon actors find difficult to master. I felt that this was the special ingredient Jonathan Miller in his production of

---

* In Eugene O'Neill's *The Iceman Cometh*

Chekhov's *'Three Sisters* ... was lunging at all night but only
occasionally grasping.

Milton Shulman: Evening Standard
23 June 1976

Betrayal

National Theatre: 15 November 1978

Harold Pinter's *Betrayal* received some very unfavourable first-night
notices; and it was left to some weekly critics, particularly Benedict
Nightingale in the *New Statesman*, to redress the balance. Pinter had
not received such bad reviews since *The Birthday Party*; and a
comparison between the treatments given to his first and his (to date)
latest, full-length plays is interesting. In 1958, the critics dismissed
The Birthday Party as being too obscure: in 1978, different critics
disliked *Betrayal* for being too banal. Had Pinter changed, or the
climate of opinion, or simply the critics?

Betrayal certainly seemed to yield its meaning more easily than
other Pinter plays. Nothing is more commonplace in the theatre than
ménage-à-trois situations, particularly among fairly well-off, even
trendy, middle-class houses. Nor did Pinter at any point try to
conceal the basis of his story, which, as several papers pointed out
gleefully, could have had an autobiographical connection. There was
nothing perplexing about what happened, no veils of cunning
ambiguity. The only superficially original feature of his play was the
way of telling the story, back to front, starting in 1977 and ending
when the affair began, in 1968.

But simplicity, of course, is not the same as simple-mindedness;
nor is it an effective stick to use against so skilful a dramatist. The
real question is – does this simplicity illuminate its theme? Is it
truthful simplicity, or plain naivety? I was one of those critics who,
on the whole, liked *Betrayal*, though less enthusiastically than
Benedict Nightingale and (in *Plays and Players*) Martin Esslin.
Perhaps the most interesting feature of its reception, however, came
from foreign critics, who were entranced by the play, and from

foreign directors, who quickly bid for the opportunity to include *Betrayal* within their repertoires. However narrow in its emotional range *Betrayal* might seem to British critics, it was not insular in its appeal.

Another factor in this comparatively rough treatment may have been the sheer familiarity of the production team, with Sir Peter Hall directing and John Bury designing. The Hall-Pinter evenings had been a well-remembered feature of the RSC's work during the 1960s, with their own particular brand of cool, poised elegance. When Hall took over the National Theatre, he staged another fine production of Pinter's *No Man's Land* with two remarkable performances from Sir Ralph Richardson and Sir John Gielgud. Hall, Pinter and Bury had set the standards by which they were to be appreciated; but in 1978, these standards were starting to be taken for granted. They had lost their immediate impact; while another director, Kevin Billington, had shown in London how Pinter's plays could be handled differently – with less 'style', but with greater realism and directness. This combination of circumstances caused a sudden and startling change in critical mood, leading to what seems to me still an unfairly cavalier treatment of a beautifully written play.

Not a great week for British playwrights. Harold Pinter's *Betrayal* ... is a woman's magazine romance that goes backwards until it disappears up its own pauses.

Herbert Kretzmer: *Daily Express*
11 November 1978

Harold Pinter's *Betrayal* has so many pregnant pauses throughout its two short acts, it would not have surprised me had the stage at the Lyttelton Theatre suddenly turned into a maternity ward.

The three-year gestation period between Pinter's last full-length play (... *No Man's Land*) and his latest offering has resulted in the birth of a very insubstantial so-what piece of work indeed.

Beginning in 1977, then hiccoughing backwards in time to 1968, the play chronicles the various stages of an affair a publisher's wife (Penelope Wilton) once had with her husband's best friend. What gives the evening its meagre narrative thrust is the fact that the friend (Michael Gambon) is unaware that the husband (Daniel Massey) has known about his wife's 'betrayal' for years.

Directed by Peter Hall in his best 'low profile' manner, and with a trio of underscored performances to match, the play is, to say the least, a far from stimulating experience.

Clive Hirschhorn: *Sunday Express*
19 November 1978

Trace backwards through a prism the bright hues of the spectrum and you arrive, inevitably, at the single originating point of colourless light. The variety and contrasts have gone. Those significant little lines which indicate the presence of this element or that are no longer to be seen. There is nothing but plain white.

This is the process that Harold Pinter has chosen for his new play *Betrayal*. Through nine short scenes moving backwards in time ... we approach the beginning of the events that have led to the situations revealed in Scene One. ...

The extraordinary thing is that Mr. Pinter has presented these nine episodes quite straight. There are no subtleties to be picked up, or at least none that I discerned, though I did think how clever I was to notice the extra emphasis put on Emma's youngest child, Ned, in the first scene. ...

'Have *you* ever been unfaithful?' Emma asks Jerry one day, as they prepare for a Kilburn afternoon. 'Who to?' he asks. 'To me, of course', she says firmly. It is not altogether a new argument: they have been faithful to each other in their fashion. What makes it such a dull one is that Mr. Pinter has made his characters such uninteresting people. There is no humour, save occasionally when Robert ventures a witticism, such as 'I've got a good mind to write to the Doge of Venice about it.' They are, I am sure, uninteresting because Mr. Pinter wants them to be so, and the colourless performances by Michael Gambon and Daniel Massey are no doubt exactly as colourless as he and Peter Hall, the director, require. Penelope Wilton, usually keeping something unspoken, is no brighter than the men.

Moreover there is the threat hanging over us all the time that we know precisely how the play must end. When it does so, in Emma's bedroom in 1968, when her husband is giving a publisher's party, it is just what it needs to be and no more, the little point of white light where Jerry, once best man at Robert's wedding, decides to seduce his wife. Well, so what? We knew that.

B. A. Young: *Financial Times*
11 November 1978

Themes, say some critics, don't matter: what counts is the skill a dramatist brings to his chosen subject. Well, the petit-point school of reviewing should have a field-day with Harold Pinter's *Betrayal* ... since it is full of technical resource. What distresses me is the pitifully thin strip of human experience it explores and its obsession with the tiny ripples on the stagnant pond of bourgeois-affluent life.

Michael Billington: *Guardian*
16 November 1978

In the first scene of Harold Pinter's new play, a man and a woman meet in a bar and start exchanging small-talk about mutual acquaintances. The familiar smoke-screen begins to gather around them. Perhaps they were once lovers, or were once married; or perhaps they are about to have an affair, or perhaps they are just old friends.

At which point, Pinter halts the game and explains everything. Yes, they were lovers. It is two years since they last met. Before that, they had a seven-year affair, which took place in the afternoons in a rented flat, and which was kept dead secret from Jerry's wife and Emma's husband, Robert. Robert and Emma are now separating. Jerry is an author's agent, Robert a publisher; each regards the other as his best friend. Both families have children; the details go on and on.

In other words, Pinter, the master of ambiguity, has laid out the facts as explicitly as a police witness; and the stark contrast with all his previous work does not end there. His obsession with the irretrievable past and the fallibility of subjective memory finds no expression in this play, which starts in 1977 and goes back, phase by phase, to show exactly what happened.

John Bury's diagrammatic interiors revolve to isolate the key moments in the trio's history: the day when Emma and Jerry gave up the flat; the Venetian bedroom where Emma confessed the affair to Robert; the honeymoon phase of the relationship; and the party back in 1968 when the betrayal began.

As Pinter and his director clearly intended, what emerges is the picture of a tiny, hot-house world of smooth London houses, Soho restaurants, and Italian holidays. The dialogue throughout is of studied banality, broken occasionally by a short-lived explosion of lust or anger, or undercutting lines like: 'That's the form: I ask about your husband and you ask about my wife'. Robert makes an off-hand reference to having beaten his wife up, there is no suggestion that the affair was to blame, and no trace of violence disturbs the blandly composed picture.

One effect this has is to throw great emphasis on conversational cliché, so as to reveal the fears of impending middle-age. 'How are you?' the characters ask each other, 'are you all right?' examining their still unravaged exterior for the first signs of decay. Another, and more typical effect, is Pinter's skill for picking up some blank conversation-stopper and putting it through spirals of invention so as to create a contest between two speakers. In this way, a weaker party can acquire dominance, or an interrogater finish up having to answer the questions.

It would be false to say that there is nothing ambiguous in the play. The contests I have just mentioned could represent genuine antagonism, or simply stand as the verbal equivalent to the squash game that Jerry and Robert are always promising themselves. Over the longer span, you could read the piece as a triumph for the unseen Casey, a creative writer who keeps the agent and publisher in bread and butter, and finally takes over the woman. But what comes over as explicitly as the biographical facts is a straight-forward view of adultery as an action begun in passion and ending in exhausted indifference.

Irving Wardle: *The Times*
16 November 1978

Seen superficially, which is precisely how most of its reviewers have seen it, Harold Pinter's *Betrayal* is a piece of shameless backsliding, a craven retreat to a theatrical period when your average dramatist was obsessed with adulterous husbands, 'other' women and triangles which, if not eternal, were certainly interminable ...

But wait a moment. Whether or not Pinter backslides, his new play positively backsomersaults. At any rate, it starts with its chronological ending and ends with the sexual serenading. To an unsympathetic critic, this is at worst a cheesy gimmick, at best an error which must drain the proceedings of any tension the oaf Pinter might otherwise have injected into them. There is, however, a less damning way of interpreting his preference for anti-clockwise. It substitutes the question 'how?' for the cruder 'what next?' in the minds of the audience. And in my view it deepens and darkens our perception of the play, infecting the most innocent encounters with irony, dread and a sense of doom.

To say, or imply, that a subject should be rejected because it was once hackneyed seems to be thoroughly defeatist. Clichés surely need to be reclaimed for reality; and by that test Pinter's play is scarcely contemptible. It is all there: the instinctive evasions, the slips hurriedly corrected, the hollow questions ('and how is Emma?') to which the answer is already known, the faked off-handedness, the suspicion and paranoia that the habit of deception tends to provoke in the mind of the deceiver, the surreptitious *billets-doux*, the fear, the panic. As the title confirms, the subject is not mainly the sexual aspects of adultery. It is rather the mechanics of cheating, the politics of betrayal.

Its reviewers, not content with coming glass-eyed and woolly eared to the theatre, have managed to sound inconsistent as well. To some, Pinter is naïvely obvious, and to others needlessly obscure. The truth is perhaps a bit subtler. He has charted the bald facts of the situation with more than his usual clarity, and then he has gone on to invite those of us with a talent for emotional map-reading to use our energies more creatively: we're to inspect and analyse the lightly-traced contours of his characters, and speculate about those motives, attitudes and feelings his cartography has left vague. To shift the metaphor, Pinter has sometimes earned a reputation for profundity simply by taking us to the edge of the psychological well and pointing out its depth. He has allowed us to hear the echoes rumbling up from inside, and even smell the rising stench, but he has not often given us a direct, detailed look at the frogs, tin-cans, used contraceptives, water-beetles, and all the rest of the mess festering in the ooze at the bottom.

Benedict Nightingale: *New Statesman*
24 November 1978

As a piece of theatre writing, *Betrayal* is a technical *tour de force*. It works perfectly on stage under Peter Hall's direction and there is not a false line in the script. It is as witty and funny as you would expect but at the same time moving and true. The acting could not have been better. Poor Pinter, or rather rich Pinter, for he is always being accused of presenting us with the wrong slice of life and of being inconsequential. *Betrayal*, it is true, has no great pretensions to universality, but I thought it dealt with its subject with the blinding honesty of a true artist. Isn't that enough or nearly enough? Long may the new Pinter continue telling us the whole truth as well as nothing but the truth.

Peter Jenkins: *Spectator*
25 November 1978

... in fact, this is a new Pinter and yet the old Pinter, the Pinter of oblique and indirect approach, the Pinter of hidden subtleties and deep layers of gradually emerging meaning. The play is beautifully written. Its only flaw seems to be a cliché Italian waiter in a restaurant scene, who is also very badly played by an actor with a fake funny Italian accent.

Martin Esslin: *Plays and Players*
January 1979

Index

Index

Index of Critics

Index